RICHARD BURTON

By the same author:

John Wayne: The Man Behind the Myth

Jimmy Stewart: The Truth Behind the Legend

Sinatra: The Untold Story

Gene Hackman

X-rated: Paranormal Experiences of the Movie Star Greats

Gregory Peck

The Hollywood Connection: The Mafia and the
Movie Business – The Explosive Story

Hollywood Rogues: The Off-screen Antics
of Hollywood's Hellraisers

Kirk Douglas

Kid from the Bronx: Life of Tony Curtis

Trevor Howard: The Man and His Films

Charlton Heston

The Sharon Stone Story

Trevor Howard: A Biography

The Hollywood Murder Casebook

Richard
BURTON
Prince of Players

Michael Munn

A Herman Graf Book
Skyhorse Publishing

For Mark and Melanie and Claire and Mike.

Visit our website at www.skyhorsepublishing.com.

10 9 8 7 6 5 4 3 2 1

Library of Congress Cataloging-in-Publication Data
Munn, Michael.
Richard Burton : prince of players / Michael Munn.
p. cm.
ISBN 978-1-60239-355-4
1. Burton, Richard, 1925-1984. 2. Actors—Great Britain—Biography. I. Title.
PN2598.B795M86 2008
791.4302'8092—dc22
[B]
2008017661

Cover design by Richard Mason
Cover photo © Corbis

Print ISBN: 978-1-63450-252-8

Printed in the United States of America

CONTENTS

INTRODUCTION

I COULDN'T CLAIM THAT Richard Burton was a close friend of mine, but he was a good friend. I couldn't boast that I was his confidant, and yet one day in 1974 in Winchester something traumatic happened that for the next several hours made me his sole confidant.

Before that, I had met him on a number of occasions, the first in 1969 when I was just 16 and still at school. I had managed to wangle myself a visit to Shepperton Studios for the day to watch the filming of *Anne of the Thousand Days*. I had the burning ambition to be a film director and, just a few years before, had been lucky enough to visit the sets of *Othello* and *The Dirty Dozen*. Those experiences made me realise that I was at my happiest on a film set, and so I wrote to the administration offices at all the studios during my last few months at school in 1969, asking if I could come and visit any of the sets. I hardly expected to be told to come down and meet Richard Burton.

Burton was, at that time, one of those mythical star actors. It was as though he didn't exist anywhere but on a cinema screen. He was as famous as any actor could be and, unlike today when every film star appears on every TV programme to plug every film, he was rarely seen on television, or anywhere else for that matter, ready to shatter the myth. I was in awe of him because I admired him enormously in *Becket* and as Mark Antony in *Cleopatra*. Oh, how I irritated him from time to time because I insisted that not only was *Cleopatra* much underrated, which is now the opinion of a good many more than just me, but that his Mark Antony was an extraordinary performance that displayed something of his power as a stage actor within the confines of the film medium.

So the idea of meeting Richard Burton was exciting enough to make me feel so nervous that I thought I was meeting royalty. And I was, because he was playing Henry VIII. I couldn't understand why he had agreed to meet me. I was taken to one of the sound stages where he sat on a kingly throne, fully dressed in his costume, sporting a thick dark beard, looking not too unlike Henry VIII perhaps but certainly looking for all the world like Richard Burton in another historical costume.

A royal ball was being filmed, and he pointed out to me his wife, Elizabeth Taylor, who was making a brief guest appearance.

'What do your friends call you?' he asked me.

I told him it was Mick.

He said, 'Then you shall be Mick to me and I shall be Dick to you.'

I was told later that nobody was allowed to call him Dick. It was a nickname he despised, even though all the Americans would insist on calling him Dick. He said it made him sound like 'a phallus'.

'We shall be Mick and Dick, and if Elizabeth comes over, we shall be Mick and Liz and Dick,' he said and laughed.

He was simply enjoying a tiny word game, but whenever I met him after that, usually when I was an extra in one of his films, I always said to him, 'Hello, Dick,' and the assistant director would have apoplexy. I would come to call him Rich, which he preferred.

Several years later, when I was with him on the set of *The Wild Geese*, he introduced Richard Harris to me and said, 'Mick, this too is Dick. I am Dick One and this is Dick Two.'

Harris said to me, 'If you call me Dick I'll knock your fucking head right off your shoulders.'

Rich said, 'It's okay, Mick. That means he likes you.' Fortunately, he was right. I got on well with Harris.

But back in 1969 there was just Mick and Dick for a short sweet time, waiting for a highly complicated set-up (well, it looked highly complicated to me) involving many people performing a Tudor dance. Richard may have been a little drunk; he was certainly very merry which, as I would later discover, was not how he felt very often during the making of *Anne of the Thousand Days*. He suffered from deep melancholy and a conviction that the screenplay was poor and his performance 'boring' – his own description. He was wrong; he was nominated for an Oscar. And it's another of my favourite Burton performances.

He told me he had been shown my letter in which I'd said that I had visited the filming of *Othello* in 1965 and had greatly enjoyed seeing Laurence Olivier performing and that shortly thereafter I had had the pleasure of seeing that performance on the screen. I said in my letter that I would like to enjoy that kind of experience again as I hoped to become a film director. That, it seems, was enough for him to decide to meet me; he figured I had to have a touch of culture to have been so impressed by Olivier's Othello.

'Larry can do what I can't,' Rich told me. 'He can become someone else. I can only ever make my characters into me. So Henry VIII will be me in tights, a codpiece and a beard.'

I hadn't learned then, as I did a little later when I began working in the film industry, to write down at the earliest convenience everything anyone of any import said to me, so I don't remember word for word all Richard Burton said to me that day. But the day itself, the feeling of excitement, and the sense of being at home on a film set has always stayed with me.

And the memory that Richard Burton was prepared to put himself out for me for just an hour or two has also remained with me. My affection for that usually high-spirited, sometimes sad but extraordinary man began that day and grew over the years.

In 1969 I was only a messenger boy at Cinerama but I was rewarded by my managing director – a wonderful man named Ron Lee – with a little work as a film extra which he was able to arrange, and one day in 1970 I was a London bobby in a scene in *Villain* with Richard Burton, who promised me that he would get me work as an extra whenever he worked in the UK, which was not all that often as he, like many of his peers, was a tax exile. But he kept his promise.

It was while he was making *Villain* that I witnessed first hand the incredible anger that could be aroused in him – I saw it both on and off the set.

Then in 1974 I went to Winchester to appear as an extra in *Brief Encounter* and spent an entire day with him, just the two of us, so he could just get away from everyone and everything. What happened there formed a sort of bond between us. It wasn't something that he ever referred to again after the event, but I could tell it was there, although a certain distance always remained, which I think he pre-ferred to keep. He didn't much care for young people, it turned out.

He was a very sick man when we last met on the set of *1984.* He was unable to even lift his right arm, but the power was still there in his acting; it was, most of all, in his voice. His voice had always been his most valuable tool. It had been the power and richness of the Burton voice that had first made an impact in his early plays. He used it to great effect in Shakespeare and even more so on radio. Even when he was appearing to do little but fight off German soldiers in *Where Eagles Dare*, the voice was paramount.

He seemed to take an immediate liking to me on the set of *Anne of the Thousand Days* because I knew whole passages from the film *Becket* by heart; I had a long-playing record of dialogue highlights from the soundtrack which I listened to over and over, so I was able to present him with a very bad impression of Peter O'Toole and for a few brief minutes I was acting alongside Richard Burton, he as Becket and I as the King. Years later I got to play the King in that play, and not too many years after that I got to play Henry VIII in *Anne of the Thousand Days*. Doing those plays made me feel very close to Richard because he was one of the few people who gave me the courage to get up and play those kinds of parts.

I seemed to go up in his estimation in 1974 when he found out I had worked on a couple of screenplays for John Huston, who was someone Rich had tremendous respect for; that seemed to make me something of a real writer in Richard's mind – he liked writers enormously. He always wanted to be a writer himself. However, he wasn't so impressed when I became a journalist for film fan magazines, but that didn't make him any less kind or considerate towards me. In fact, I may have been the only film fan magazine journalist he ever allowed to interview him (I only did one formal interview with him).

So that's something, in brief, of the kind of relationship I had with Richard Burton. And in writing this biography of him I have my chance to set down some of my own personal memories of him, of the things he said to me, and also the memories of many who had known and worked with him and who I had either met briefly or had got to know during the years I was working my way through the film business.

I remember he once said to me, 'I always believe that if something's worth doing, it's worth doing well.'

I replied, 'That's like a line out of *Becket*.' (Well, it was almost a line out of *Becket*; it was actually, 'I love doing what I have to do and doing it well.')

He said, 'And it's true. So even when you don't feel much like it, try and do it well, whatever it is. And do it in as quick a time as you can, before you get bored.'

There was one particular thing that Richard did very well indeed: he *lived.* He enjoyed living and doing it well. What he hated was being bored and being a bore. In his later years he endured sciatica, arthritis and chronic depression but he continued to live life to the max before he got bored or boring.

He always said that his lifestyle would kill him, so when the end came, I think, perhaps, he didn't feel that all he had enjoyed had been in vain. Alcohol was one of his great pleasures. So was sex. Reading was one of his greatest pleasures, and that surely came with no threat to his health. Acting, though, was not one of his greatest pleasures. It was just something he discovered he could do which earned him good money, but he would have preferred to have played rugby for Wales, or have been a great writer. Nevertheless, when he acted, he tried to do it as best he could, and when he had done it as best he could, especially on the stage, he then grew bored with it. He had done it well and that was all that mattered. He looked for the next challenge.

From time to time he spoke of death. He said he could sense it would come sooner to him, before he grew old. He knew that alcohol was gradually killing him. He told me once, 'Most people are afraid of dying. The trouble is, they are also afraid of living. Don't be afraid to live, and then perhaps you won't be so afraid of dying.'

He lived, loved and lusted his way through his mortal existence, all the way to the moment he died. That, in itself, was a considerable achievement. But he achieved so much more. There are those who maintain that he squandered his talent. I think they're wrong.

I'd like to add a quick note about someone who was a great friend of Richard's and a friend of mine too. He was Brook Williams, son of actor/writer Emlyn Williams; Williams senior was one of Burton's greatest friends and mentors. Brook was almost like an adopted son to Rich. He appeared in many of Burton's films, always in bit parts, his name often not even appearing on the credits. Brook became a close friend, confidant and virtually a personal assistant to Rich.

In 1987, three years after Richard's death, I sat with Brook to do a lengthy interview for a book I always hoped to write about Richard Burton. Every now and then over the years he'd ask, 'Written that book yet?' and I'd say, 'Not yet, Brookie. Hope to do it soon.'

It's now 20 years since that interview, and Brook is no longer with us; he died in 2005. Two years since his passing, I can at last say, 'Done it, Brookie.'

Michael Munn, 6 June 2007

Chapter One

FROM THE LAND OF HEROES

R ICHARD BURTON WAS proud of his surnames – both of them. He was Burton and he was also Jenkins. Both names meant much to him.

He was born Richard Walter Jenkins on 10 November 1925, in the mining village of Pontrhydyfen. He was the 12th child of miner Richard Walter Jenkins, nicknamed Dic (the Welsh abbreviation of Dick), and even better known as Dic Bach, meaning Little Dick, because he hardly stood more than five feet.

'My father looked a lot like me,' Rich told me one day when we were lunching at a pub in Winchester in 1974. He'd opened up, without too much prompting, about his father and of his early life as a coal miner's son.

Dic Bach had always lived in Pontrhydyfen and had worked in the mines since he was a lad. His family, friends and neighbours knew him as a bit of a scallywag who drank too much and kept everyone entertained with his hilarious tales told over a dozen or more pints in the Miner's Arms.

His wife was Edith, 'a religious soul with fair hair and a beautiful face', said Rich, although he only knew that from a few photographs and the hearsay of his friends and family; Richard hardly knew his mother for she died when he was not yet two. She was liked by everyone, and in common with most of the locals, she was a strict Methodist who went to chapel every Sunday.

She had been a 17-year-old barmaid at the Miner's Arms when she married 24-year-old miner Dic in 1900. There was a class distinction even in that part of Wales at that particular time; Dic was a Jenkins and Edith was a Thomas, and the Jenkinses were

1

beneath the Thomases, so her parents disapproved of Dic.

'My parents could sign their own names,' Rich told me. 'They were the first in either family to not sign with an X on the marriage certificate.'

Edith had not been married a full year when she gave birth to their first son, Thomas Henry, in 1901. Then Cecilia arrived in 1905, Ifor in 1906, and then a girl, Margaret Hannah, who died a baby, followed by another girl, also named Margaret Hannah, who also died. Such were the risks of childbirth at that time in that place. Children were born at home, and some died there. William was born in 1911, then David in 1914, and Verdum in 1916, Hilda in 1918, and then Catherine in 1921, Edith in 1922 and Richard in 1925.

From the moment he could crawl, Richard was on the heels of his mother wherever she went, and if he lost sight of her, he cried. Despite her many children, Edith kept the house clean and everyone fed, and she remained outwardly cheerful. But she aged quickly, losing her pretty looks through constant childbearing and working too much for too many hours each day, not just in the care of her own family but also doing laundry for others as a means of supplementing the family income, which was whittled away too often by Dic Bach's heavy drinking.

Rich remembered how his father 'used to go off on a "bat"'.

I asked him if he meant his father went off to play cricket.

Richard laughed and then explained:

'A "bat" is a bender of legendary proportions. He would be gone for up to three weeks. He'd disappear on a Friday and sometimes for a week, two weeks or three weeks and then he would turn up all of a sudden. He'd be standing in the kitchen door, covered in chicken feathers because, you see, his last bed before coming home was some chicken coop. But he would smile as his anxious children tried not to look so delighted to see him for our mother had told us to look helpless and hungry and sorrowful and to make him feel the guilt of the world. But he only ever smiled effulgently.

'His oldest children would put him to bed and he would whisper, "I've got children in a thousand. Good as gold they all are." My oldest sister, Cis (Cecilia) nursed him when he was ill so my mother could take care of the rest of the family.

'Another time he came bursting again into the kitchen where we all lived, all thirteen of us [children and mother], and he held an orange rope and on the end of this orange rope was a greyhound so old it had no teeth and could barely walk without fighting for breath. The miner's loved greyhound racing. It was forever the way to everlasting fortune. And my father had bought this dog believing it to be the solution to our everlasting poverty, and announced, "Boys and girls, our troubles are over." The dog dropped dead a few weeks later.

'He loved watching rugby, but he rarely made it to the match because he'd visit every pub en route.'

Rich, like his brothers, like all the boys of the village, grew up knowing that they would probably all follow in the footsteps of their fathers by leaving school and heading straight down the mines. Or they might find work in the steelworks of nearby Port Talbot. They might then become victims of pneumoconiosis in the lungs, which was common to the miner, or tuberculosis, or crippling injuries sustained in pit falls and explosions.

Dic Bach was himself a victim of an explosion. Burned all over, he came home wrapped in bandages from head to foot with only his eyes and nostrils left uncovered. His daughters nursed him, bathing his body in olive oil.

The girls would be just like their mother; they would marry and have children. Life was not intended to be easy for any of them. So the men drank and sang and told stories. And that's what Richard Burton grew up doing. Rich forever drank and told stories – the same stories over and over – like the one about the day Richard's grandfather had picked the winner of the Grand National. He used his winnings to buy drinks for everyone at the Miner's Arms. Said Richard, 'They sang and drank and it was a mighty and legendary celebration and the winnings were tipped down the throats of happy miners that night. Then my father got behind my grandfather's wheelchair and began the long climb up the hill to the house. It was an heroic ascent, but they reached the house where my father reached for the front gate, and in a moment he had let go of the wheelchair, and suddenly my grandfather was careering down the hill and he was crying, "Come on Black Sambo! Come on Black Sambo!" until he was brought to a sudden and permanent silence when he hit a brick wall. I am sure when they buried him, he was still smiling from his triumph with the horses.'

I couldn't help but laugh when Rich told me this really very tragic tale. His stories were pure entertainment. He couldn't bear the memory of it as a tragedy and so he had told it as a humorous and heroic tale. Heroes were important to the Welsh.

Perhaps he preferred to dwell on the heroic memories because his earliest memories were more about death than life. His mother, Edith, gave birth to a 13th child, a boy called Graham, in October 1927, and a few days later she died. It was a miracle she had survived the birth of 12 previous children. She died, Richard said, of 'puerperal fever', or more bluntly, lack of hygiene. She wasn't a dirty woman. She was fastidiously clean. The coal dust from the mines got everywhere. The men trod it in to the house and breathed it in; the air and the ground were peppered with it. Edith fought a losing battle against grime and dust and muck, that 13th birth stole her last ounces of strength and infection set in. She was 42.

Richard always felt that the doctors failed her and he rarely trusted doctors ever again. Through his life, despite his many illnesses and ailments, he resisted seeing doctors.

He grew up frustrated that he had so little to remember her by, but he was told by his family and others who knew him that he cried endlessly for his dead mother. So he concentrated on recalling how his father was a lovable rascal; he wasn't, of course. Dic Bach neglected his family before and after Edith died.

Because Dic Bach was unable, or unwilling, to take any kind of responsibility for all 13 children, the two youngest boys moved in with older siblings who had already moved out to make homes for themselves. Graham went to live with the oldest brother, Tom, who was 26 and working as a miner and was married and living in Cwmavon, a few miles down the valley.

Rich went to live with his oldest sister, 22-year-old Cecilia, or Cis as he liked to call her. Cis was married to miner Elfed James, and they lived in Taibach, a district of Port Talbot. 'I'm told that from the time I moved in with Cis, I never cried again for my mother,' he told me.

A good deal of English was spoken in Port Talbort where Rich learned to speak it. His first language was Welsh; few people spoke English in the valley. It might have been a toddler's version of Welsh, but it was unquestionably Welsh.

Cis and Elfed had no children. Elfed was a fine, solid father-figure, although Rich would grow to give him merry hell. Cis loved her little brother deeply. He could do no wrong in her eyes. He adored his sister, never confusing her for his mother; she always remained his beloved sister. She bore up well for Richard's sake, but she was grief-stricken over the loss of their mother. Being the oldest sister, she did all she could to maintain the Jenkins home back in Pontrhydyfen.

Cis, Elfed and Richard lived with another family, the Dummers. Margaret Dummer was Elfed's sister. The house where they all lived in Caradoc Street was full but happy. Elfed was, unlike Dic Bach, a responsible man, and his sister became 'Aunty Margaret' to Richard. He remained close to her until she died.

The Dummers had a son, Dillwyn, who was about the same age as Richard, so the two grew up like brothers.

'We shared everything,' Rich told me about his adopted brother. 'If one of us was ill, the other would share his bed so he would catch the same disease. We kept nothing for ourselves: our bicycles, our illnesses and our relatives. Elfed's parents lived very close and so did his other relatives, and so I had more uncles and aunts than I could have ever needed. It was even slightly incestuous because my grandmother on our mother's side and Elfed's grandmother were sisters. That made for one happy family.'

Richard didn't lose contact with his other siblings or his father because he visited the Jenkins household in Pontrhydyfen as often as he could, and his siblings would often take turns to come and visit the James family. Dic, without Edith, was even less of a father, neglecting his children and yet always loved by them; he shifted between his older daughters who had homes of their own.

'My sisters raised themselves,' Rich recalled. 'My brothers did as they pleased, able to care for themselves. It was a strong family of strong people. My father was the weak one. The chapel in Pontrhydyfen was maintained and cleaned by the family. I am proud that my family were always well thought of in the village, and always remembered. I may have become the one with the fame and the success as well as the failures and the excess, but my brothers and sisters were heroes.'

Living next door to Cis and Elfed was Margaret Dummer's mother-in-law, Dillwyn's grandmother. She was, he recalled, the most 'terrifying member of the entire extended family. When she caught Dillwyn and I telling lies, she held our hands on the hot iron gate of the fire'. She was a devout Welsh Christian; her method of punishment must be regarded as highly questionable. 'Very quickly I learned how to act my way out of trouble and often avoided getting my hand burned by declaring with absolute conviction, "Dillwyn did it, Grandma."'

Understandably, Rich and Dillwyn preferred to get a straightforward beating from their respective male guardians.

The two boys had the job of carting coal through the house to the back yard. Coal was the one thing that was never in short supply; the local mines ensured all the families in their employ had plenty to keep their fires burning through the winters. But the one small fire in each house was hardly enough to warm every room, and Richard recalled, 'I remember the cold. I remember how the bedrooms were as cold as ice. The condensation on the windows turned to ice. I'll never forget how cold I was at times. I can't bear the cold now. I can stand being out in the cold but only when I know I can go inside and be as warm as toast. Whatever happens to me in life, I will never be as cold again.'

There was little money to go round, even though the men of this household didn't drink away their earnings the way Dic Bach continued to do. Nevertheless, nobody went hungry. They lived on sausages, pies, cheap meat, faggots, plenty of potatoes, bread and cawl which was a Welsh dish made from lamb chops and vegetables. Later as a millionaire, Richard often preferred to eat a dish made from seaweed called lava bread; he called it 'colliers' caviar'. But his favourite meal was always sausages and mash, as Susannah York discovered many years later when the Burtons came to call on her.

Susannah told me this story over dinner one evening down in Devon during the filming of *The Shout* in the late summer of 1977:

'My husband Michael and I invited Elizabeth and Richard down to our house for the weekend. Richard said he had a better idea. Why didn't we join them on their yacht? I was relieved, really, because how do you entertain the world's greatest entertainers? Unfortunately, Elizabeth phoned to say there was something wrong with the yacht and could they come and see us after all. I tell you, I just didn't know what to expect. I thought they'd turn up with an entourage. Fortunately, only one car turned up – their Rolls. Elizabeth stepped out carrying four bottles of Jack Daniels rye whiskey, and then they sent their chauffer away. It was pouring with rain and the first thing Elizabeth wanted to do was go for a walk in the woods. When she came back she was soaked. I couldn't think what to cook them for dinner until Richard asked for bangers and mash. That's what he wanted, and to him it was like a gourmet meal. There was still a lot of the Welsh child in him.'

Even then, as a millionaire with a Rolls-Royce, Richard harked back to his childhood by demonstrating his singing, and also by showing off with a special party trick. Susannah told me, 'I invited a few of my friends over and after dinner we sang Scottish songs. Richard was boasting that he was the only person he knew of who could put a whole egg into his mouth, close his mouth and not break the egg. It had been his very special party piece for years until this night when a few of the other men proved they could do it also.'

Cis and Elfed, being strong Methodists, took Rich to chapel every Sunday. He told me, 'You haven't heard the real beauty of the Bible until you have heard it in Welsh.'

He sang at the top of his voice. The hymns were all in Welsh; throughout his life he continued to sing those Welsh hymns. He was always proud of his blood heritage. He said, 'There is nobody like the Welsh. We were oppressed and exploited, poor but rich with our language, suppressed by the mighty English. I grew up among heroes who went down the pits, who played rugby, told stories, sang songs of war, composed the greatest poetry.'

Eventually Cis and Elfed moved into their own house, where Cis gave birth to a girl. Life wasn't easy for them, as indeed it wasn't for anyone in that community, but Richard had no complaints about his childhood. Elfed treated him like a son, but while Cis forgave Rich any indiscretion or sin, Elfed found himself increasingly having to punish Richard who was always tearing his clothes which Cis had to mend because they couldn't afford new ones. And he was always wearing out his shoes too.

At the age of five, he began school at Eastern Infants School, which was just around the corner from his home. When he was eight he was sent off to an all-boys school where 50 children packed into a classroom.

After school, he would stop to play football without first going home to change his clothes. Elfed impressed upon him how expensive those clothes were to replace and would attempt to punish him, but Rich would tell his sister, 'Sorry, Cis, I just got carried away,' and he'd

7

promise to come home and get changed in future. But he rarely, if ever, did. Nevertheless, Cis would defend him because, as Richard would say, 'where I was concerned, she couldn't help herself.'

Richard's great hero was his brother Ifor who continued to live in the Jenkins household and was one of the village's great rugby players; a good solid Welsh hard man. 'Heroes were vital to our way of life,' Rich said. 'To play rugby as well as carving out the mines was a sign of great heroism, and my older brother was my greatest hero. I worshipped him.'

Ifor was someone all of Richard's later, rich friends would know and admire. Sir Stanley Baker told me, 'Ifor was a wonderful brother to Rich and a fine man. He had to leave school when he was 13 to go down the mines. But he could do anything, and he escaped from the mines and became a builder. He was strong, very fit. And like Rich, he loved poetry. I think maybe Ifor influenced Rich in that way. He was Richard's hero, and if the hard man of the family could read poetry with great beauty, then that was good enough for Richard; he would read poetry too.'

One of Richard's most treasured Christmas presents was a bicycle from Ifor. 'It was a thing of beauty and I went everywhere on it. It opened up the world for me. I went to Swansea and Newport and Aberdare and Mountain Ash; just me and my bicycle. I was so proud of that bike, and I was so proud of my brother who gave it to me.'

Rich came to the notice of a teacher, Meredith Jones, because he had become an avid reader. Some boys thought Jones was a rather tough bully of a teacher, but Richard wasn't afraid of him; Rich was quite fearless and always remained so.

He might have been developing a taste for culture, but at the age of eight he was as naughty as any of the boys, getting up to typical schoolboy pranks. He was quick witted and eager for fun, no matter how mischievous. One day he and Dillwyn borrowed one of Dillwyn's grandfather's pipes that still had tobacco in it, and they set up a tent in a field and sat inside to smoke for the first time.

After that they would buy a pack of five cigarettes on their way to the local cinema. It was called The Cach – or 'shithouse'. The Cach had to be regularly doused with insecticide. Watching a film on a Saturday afternoon was the highlight of the weekend. The cost of admittance was paid for by Richard's and Dillwyn's guardians, and they always had a little extra money to buy sweets which they usually spent on cigarettes.

In his prepubescent years, Rich drank and smoked. Elfed was teetotal, so he frowned upon the youngster's boozing. There were arguments. Rich admitted he showed little respect for Elfed, a good man but one overruled by a wife who doted upon her little brother.

By the time Rich was 12, most of the girls of the town seemed to be in love with him. Stanley Baker said, 'I heard how he would come home from playing football and find Cis dealing with a girl crying because Rich had promised to meet her. He liked the girls but he loved rugby football. That was his great passion. He told me he would have preferred to play for Wales at Cardiff Arms Park than play Hamlet at the Old Vic.

When Rich was 11, Meredith Jones coached him through his scholarship exam which gained him entry to the Port Talbot Secondary School in 1937. There he excelled at rugby. Unlike most of the young big-built men who played rugby and were generally well over six feet tall, Rich stood only five feet nine and a half inches, short by rugby standards. 'What I had was speed. I could run fast. I had to because if I wasn't fast enough, heavier and bigger men would bring me down and crush me.' He developed back trouble early on in life because of being occasionally crushed beneath a pile of heavy Welsh rugby players, and it was something that plagued him all his life.

It was common for the men from that environment to develop problems with their bones, either from playing rugby or simply working in the mines. Ifor also suffered from back problems, and it was further damaged during the Normandy landings.

Brook Williams told me, 'It was on the rugby field that Rich displayed his growing ability to land a good punch. He saw a friend being picked on by a much bigger opponent and when the referee wasn't looking, Rich, despite being towered over by the bully, punched him hard and laid him out. He was now a hero to others; not only could he play rugby but he could fight too. But he was never a bully. He only picked on the bullies.'

And that was something he did all his life. He didn't stand for anybody picking on somebody less able to take care of themselves. In fact, he once stood up for me.

It happened when I was an extra on the film *Villain*. I was given a policeman's uniform to climb into and very strict instructions given by an assistant to the assistant of the assistant to the assistant director, which was, 'Under no circumstances speak to the star of the picture. You are just an extra.'

We stood about for a long time. I remember the sun shone but it was cold. For us mere extras, there was no hiding place. But for Richard Burton there was a caravan.

For some reason he chose not to stay inside it and I watched him emerge from his caravan. There was the man I had met a couple of years earlier when he was playing Henry VIII. I'd talked with him for a couple of hours on that day, but I knew I wasn't to say a word to him on this day. Then, suddenly, I noticed that I had caught his eye. I was sure he couldn't have remembered me from my day on the set of *Anne of the Thousand Days*, but he began to walk towards to me.

I reached into my pocket for one of the cheap cigarettes I could afford, put the wrong end in my mouth and lit the tip. I realised my mistake just as he reached me and he was immediately holding out a packet of what were obviously very expensive cigarettes.

'Here,' he said, his rich voice giving cadence to a mere word, 'have one of these.'

I had been instructed not to talk to the major star under any circumstances, so I shuffled my feet and looked in another direction.

'I'm offering you a cigarette.' His rich voice was louder and just a little irritated. I ignored him.

He suddenly said, 'Parla inglese?'

Very slowly and patiently, he said, 'Do – you – speak – English?'

I have Italian blood and look slightly Italian; I looked even more so when I was young.

I glanced at him quickly and nodded.

'Then bloody well say something.'

Making sure the assistant director wasn't looking, I said with lips that barely moved like a bad ventriloquist act, 'I can't.'

'Why the bloody hell not?'

'I'm under orders.'

'What orders?'

'From that man.' I made a sly nod towards the assistant of all the other assistants to the assistant director.

Richard Burton grabbed my arm and firmly but gently dragged me over to the accused and said, 'Did you tell this young man not to speak to me?'

'Of course I did,' replied the assistant.

'Why?'

'Because he's just an extra.'

'And that makes him – what – a *turd*? Which is exactly what *you* are.' His rich voice cut through the air.

The assistant director to all the others opened his mouth to protest, but Richard cut him dead. 'Let me make this clear, if you treat any . . . *any* of the extras here like *turds*, I will *personally* see to it that you are removed from the set and you will never, *ever*, work in this fucking business *again.*'

The assistant to all other assistants retreated.

Richard Burton said to me, 'What an incredible arsehole he is. Now, take one of my cigarettes and smoke with me.'

I took one his cigarettes and reminded him that we had met before. He quickly remembered. 'Ah, yes, you are Mick and I am Dick. Well, Mick, let me buy you a coffee.'

I suddenly felt on top of the world. The assistant must have felt under it. From a distance, he gave me a glare that told me he would hate me for the rest of his life as I strolled off with Richard Burton towards the catering truck where he didn't actually buy me coffee because it was free, but he nevertheless said, 'A coffee for my friend here, and one for me.'

We stood in the sunshine, smoking expensive cigarettes and drinking good coffee.

'Of course,' he said, 'extras aren't supposed to talk to the principal actors because we're supposed to be *the stars*. But I try not to be up my own arse. But I saw you and wondered if you were an actor doing extra work just for the money.'

'Me? An actor? Oh no. I'm going to be a film director.'

'I see. Well, I'll tell you what. When I come back for my next film, if you're not directing pictures, I'll see to it you get work as an extra, if you'd like. You may well find you'll fall into acting that way. How does that suit you?'

I couldn't believe that Richard Burton was offering me this opportunity. 'I'm very grateful,' I said. 'But I think I'll probably be directing films soon.' There is nothing like the optimism of youth.

He, of course, knew more about his business than I did, and he said, 'Well, I'll make a deal. If, by the time I come back here to make another film, you're not *busy* directing anything, let me find you some work.'

And at that point the assistant to whoever called me away to be herded with the rest of the extras, while the principal director came over to talk to Burton. But before we parted, Rich shook my hand. And he was as good as his word. He was a hero to me – from Wales, a land of heroes.

Chapter Two

THE TURNING POINT

A T SCHOOL RICHARD JENKINS became the kind of hero for others that Ifor was for him. He became captain of the school cricket team, did well at table tennis and also played court tennis, coached by Ifor. He was, apparently, thought to be destined for an international cap as a rugby player.

But his academic achievements were a lot less. He wasn't a failure, but he was never able to reach the heights that he achieved on the sports field. However, he did prove he had a brain when he began answering back to one of his teachers because he quite simply felt that he was in the right and the teacher was in the wrong. Such behaviour was frowned upon, but nobody could claim that Richard didn't answer back politely.

In January 1941, he landed the role of Mr. Vanhattan in the school production of George Bernard Shaw's *The Apple Cart*. 'I was terrible,' he told me. 'I was playing an American and had a thick Welsh accent which I couldn't disguise. I tried an American drawl, but it only made me sound like a Welshman with a stammer. It didn't spur me on to want to be an actor.'

Cis and Elfed now had two daughters as well as Rich, who was becoming more of a handful for Elfed. Richard said, 'The allowance I got each week would mainly go on cigarettes and beer. When I needed extra cash to take a girl out, I borrowed from Cis.' The money Cis loaned him came from her housekeeping and he was never able to repay her. He would take girls to the pub or sometimes to a dance, but he was not, as his image as a womaniser might suggest, a young man keen to sow his oats. Rather than ravishing the local girls, he treated them with great respect and they swooned as he spoke poetry to them. That's what attracted the girls to him; he had natural charm and a certain elegance. He may have had a handsome face, which grew more

13

handsome with age, but in his teens his neck was constantly breaking out in boils and his face became increasingly pockmarked, but none of that put the girls off one bit.

He seems to have held back from being sexually active too soon; he said that he didn't lose his virginity before he was 16. Maybe part of the reason he was not as active as one might suppose was because a simple caress from a girl that passed over one of his boils made him scream in pain, and that was often enough to send the girl fleeing home in a panic.

Elfed was doing all he could to keep his family clothed and fed, but Richard was squandering money on tobacco, booze and girls, and making no effort to earn a wage of his own. Elfed had just cause to be angry but he couldn't count on Cis to back him up. 'My dear sister thought I could do no wrong, even though she knew I did enough wrong to warrant the verbal lashings of Elfed,' said Rich. 'He knew, I should think, better to try and lay a hand on me. I would not have stood for that.'

In 1941 Elfed became ill and was laid off work. He had no choice but to take Rich out of school and get him a job by using his influence with the local Co-operative committee and thereby landing Rich a job at the local Co-operative store. At the age of 15 Rich became an outfitter's apprentice in the men's clothing department, earning 28 shillings a week. He said:

'I was humiliated. It was not the kind of work a miner's son should have been doing. I hated it and took every opportunity to break all the rules. When I had a delivery to make, I spent hours out of the shop, stopping off to chat with friends and family, or to pop into the pub. Everything was rationed – the war was on then – and everyone had clothing coupons which they had to offer up along with their cash. I pretended to forget to take coupons from many of my customers, allowing them to come back another time and buy more than their rations allowed.

'The only benefit I got from that job was learning how to fold a suit properly. I still fold all my suits properly . . . professionally. I can't bear to see someone do it badly, and I have to show them how it's done.'

14

Meredith Jones opened a youth club in Taibach, having secured funds from the Glamorgan Education Authority. Rich was encouraged to join and it was, in his own words, 'the turning point in my life'. He recalled:

'The club met in the Eastern Elementary School, a building which had been condemned. The gloomy lighting was gas and the roof leaked. We – the boys – did what we could to fix the place up, mending the skylight blinds so they could be drawn during the nightly blackouts.

'We even managed to open our own canteen, supplied largely by the American military which was stationed nearby at Margam Castle. We also learned to box. I could already use my fists. We found a pair of boxing gloves, and my friends Gerwyn Williams [who later became a Welsh rugby international] and Trevor George started boxing with them. Just the one pair between us.

'Then I did my first play. Leo Lloyd, who ran the club for Meredith Jones, put on a production called *The Bishop's Candlestick*, a one-act play adapted from *Les Miserables*. It was all done in mime, and I got the role of the Convict. The stage was created by laying blackboards across tables and desks. I was persuaded by Leo Lloyd that acting was infinitely fascinating. I had never thought of it before, but he taught me the fundamentals of acting. He was quite tough on me because, perhaps, he could see the potential in me which I didn't see at all at the time. I had anger and discontent in my life, and he channelled all that into making me do plays. I could see that acting was a way to escape not just from my environment but from real life which, when you're 15 and 16, seems so bleak and uncompromising. I learned that becoming someone else somewhere else in a different time was an escape.'

In April 1941, a local cadet force, Port Talbot 499 Squadron of the Air Training Corps, was formed. Meredith Jones became a flight officer and coached the squadron rugby team which included Richard. Having learned how to play on the streets, Rich now began to learn how to play on the field, according to the rules.

The commanding officer, Philip H. Burton, the English teacher from the secondary school, was someone who would become the most influential person in Richard's life. He was considered to be something of an eccentric bachelor, living alone in lodgings, and speaking clear English with just a hint of a Welsh accent which made him odd indeed, being the son of a miner from Mountain Ash. His parents were actually English and he had to learn to speak Welsh at school. He, like his parents, was an Anglican, not a Methodist like most of the locals.

He was 14 when his father was killed in a mining accident. With a keen intellect and no wish whatsoever to go down the mines, he graduated from the University of Wales at Cardiff with a double honours degree in mathematics and history, and in 1925, at the age of 20, he began teaching at Port Talbot Secondary School. He started as a maths teacher but realised he preferred to teach English. He also had a great love of theatre and would later have success as a writer, producer and actor at the BBC Radio studios in Cardiff.

Brook Williams told me, 'Philip Burton had a Pygmalion complex. He sought to find those who were in need of him.'

Richard said, 'I had become impressed by Phil. I admired the way he spoke English, and he wasn't afraid to demonstrate his love of books, poetry and plays, and that struck a chord in me.'

Philip Burton had no girlfriends. He was a very private person and something of an enigma to all. He took it upon himself to take boys under his wing from time to time and nurture them, such as Owen Jones who, with all the help and support of Philip Burton, won a scholarship to the Royal Academy of Dramatic Art (RADA) and from there played Shakespeare at the Old Vic. During the war Jones enlisted in the RAF and was killed in 1943.

Despite the enjoyment Richard got from the club, he was growing ever more belligerent at home. He hated working in the store and blamed Elfed for his misfortune. When he wasn't at the club, he was at the pub drinking heavily. At the age of 15, he was learning how to consume large quantities of liquor. 'I wasn't unusual,' he said. 'It's what all the miners did.'

'But you were not a miner,' I said.

'I should have been; I was a miner's son.'

So I asked Richard, 'Why didn't you get yourself a job down the pits?'

'Maybe I would have, but suddenly I was back at school.'

Actually, it wasn't all that sudden. Richard worked at the Co-op for about a year before Meredith Jones took steps to secure him an education which Jones felt Rich would need if he was going to go on to acting. 'Acting seemed as good as any idea,' Rich told me. 'I went along with it, and for a while that was my ambition. Or maybe I just pretended it was; anything to get out of working at that bloody store.' Rich swore that he couldn't remember if he really had ambitions to act back then.

Jones and Llewellyn Heycock, a local county councillor and the Chairman of the Glamorgan Education Committee who had provided the funds for the Taibach Youth Club, recognised that with his love of culture and his resourcefulness Richard was totally wasted at the Co-op where he would undoubtedly be spending the rest of his working life. He was as tough as any of the locals and could box and play rugby, but he also had a great mind and he read avidly; he possibly also had a vague idea that he might become an actor. It was a mind, Jones and Heycock reasoned, to be nurtured, and that meant Rich had to go back to school in 1942.

He detested the idea of going back to school at the age of 16. He had been humiliated enough by being made to work in a shop, but to go back to school was, to him, a far greater humiliation. And the school wasn't keen to have him back, but Jones and Heycock persuaded the reluctant headmaster to readmit him.

Rich found himself in a class of children a year younger than him, and so he saw himself as a man among boys. His disapproval was displayed in a moment of frustration on his first day when he hurled a gym shoe across the classroom and smashed a window.

He said, 'I think that being sent back to school made me more rebellious than ever.' He would sometimes turn up in the morning reeking of the beer he had consumed the night before, and then he'd be sent home. His behaviour didn't impress his teachers, so he told them he had decided on becoming a teacher. 'I had no intention of really being a teacher,' Richard said. 'But it was a good move to say I was. They went a little easier on me.'

He had come to realise that life seemed to rely on a series of networks. His family was a network in itself, and during his childhood years that network served him well. But it let him down when he most needed it, or so he felt, when he was made to work in the Co-op. That job was itself the result of a network of which Elfed was a part, and it did him no good. Then he realised that Meredith Jones was part of another network which got him back into school, a move he couldn't see the value of at the time, but he would later.

When he finally became an actor he would discover that there were networks that he had to use or avoid depending on the desired outcome. He still had no real ambition, although he did have dreams of playing rugby for his country. What he wanted most of all was to be his own man and be independent. He would take care of himself, but more important still, he would, when he could, take care of others.

Philip Burton was still teaching at the secondary school and he was asked by Jones to keep a special eye on Richard. Philip Burton detected a considerable sense of culture and intellect in Rich where others saw only the rough boy who drank, smoked and played rugby like a champion.

Chapter Three

PHIL

PHILIP BURTON SET his sights on nurturing young Richard Jenkins; Phil, as Rich always referred to him, was to become his Svengali. Rich, recognising that he had been singled out and seeing his chance to find a way out of the valleys, began staying behind after class to discuss the poetry of Dylan Thomas, Gwyn Thomas and R.S. Thomas, and the plays of Shakespeare with Philip Burton.

'I don't think I really knew then that I wanted to be an actor,' Richard told me. 'But it was an idea that appealed, and it was something that I thought might be a way out of the poverty trap one finds oneself in living and working in the valleys.'

They seemed an unlikely pair. Philip was very clean and tidy, and Richard was always a mess with socks that stank of sweat.

'I was quite calculating,' said Rich. 'I told him that my mother had died and I was living with my sister and didn't get on with her husband. I felt that this was the one person who could help me. If I went back to working at the store, I would drink myself to death, and if I went down into the mines, I would never escape.'

The irony of what Richard told me – that he might drink himself to death if he stayed in the valleys – was not lost on himself, and he added, 'So I got away from the valley and proceeded to drink myself to death elsewhere.'

Philip Burton began inviting Rich home for tea each evening and they would spend hours talking about books, poetry and theatre. 'The seeds of culture were already there,' Richard said. 'That wonderful man made sure they grew into something lasting.'

In 1943, one of the lodgers in the house was called up for the war and a room became free. Philip suggested that Richard might like to take the room. He talked it over with Cis and Elfed, saying that he would take Richard into his own personal care.

Before long Philip Burton was calling Richard 'son', and Richard was calling him 'father'.

Immediately, this scenario begins to sound highly suspicious. Philip Burton had no girlfriends. He lived to find boys who would become his personal protégés. And he was suggesting that Richard move in with him.

Cis was delighted that Richard might find a way to better his life, and Elfed was relieved that he would no longer have to endure Richard's difficult behaviour, and so they consented. Rich was ecstatic, and in March 1943 he moved out of the home he had known for so many years and into a room next to Philip's.

You can't help asking the question: was there more to it?

Richard's own explanation was that the poverty that engulfed virtually all who lived in Port Talbort was such that an arrangement whereby professional men, such as Philip Burton who had risen out of the working class and attended university, could personally give something back to their community by helping others escape the cycle of poverty that was the Welsh miner's life. It was, said Rich, 'not an unusual arrangement in Wales during the first half of the 20th century'.

Richard said often, sometimes without prompting, 'I'm not a homosexual', as if the question hung over him.

As far as Richard's sexuality goes, those who knew him recognised that he was a prime example of sheer heterosexuality. A long series of conquests with women, famous and not so famous, have accompanied his journey from his days in the valley, through Hollywood and beyond. He exemplified a certain kind of manliness that sprang, perhaps, from the mining community where only the most rugged men were completely admired.

Men like Philip Burton could be admired for their intellect and sense of culture, but he impressed the common Welshman far less than the man who could endure the mines or walk away from a bone-breaking rugby tackle. Richard had intellect but could also take the body wrenching. He could also drink and smoke heavily along with the men from the pits, and he was something of a womaniser even at an early age. He was a little like all things to all men – or all Welshmen.

When he took a girl out, he was less likely to have his way with her and more likely to spout Dylan Thomas. The Welsh always liked their cultural heritage, and Rich made good use of it when pursuing the girls.

His voice was beautiful even as a teenager, and his native accent was broad. He could recite poems in Welsh, and the Welsh girls loved him for it.

Philip Burton decided that he would mentor Richard who was reading a book each day, or so he claimed. He learned from Philip how to lose his Welsh accent, or at least speak with a theatrical English accent. Philip taught him how to breathe, how to project, how to appreciate Shakespeare.

But what did Philip expect in return? He certainly hoped to see Richard succeed; that's without question. But did he require something more than dedication and ambition from his young protégé?

There were some who thought so. Perhaps most outspoken among them was Sir John Gielgud. I was acquainted with Sir John for a number of years, and we often talked of the actors he had known, worked with and who were generally his contemporaries, such as Laurence Olivier and Ralph Richardson. And Richard Burton, who was not so much a contemporary but a star pupil.

Gielgud once told me, 'Philip Burton was a very decent man with the most honourable of intentions for Richard. Richard *must* have known, as I am sure he did, that Philip Burton was a homosexual.'

This topic came up over lunch in a Norfolk restaurant in 1979. Sir John didn't talk openly with reporters about his own sexuality, even though it was a matter of public record after he was arrested in Chelsea for soliciting a homosexual act in a public lavatory in 1953 for which he was fined £10. But by 1979 I wasn't interested in a journalistic career – and never had been – and my relationships with theatre and film people had become considerably more casual than a show biz writer might have expected. I didn't record anyone on tape unless it was a formal interview. But if it was a casual conversation, I made notes of what was said, not for publication, but for my own sheer delight and pleasure; for me, knowing people like Gielgud, Olivier and Burton was like mingling with demi-gods. I have the greatest admiration for their talents.

And so Sir John and I chatted about Richard Burton and his mentor, and somehow the subject of homosexuality in the theatre world came up, and Sir John was quite frank in telling me, 'I made an approach [to Richard Burton] and he very kindly and gently rebuffed me.'

I asked him if he knew for sure if Philip Burton was a homosexual, and he said, 'Oh I *know* he was.' And when asked how he knew, he said,

'There is a network. There are all kinds of networks. If one is Jewish, there is a Jewish network and somebody who is Jewish can make his way, and everybody in that network will know. And if one is sexually inclined in some way, there is a network of like-minded people they can trust and who will help.'

One of the great theatrical managers was Hugh 'Binkie' Beaumont, a homosexual, as many of the leading figures in British theatre were – and are. Today they are able to be more open about it than in the past. Beaumont gave chances to many actors, gay or straight, including Richard Burton. Homophobia was not something any aspiring British actor should suffer from.

'I know Philip Burton was homosexual because he was a part of this network,' Gielgud told me with characteristic gentility and a gracious smile as he so often gave. 'My dear, there isn't anyone who isn't homosexual in theatre that I do not know about.'

So Philip Burton was homosexual, but did that make his relationship with Richard in any way salacious?

The actress Mary Ure, with whom Rich had a very casual affair when they made the 1959 film *Look Back in Anger*, once confided in me that Rich had told her that Philip had made a pass at him. She said it was a very offhanded, casual sort of pass, and that Richard had simply made it clear that he was not inclined to accept.

Even Stanley Baker, who I knew briefly in the early 1970s before lung cancer finally took him, had referred to Philip Burton as 'Richard's adopted father who wanted to be much more'.

How, then, did the young Richard Jenkins cope with being in close proximity with a man who was attracted to him? I can only hazard a pretty well-educated guess because of the various things Richard said to me. For instance, he said that many in the world of English classical theatre were homosexual and bisexual. 'What is it to me what they do in their beds as long as they give pleasure in performing on the stage where it counts. I don't bloody care about their sex lives, and I hope they wouldn't care about mine.'

Richard, then, believed in live and let live, and even said to me on that day in Winchester in 1974, 'We should never judge others. We have enough sins of our own, so I try not to cast stones. We all have to work together, and as long as the work is good, then John Gielgud could be a cat burglar for all I care.' He was talking in general terms, saying that it didn't matter to him what people did in their lives outside of work, and I take that to mean it could just as well apply to people's sexual preferences.

He was very aware that he was attractive to some men; he had first noticed it, he said, when he was at college in Oxford. There were men who just wanted to be his friend because he was a good storyteller and a great drinker, and then there were some who simply found him attractive. He told me, 'I was different and attractive; that's no idle boast. There were young men who obviously liked each other's company, and they sought mine too. Later I would discover how important it was to be attractive to women *and* men, not for personal reasons but because when you are on the stage or on the screen, you have to *appeal* to all – men and women. Maybe that's to do with looks, or maybe it's what they call star chemistry. And if you have talent and some luck, you can have success. Never underestimate physical attraction. It opens doors.'

So he had no prejudice about gays, despite having come from a Welsh Methodist background where homosexuality would have been heavily frowned upon. In fact, as Stanley Baker told me, it would have been 'invisible to them because they wouldn't believe that such things went on'. So Cis and Elfed most likely never even questioned what Philip Burton may have secretly desired; all Cis knew was that he was a man who could help her beloved brother, and all Elfed cared about was that he wouldn't have to put up with Richard's belligerence towards him any longer and he would no longer have struggle to feed and clothe Rich ever again.

But it must have come as a shock to Richard when he discovered that his mentor had more on his mind than mentoring. I never asked Rich about that, but I did ask Brook Williams who said, 'Rich was very smart. Very sharp. He knew Phil was his ticket to something better, and he had the charm and kindness not to reproach Phil but simply deflected his suggestion or pass or however it came – because Rich never elaborated it to me – in such a way that Philip would have not felt ashamed and Rich would not have felt threatened. Anyway, Rich was a fine boxer even at that age and he could have dealt a blistering blow to anyone, but that wouldn't have been his way. He would have dealt with Phil with kindness and real affection, for he was fond of, immeasurably fond of Phil.'

Rich, though, was only 17, and I wondered how at that age, he could have behaved so maturely. Sir Stanley Baker told me, 'He may have been young in years but his mind was years older. Getting to know Shakespeare as a boy will do that, I think. He looked and behaved older than he was, and maybe he had an old soul within him. At 17, Rich was a man, not a boy, and a very clever man.'

He was certainly clever enough to know that he could maintain a relationship with Philip Burton so he could learn all he could from him and escape from the valleys. It was in part manipulation but it was also true affection. The intellectual Richard Jenkins obviously had power over the physical Richard Jenkins.

But that still didn't explain everything about Richard's sexuality. Too often I heard him say, and so did others, 'I am not a homosexual'. Was he protesting too much?

Richard explained it, I think, without my asking the question when he told me, 'When I became an actor, everyone – men and women – looked at me like I was a potential conquest. You understand?'

I didn't, so he added, 'Acting is what homosexuals love to do. I think perhaps that acting is something that appeals to the latent homosexual. I did not wish to be a homosexual and I bloody well wasn't going to be one. The truth is, I was afraid of it. I drank because I was afraid of being a homosexual. I drank because I hated wearing make-up. Make-up isn't for men, but it is for actors. I find myself telling people over and over, "I'm not a homosexual", so there will be no confusion.'

There could certainly be confusion to the women whom he bedded and some he wedded, like Sybil Williams who became his first wife and endured his many affairs with leading ladies such as Jean Simmons, Lana Turner, Claire Bloom and Mary Ure, as well as those who were not his leading ladies, like Marilyn Monroe. And there was, of course, Elizabeth Taylor, his second – and third – wife, followed by wife number four, Susan, and wife number five, Sally. Not to mention God knows how many theatre usherettes and studio office girls.

Sex, for Richard, was, as he put it, 'one of the greatest pleasures life has to offer, and I enjoy getting as much of it as possible'. He was testosterone-driven, being a true man of the Welsh mining communities. But he was not a typical one-night-stand kind of man. Well, not often. He retained some of that Methodist morality, in his own kind of way, and he made every girl feel like they were the only one for him . . . at that time. Mary Ure told me, 'Richard didn't just want to fuck. He liked to wine and dine and recite poetry and make it memorable. He was irresistible. You knew you were only in it for the short haul, but he made you feel the most special thing in his life at the time.'

Rich elaborated on this for me: 'It must be the greatest pleasure, and to be with a woman makes me feel special, so I want her to feel special too.'

I asked Mary as someone who would have been considered an authority on the subject if Richard was a great lover. She laughed and replied, 'He is not the best lay I ever had, but he was the most charming. He has great charm and wit, and he has no hesitation in propositioning a girl. Other men can spend days or weeks getting to the point even if they know they haven't a chance, but not Rich. He has a system which always gets results.'

It might be assumed that women were the only ones who ever provided Richard with his greatest of pleasure. But that didn't stop him experimenting. In Winchester, during a discussion about how he perceived acting to be a primarily homosexual craft, he told me out of the blue, 'I gave it a try once.'

'Gave what a try?' I asked.

'Intimacy with a man. How can you know you don't like caviar if you never tried it?'

He didn't like it. I asked him when his act of intimacy took place; he said it was during his time in the RAF. 'There develops a special bond, you know. I have heard actors say they find it when they do a play or a film, but I've never known the bond to be as strong as when I was in the RAF.'

When he was stationed at an RAF base at Babbacombe, on the south coast near Torquay, in 1944, he was able to secure single sleeping quarters for himself, while all the other recruits had to share. One night Rich burst into the quarters of Tim Hardy – later well known as actor Robert Hardy – in a state of panic and told him that a terrible thing had happened and that he was sure he would be court-martialled.

Legend has it that Richard had been caught entertaining the wife of a senior officer. But that version of events was never confirmed, and Rich certainly never dwelt on it. But that day in Winchester he told me that it hadn't been the wife of an officer he had been caught with, but the officer himself. Richard Burton had his one and only homo-sexual experience. It was probably his last because, he said, he hadn't enjoyed it.

'I was scared to try it again,' he said, 'because what terrified me most was that I might have come to like it. Many do. But even those who do, like Olivier, suffer tremendous guilt about it, so what's the point if you are going to suffer from guilt? And then there are those who have to keep it secret, like [Michael] Redgrave and dear Alan Bates. Denholm Elliot is another.' Those Rich mentioned are gone now. Their sexuality made for good gossip fodder, but in the theatrical world that they inhabited, nobody cared, and a later generation of actors have not felt the need to hide their sexuality, such as Sir Derek Jacobi and Sir Ian McKellan.

Back in 1974, when Rich was referring to the likes of Olivier and Redgrave, he said: 'They are people in torment. I never want that torment. And frankly the idea of being a homosexual scared me. But I was saved by a profound knowledge which is that women are the only beings on God's earth that drives my lust. Now isn't that a wonderful thing?'

If Sir John Gielgud was right and Philip Burton was a homosexual, it made no difference to his relationship with young Rich. Phil was not the man Rich wished to experiment with, and when the experiment came with an officer in the RAF it only served to prove to Richard Burton that he was not a homosexual.

Chapter Four

FROM JENKINS TO BURTON

BEING MENTORED BY Philip Burton was not an easy ride for Rich. Burton demanded his full attention to details such as diction, interpretation and delivery. The rich tones that became Richard Burton's trademark were always there but they only rang clear when he recited poetry, which was the foundation that Philip Burton built upon. He coached Rich through long passages of Shakespeare, particularly the monologues, often late into the night.

'Shakespeare was the best way to learn English,' Rich told me, 'and the best way to learn all about acting.'

He also had to learn to curb his temper. Philip must have impressed upon him how lucky he was to have a second chance at school, and Rich began to behave himself. Behaving didn't include stopping drinking or smoking. They were social habits. It never occurred to anyone that at such a tender age Richard was on his way to becoming an alcoholic.

Philip produced two plays in 1943, one at the school, *Gallows Glorious*, and one at the Air Training Corps, *Youth at the Helm*. He cast Richard in both and gave him private rehearsals in the front room that went on late into the night. With two plays to rehearse as well as lessons in Shakespeare, Richard Jenkins had little opportunity to be out drinking and wenching, so in a way Philip did manage to curb some of young Richard's habits.

In August 1943 an advertisement appeared in the local paper: the Welsh writer and actor Emlyn Williams was seeking Welsh actors, including a boy, for a new play, *The Druid's Rest*, to be produced in London by H.M. Tennent Ltd, run by the legendary Hugh 'Binkie' Beaumont.

Philip put Richard's name forward, and Rich was duly given an audition in Cardiff. Philip went with him and, among scores of other hopefuls, Rich had a meeting with Beaumont's casting director Daphne Rye. She was, apparently, struck by his riveting eyes set in a pockmarked and boil-scarred face that looked like it had been purposely sculpted as the epitome of a Welsh boy.

She selected him to go forward to the next interview to be held by Emlyn Williams. Another Welsh boy at those auditions was Stanley Baker who told me, 'Rich had such audacity. When Emlyn Williams asked him what he had just done on the stage, Rich said that he had just played Professor Higgins in *Pygmalion*. He still had a thick [Welsh] accent and he passed the audition.'

Years later, Emlyn Williams told me that he felt any young man 'who could lie so convincingly had to be a talented actor'.

There is actually some confusion over whether Richard did or did not perform in a production of *Pygmalion* directed by Philip Burton. It's very possible that Philip coached Richard in English by getting him to perform scenes from *Pygmalion* in their home, and maybe Philip was Professor Higgins and Rich was Eliza Doolittle. The true situation was, after all, not unlike that of Higgins and Eliza, the main characters in *Pygmalion*. Or it may be that there really was a school production of *Pygmalion* in which Richard played Professor Higgins; the record is unclear. Emlyn Williams believed there had been no such production.

Richard got the part in *The Druid's Rest*, playing Glan, the elder son of a publican. Before rehearsals began, Philip had embarked upon a course of action that would, he hoped, allow Richard to go to university. He was convinced that Rich had improved enough academically to succeed at university, and sure enough, when it came time to take the final exams at the secondary school, Rich passed in seven subjects.

The problem was how to pay for Richard's university education. The war proved to be the solution. The RAF ran a scheme whereby they offered suitable recruits a short university course at Oxford or Cambridge. Most recruits came from the Air Training Corps, so the commanding officer of the Port Talbot 499 Squadron, Philip Burton, was able to put Richard Jenkins' name forward.

As a recruit in the Air Force, Richard would not only go to university but he would be paid as well. The only drawback was his background. No university was likely to accept a working-class miner's son.

So Philip came up with a solution. He sought to adopt Richard as his legal son.

Dic Bach approved; he had hardly taken any active interest in Richard's upbringing. Cis and Elfed and the rest of the family also agreed. But there was a major problem that Philip came up against. By law there had to be a minimum of 21 years between the age of the adoptive parent and the child, and Philip was 21 days too young. There was a solution. Philip could make Richard, who was still a minor until he reached the age of 21, his ward, thus giving him custody of Richard with the requirement to feed and clothe him, and give him the right education.

While the legal process went ahead, Rich reported to the Haymarket Theatre in London in October 1943 to start rehearsing. So did Stanley Baker, who was given the job of understudying Richard. Baker said, 'We were both away from home, and the war was still going on. Both of us were as green as grass and felt like foreigners in a strange land, and we hit it off immediately. He's two years older than me, but we were the best of friends.

'When we began rehearsals, Rich shone. I mean, *really* shone. Emlyn Williams was immediately aware that he commanded the stage, even without trying. One time Emlyn saw he had a book and asked what it was. It was Dylan Thomas. Without opening the book, Rich began to recite. It gave me goose bumps and I knew that he was going to be a great actor.'

The play went on tour in November for two months. Rich and Stanley were generally left to their own devices; sharing shared digs, drinking – 'far too much booze for working actors in a play,' said Baker – chasing girls, and fighting with each other. 'We were wild boys. We had some terrible fights, even in the dressing room, smashing the window in the process.'

The fighting was a part of their developing friendship because they competed on every level; Rich was always the more determined one and wanted to beat Stanley at every game, including the game of womanising.

Sir Stanley recalled, 'Rich took a fancy to one of our landladies. She was much older than us. He said, "I think I've got a real chance with her." I told him he was deluded. Then one morning he said, "I did it. I had her last night. In front of the fire."

'I thought he was making it up. But then he said something that made me think it had to be true. He said that halfway through he felt as though his feet were burning. He said he thought he must have gone to hell for such a sin. Then he realised that he was too close to the fire and his socks were burning. That convinced me it had to be true. I mean, nobody could make that up.

'About 20 years later, he said to me, "Do you remember that time I told you about the landlady and how my socks nearly caught fire?" I said, "Yes. You fucked the landlady, you sod." He said, "I didn't. I made it up." And he laughed. He thought it so funny that I had believed him for all those years.'

The play ran in London just about the time Richard became a ward of Philip Burton. On 17 December 1943, at the age of 18, Richard Jenkins abandoned his surname, as required by law, and took on the surname of his legal guardian, and became Richard Burton.

The Druid's Rest gave Richard his first good review, and one he never forgot. 'In a wretched part, Richard Burton showed exceptional ability.'

His papers for admission into the RAF were completed and he enrolled at Exeter College in Oxford for a six-month course in RAF training and English; one academic subject had to be included. He undertook both his RAF training and his English studies with enthusiasm.

But at first he felt 'like a foreigner' at Oxford. 'They were a bunch of toffs,' he said, 'who didn't seem to want to be around me and I certainly didn't want to be around them. They were ex-public schoolboys and I sensed a great deal of prejudice against me because I was a miner's son from a poor and very rough part of Wales.'

That experience taught Rich something he would never forget. 'I know something of what it's like to be a minority. I know something of what it's like to face racial prejudice. I won't stand for any kind of prejudice. I don't care what colour people are, or what their sexual orientation is. The only kind of people I don't like are fools.'

He may have been like a fish out of water to start with, but gradually his fellow students began to take an interest in him as he regaled them with stories of his home, his family and of the exotic ancestors he either dreamed up or had discovered he really had – or just wished he had. No one could ever be quite sure if the stories he told were true or not. Stanley Baker told me, 'He goes off into wild tales when being interviewed. I heard him once tell a journalist, from *Cosmopolitan* I think, how his father was a one-legged miner. I told him, "Hey, that's not your father. That's mine." He just said, "What does it matter whose father it is?" To Rich, the point of a story is not to inform but to regale. That's what he did; regale. It was the telling of a tale that gave him pleasure.'

Shakespeare was his great passion, and he knew whole chunks of it by heart. So too did another fellow student, Tim Hardy, who was, Rich observed, 'a toff'. Later Tim Hardy became actor Robert Hardy, one of our greatest actors, but best known to British TV audiences as Siegfried Farnum in *All Creatures Great and Small*. It was during a rehearsal session of that series at the BBC rehearsal rooms in Acton, London, that I interviewed Hardy in 1977; the subject of Richard Burton naturally came up. Hardy remembered:

'We were both in the Experimental Theatre Club in Oxford where we were going to do *The Dog Beneath the Skin*, and we were all arguing about who would direct the play. There were quite a number of us, maybe 30 or so, a lot from public schools, and everyone was suggesting this and that person to direct. Then Richard stood up and in that rich voice of his said, "If you want this play directed properly I will get you the best director in the country." And everyone stopped and listened. He had such command. There was silence while we waited to hear who this great director was. He took a dramatic pause, said "My father", and sat down again.

'Later we were studying a navigational map. I was just a "toff" to him, and I can see why, so there didn't seem any likelihood that we would ever become friends. I said to him, "So who is this father of yours – this wonderful director?"

'He said, "He's not my real father. He's my adopted father. My real father is a Welsh miner." It's funny that he only ever referred to Philip Burton as his "adopted" father, which is understandable. Why should he explain?

'Anyway, we got to talking and I told him I was going to be an actor, and he said, "Do you know Shakespeare?" I said, "Shakespeare is my subject and I am going to major in it after the war."

'He said, "What do you think of *Henry IV Parts I and II*?"

'I said, "They're the greatest plays ever written," and he agreed, and that broke down the barrier, and we became great friends and still are.'

Describing Richard during those college days, Hardy said:

'I had never met anyone like him – not before or since. He liked to hold court, maybe in a pub or at a party where he could tell his stories and people would love to hear him. He was a genuine leader. You could put half-a-dozen hellraisers in a room with him, and in ten minutes he will be their leader. You could have the best minds in the world around to have dinner with him, and he will wipe the floor with them. When we went after girls, Richard always got the girls. When we all drank, Richard out-drank us all. There was so much danger about him back then. He drank an awful lot. Pints and pints of beer. Men couldn't resist trying to compete with him. He could drink far more than anyone else, and they would just get drunk while he appeared to be sober. He was, I realised, emulating his [real] father. He drank and told stories that could be tall or slightly expanded and maybe even true, but it was the telling of them and the enormity of them that made him the centre of attraction. Before long everyone wanted him at their party. The girls certainly loved him. And the men wanted to get to know him, to be his friend. He was someone you wanted to be connected with. He was an outstanding personality.

'You couldn't help but look at him. There was an Air Force Day and we were putting up stands for a show, and he just leapt up and did half-a-dozen speeches from *Henry IV* and *Henry V*. I couldn't believe it, and I looked at all the other men who were a tough lot, and they couldn't believe it either. I tell you, they were intoxicated by him.

'But he liked to keep his distance too. I don't think he trusted a lot of the people, and he was out to show them that he was as good if not better than them. You couldn't get close to him if he didn't want you to.'

Remembering Robert Hardy from those days, Richard said to me, 'I thought that anyone who spoke as though they had been born with a silver spoon in their mouth must come from a family with exorbitant amounts of money at their disposal, so I was very glad to discover that

Robert was as hard up as anyone, although he had expensive tastes. He wanted to go to Paris for the weekend, and he asked me to lend him the money – a hundred pounds. Of course, I obliged, but I gave him the amount in £5 cheques and told him that in the event that he didn't spend it all, it would be easier for him to repay it if he had uncashed cheques rather than cash.'

When you were Richard's friend, you could certainly count on him to be helpful and generous. And that continued to be a personality trait through his life. When I went to Winchester, he paid for my bed and breakfast, and gave me money for the petrol, as well personally paying me out of his own pocket for a day's work as an extra because I wasn't on the payroll. He knew that people, individually or through whatever network they belonged to, had helped him, and he helped others. He enjoyed becoming a benefactor.

Perhaps having taken on the name of Burton, he had also taken on the responsibility that came with the name of his 'adopted' father. I think it meant something for him to be 'Richard Burton'.

Something happened during his time at Oxford that was to affect him for the rest of his life; a stupid prank that would, towards the end of his life, threaten to cripple him. Somebody at the college spiked Richard's pint of beer with wood alcohol stolen from the laboratories. The result was that Richard fell down a flight of stairs and landed in such a way that the base of his neck was badly hurt. His back was already weakened by the blows he received in rugby, but this prank was probably the cause of a lifetime of suffering which intensified in his later years.

'My shoulder freezes and sometimes the pain is so acute that I can't raise my right arm,' he told me in 1974. His suffering was hardly noticeable then; he had concealed it well for many years.

By 1978 when he was filming *The Wild Geese*, I noticed that he used his right arm a lot less than usual. 'It's not so bad,' he told me when I saw him wince with pain on the set. But it was bad. And it was getting worse.

When I saw him for the last time, on the set of *1984*, he said, 'Today I could happily murder the bloody bastard who spiked my drink and made me fall.'

Chapter Five

THE MYTH MAKER

WHEN RICH DISCOVERED that his English literature tutor, Nevill Coghill, was producing Shakespeare's *Measure for Measure* for the Oxford University Dramatic Society in the summer of 1944, he asked Coghill if he could have a part in it. All the roles were taken but Rich persisted and Coghill allowed him to audition. Rich launched into 'To be or not to be', and gave what Coghill would describe as 'the most perfect rendering I had ever heard except that given a short while before by John Gielgud'.

Not to be quite as good as Gielgud was no bad thing, and Coghill gave Rich the job of understudying the actor who was playing Angelo. Richard attended rehearsals and learned the part and, in the best, almost clichéd tradition of theatre, the actor playing Angelo was unable to go on, either because he was sick during rehearsals or was called to active service – depending on which account you hear – and Richard took over the role.

The spell he seemed to cast over the older men who tended to mentor him landed on Nevill Coghill, who managed to get the University Air Squadron to free Rich from many of his duties so he could concentrate on the play. Coghill also got permission from the Air Corps for Richard to forgo the usual short back and sides so his hair would be longer for the play.

His Angelo was a hit.

'The first thing you noticed about Richard was his enormous power,' Robert Hardy told me. 'There were moments when he totally commanded the audience by his stillness. It was sheer, raw talent. There was much to be honed. He moved awkwardly. But when he found his mark he delivered his lines and he could shake the floor.'

Richard displayed such passion that on one occasion he clawed at the stone arcade and it literally crumbled in his hands.

Hugh 'Binkie' Beaumont came up from London especially to see Richard's first night. He told Rich, 'If you've made up your mind to be an actor by the end of the war, look me up.'

Brook Williams told me that Philip Burton also arrived for opening night. 'After the play, he went to Richard's rooms at the college to await him. He was looking forward to celebrating with him, probably by discussing the whole experience. That was Phil's way of celebrating. But Rich didn't turn up until the morning. His trousers were torn and his leg was bleeding because he'd got caught on a spike while climbing over the college railings. He'd been at a party at some rich woman's house all night and had drunk so much that he'd passed out. That's what he told Phil and said he was sorry to have forgotten him, and Phil as always forgave him.'

When filling in Richard's student record card, Nevill Coghill wrote, 'This boy is a genius and will be a great actor. He is outstandingly handsome and robust, very masculine and with deep inward fire, and extremely reserved.'

The initial six-month course at Oxford over, Richard and the other recruits, including Robert Hardy, reported to RAF Babbacombe on the south coast of Torquay where they were to train for the next two months. There Richard was again faced with prejudice from ex-public school types, but before long, with no determined effort on his part, his company was gradually sought. His personality, his tales, his epic drinking won over many friends, and the toffs decided to make him one of them by inventing a public school for him to have attended called Blundles, and so he became 'Burton of Blundles'.

'They wanted me to be one of them' he recalled. 'It meant more to them than it did to me. I remained as I was. I wouldn't change for anyone.'

He became hugely popular for his talent as a raconteur. When a lecturer once failed to turn up on time, 200 impatient men began chanting for Richard who finally, and quite happily, rose to his feet to deliver his amusing tales until the visiting lecturer finally arrived.

'He didn't so much relate stories as create myths,' Hardy said. 'I heard him regaling a captive audience once and I said, "Come off it, Richard, you know that's not what happened." He said, "Never forget, we are the myth makers."

'There was something very commanding about Richard, even so young. He could command almost anything or anyone. He was the only one of us who was able to get a single sleeping accommodation for himself. The rest of us had to share.'

Richard thereafter was discovered entertaining an officer in his room, and the following day he was ordered out of line while on parade and marched off to face the music. No one knows for sure what happened, and Richard never elaborated, but ultimately nothing came of it – or nothing that anybody knew of.

While at Babbacombe, Rich made his directorial debut with *Youth at the Helm*, which Philip Burton had directed him in the previous year. Robert Hardy was given the leading role, and Rich played a small part, that of a janitor, complete with a blacked-out tooth. 'He would have made a marvellous director,' said Hardy, 'but then we would have lost an even more marvellous actor.'

He also performed in a radio production of *The Corn is Green* for the BBC in Cardiff. It was adapted from the play by Emlyn Williams about a boy from the Welsh pits – as Williams himself was – who is discovered by a schoolteacher and manages to get into Oxford and goes on to become an acclaimed actor and playwright. Williams was writing about his own life, but it was amazingly close to Richard's too.

Rich had not quite committed himself to becoming an actor at this time. To him acting was a way of getting time off from the RAF and getting paid extra for it. He wanted desperately to be a pilot but his eyesight proved to be inadequate, so he was eventually assigned the grade of trainee navigator and sent to his first posting, in Canada, early in 1945. 'It was just as well the war was almost over,' he said. 'I wasn't a very good navigator. I could have lost the war for us single-handed. I would find myself over Winnipeg when we should have been over Toronto.'

Robert Hardy saw for himself just how hopeless Richard was as a navigator: 'We were on a regular exercise, up in the clouds, and I heard him saying over the intercom, "Sorry, Oggy, I forgot my ruler." He's the bloody navigator and he forgets his ruler!

'We had to do an aircraft recognition test. The maximum score was a hundred. You lost six points if you shot a friend, eight if you failed to shoot an enemy. The CO said, "Burton!" "Yes, sir?" "Your score, Burton." "Minus 254, sir." I'd hate to think what would have happened if he'd ever been in a real aerial fight.'

With the war over, Richard was posted back to England where he was sent to an old bomber airfield, RAF Docking, in Norfolk. The men were allowed to do pretty much what they wanted while they waited for their discharge, so Richard took command and secured lodgings for himself while everyone else remained in their cold Nissen huts.

Also stationed there was actor Warren Mitchell, then under his real name of Mick Misell. I interviewed Mitchell in 1976 at Elstree Studios (where he was making a terrible military comedy called *Stand Up Virgin Soldiers*). When we got to talking about Burton, he said, 'Oh yes, Richard was in residence at the local hall because he was going to bed with the cook.'

Mitchell recalled an incident that almost contradicted Richard's hatred of racial prejudice:

'I was really upset when I heard an officer ask Burton if he was going to be an actor, and Burton replied, "Probably not, sir. You see, the trouble is the theatre's controlled by Jews."

'I bristled at that. I told him that sort of remark was what we were supposed to be fighting the war about. I really went for him, and he backed down, there and then, in front of others. Normally he would have argued until he had won if he had known he was right, but he apologised and said he had been stupid, and that way we became friends.

'I think it was something he had heard some old actor say, and he just said it on the spur of the moment. There was no prejudice in him. Well, there was, I suppose, because he thought the Welsh were marvellous, especially the Welsh-speaking Welsh and most particularly those from Pontrhydyfen and most of all the Jenkinses. That's as far as his prejudice went. He had a black dresser [Bob Wilson]. He couldn't give a damn about somebody's colour. He couldn't give a damn about *anybody*. That's what was so attractive about him. And frightening. What was sometimes frightening was what he could say, like his remark about the Jews. But it meant nothing, you see. When he knows he's offended someone, he apologises. And if he feels strongly about something, he speaks up and doesn't back down.'

Rich had no prejudice for the enemy either. When an Italian POW was accused of raping a local girl, Richard volunteered to defend him; Rich knew a little Italian from his studies at Oxford. He also knew the girl and, as it turned out, so did most of the other men from the base. He was able to get the POW acquitted and then asked the Italian to sing an aria, following which Richard sang a Welsh song.

He was called 'the Squire' and held court in the local pub, drinking and womanising. Robert Hardy told me:

'I had managed to pull some strings and get myself billeted in London where I did some typing during the day and plenty of socialising at night. I offered to get Richard transferred to London, but he was having too much fun in Norfolk. So from time to time I went up to Norfolk to visit him, and the two of us wandered over the freezing airfields of winter, talking about Shakespeare.

'When I went up to see him, it was like visiting a Tartar camp. It was chaos, and Richard was at the centre of it all. The men would go to the pub with Air Marshal's rankings chalked on their uniforms. He lived in the local hall. He was having a wonderful time. No wonder he wanted to stay there.'

Rich had a steady girlfriend for a while. She was actress Eleanor Summerfield. He must have thought a great deal of her because when she was performing in rep, he'd get however many trains he needed to reach wherever she was performing, just to spend a little time with her. They apparently regarded themselves as engaged, but when she took him to meet her middle-class mother in London, Richard was disapproved of and the engagement was cancelled.

He had maintained his friendship with Emlyn Williams and stayed with Williams and his wife Molly when he could get a weekend pass. Emlyn and Molly had two sons, Brook and Alan; Richard became Brook's godfather.

Brook, born in 1938, was delighted to find in Richard something of an older brother who looked out for him. Brook told me:

'When I was ten, I used to watch him shave. So he'd foam up my face and he taught me to shave. We'd stand side by side in front of the mirror as he showed me how to shave. He made it seem like a great art, something to take care over.

'He was always giving me tips. He'd say, "Do you know how to immobilise a man, Brookie?" "No, Rich, how do you do that?" "You pull his jacket over his arms and then – bop!" He taught me how to do a cannonball serve in tennis, and he said, "That's all you need to learn about tennis, Brookie. Give them the cannonball serve and they never get it back."

'He often came to see me in school plays and would bring a tea flask which was full of beer or martini. He'd pour it into a plastic cup and blow on it, pretending it was hot tea.'

In 1946 Rich received special permission to perform in a BBC television production of *The Corn is Green* in London. He was also allowed to record radio plays for BBC Cardiff where Philip Burton had, by then, become a full-time producer, having given up teaching. His house in Cardiff was now Richard's official home. When Rich turned 21 on 10 November 1946, he was officially no longer Philip's ward. But the two always referred to each other as 'son' and 'father' and Richard visited him whenever he could. By this time, Rich was considering becoming a writer, influenced no doubt by his guardian's success. In fact, he had written a couple of plays which were rejected; one was turned down by the BBC. Philip encouraged him to make up his mind about the future, and around this time Richard finally decided to become an actor.

His discharge came through towards the end of 1947. The original plan was that he would go to university at Oxford, as did Robert Hardy, but now that he was free he wanted to make money doing what he did best. So instead of moving in with Philip in Cardiff, he went to London to make contact once more with H.M. Tennent Ltd in the hope that Binkie Beaumont would be able to offer him work. He was put under contract at £10 a week for a year.

Now employed, although not always working, Rich sought out Stanley Baker. 'We shared cheap digs in Streatham,' Sir Stanley told me. Streatham is on the edge of south London, which meant it was inexpensive but quite a distance to travel to the West End. 'We could spend our money on having a good time. There were dance halls where we met girls – *lots* of girls – many of them Irish nurses. We earned ourselves something of a reputation. We became known as the *Palais de Dance Kings of Streatham.*

'We had one rule. We never shared a girl. If one got lucky and the other didn't, that was tough on the other. But mostly we had a girl each. We didn't always want to take them back to our place. It didn't seem a good idea to let the girls know where we lived. So we took them to the common and sowed our oats there.'

Richard did a radio play, *In Parenthesis*, for the BBC Third Programme. It was based on David Jones' book set during the First World War, delving into Welsh military history. It was a somewhat mythical epic poem which Richard thought was one of the finest things he ever did. Also in the cast were Philip Burton and poet Dylan Thomas.

Thomas used to act occasionally to earn the money that being a great poet didn't bring him. To Rich he was a *true* poet, the only kind; he was Welsh, and he drank. Rich was proud to have become the friend of Dylan Thomas who was just a few years older than he was.

Rich landed a small part in the play *Castle Anna* at the Lyric Theatre in Hammersmith in February 1948. Daphne Rye directed it. She probably did more to help Richard get started as an actor than anyone else.

Bryan Forbes, actor, screenwriter and director, also began working in London's theatreland around that time. 'I knew Richard well,' Forbes told me (in 1975 when he was directing *The Slipper and the Rose*). 'The West End belonged to Binkie Beaumont who controlled or had influence over about a dozen theatres. You had to be with Binkie if you wanted to work. It probably helped if you were homosexual. Richard, I think, went out of his way to prove he was not a homosexual and could make it on his own terms. But people like Binkie weren't idiots and they could see Richard had talent. Daphne Rye was the one who really made it happen for us.'

Daphne Rye got Richard out of Streatham and into the top floor of her house in Pelham Crescent in London; Emlyn Williams lived just a few doors along. Daphne put Rich into a tour of *Dark Summer*. 'Those plays were great experience for an ambitious actor but he just wasn't ambitious,' Brook Williams said. 'What he wanted to do was earn good money. He was beginning to wonder if he had made the right decision to become an actor because the plays had not been successful and he wasn't making good money. He decided that if he couldn't earn a decent salary from acting, he would quit. He was never obsessed with acting and he was not prepared to suffer for his art.'

Said Brook Williams:

'It might be that Rich may have quit acting but his career was saved by my father [Emlyn Williams] who was going to direct and act in a film he had also written, *The Last Days of Dolwyn*. My father was playing a Welsh businessman who plans to transform a Welsh village into a reservoir to provide water for England by flooding it. He wrote a part especially for Rich, that of the foster son of an old lady, played by Edith Evans, who refuses to leave the village.

'My father had to arrange for Richard to do a screen test for the producers [Alexander Korda and Anatole de Grunwald] because they weren't convinced about him. In the event, the producers were impressed and so my father sent Rich a telegram telling him he had the part. Rich was still touring with *Dark Summer* and didn't bother to reply. He told me later that by then he'd lost the heart for acting and he screwed up the telegram and kicked it into the waste bin, then went out for a drink.

'My father heard nothing from him until he turned up months later on the first day of filming. He'd obviously had second thoughts.'

Interiors were filmed at the London Studios in Isleworth, with locations shot in North Wales in the autumn of 1948. 'My father had some concern about the amount Rich smoked and how it could ruin his fine voice,' Brook told me, 'so he said he would give him a hundred pounds if he didn't smoke for three months. After two months, Rich owned up that he had given in and smoked. Smoking was one thing more important to Rich than money.' But that is, perhaps, putting it too simply. Richard smoked up to five packs a day. He was addicted, so no matter how hard he might have tried to last the three months, he needed the narcotic effect of tobacco. Although he hardly showed it, he was given to moments of nervousness. Some have said he was often insecure, but that isn't what Robert Hardy thought. 'I've never known anyone as secure as Richard,' he said.

But much goes on inside someone's head that can't be easily known by all and sundry. Richard kept a lot of things that troubled him from his closest friends for many years. He would become affected by mood swings. He could go from being on top of the world to becoming hammered into the ground by deep dark depression. It may not have been so evident in those early days, but it was there.

'There were days when I couldn't see the sun no matter how bright it shone,' he told me.

Although he lived a somewhat manic depressive existence

throughout much of his life, he never sought either a diagnosis or a treatment. He was terrified that he might be diagnosed with some kind of mental illness. But it wasn't just the depression that gave him cause to fear, but something that he tried to keep secret from all but the closest to him. It was epilepsy. Few things, it seems, scared him more than epilepsy. It was what he called 'this thing in my head', and he feared that it was the one thing that would define mental illness.

Chapter Six

THE THING IN HIS HEAD

Iᴎ 1974 I was alone with Richard just outside of Winchester. We had enjoyed a fine time in the morning, driving aimlessly in my father's old Morris around the countryside, looking for a pub where we might get a decent lunch. We had no map and I didn't know the area at all so I had no clue where we were going. Richard was in good spirits and there was nothing to suggest anything was untoward with him. He was tired and wanted to get away from everyone and everything connected with the film just for a day, and I was making that happen for him.

We found a country pub where Rich enjoyed a simple dish of sausages and chips and fruit juice; no alcohol. He was on the wagon. It was one of the many times he gave up drink for limited periods of time in his life. He apologised for being 'so boring'. He said he wasn't very entertaining when he was sober. I didn't agree. He was full of interesting and funny stories, and as usual I was full of questions. He spoke in a quiet tone; had he been drunk he would have talked out loud and would no doubt have gathered an audience about him. But in that country pub that day nobody seemed to either realise it was him or cared. He was left alone. Not even an autograph was asked for.

I was working for Warner Bros. at the time but had no connection to *Brief Encounter*, which Rich was making with Sophia Loren. I hadn't yet embarked on a journalistic career so I wasn't even attempting to interview him. It was just a casual conversation.

During lunch he appeared to be unsettled. His hands shook just a little. He said he felt a little 'out of sorts' but was sure he would be all right. As soon as we had finished eating, we left the pub.

'Just drive,' he said. I could see he was feeling increasingly unwell, but he didn't complain. He just sat quietly and closed his eyes.

Then suddenly he said, 'Pull over.'

I stopped the car. He opened his door and literally staggered out and dropped to the ground. It scared me to death. I didn't know where we were and saw no sign of a public telephone, although there were some cottages nearby. I crouched beside him and said, 'You're ill. Let me get some help.'

'No,' he said, grabbing my sleeve.

The shaking was worse and I thought then that he might be having a fit because I had seen a boy at school have an epileptic fit in the playground. But nothing I knew about Richard or anything he had said suggested he was in any way prone to such seizures.

He hung on to me at first, and I held him, and then he just seemed to black out in my arms while his body still shook. I really couldn't tell if he was conscious or not. I kept saying, 'Rich! Rich, can you hear me?' He just continued to shake. I sat there, cradling him, not knowing what to do; I was just 23 years old, basically lost in the countryside with one of the most famous men in the world who, for all I knew, might be about to die.

The seizure seemed to last for ever, but I think it was really just a couple of minutes. He began to come round. His eyes looked up at me and he just lay there as I held on to him. He actually hated physical contact as a rule; hugging was not something he did. He even admitted to me that he felt awkward about love scenes. But there he lay, his head in my arms and on my lap, trying to smile.

Eventually he said, 'I am sorry, Mick.'

I told him he had nothing to be sorry about.

Probably no more than five minutes after he came around, he sat up warily as he realised that he had been cradled by me, and then he got to his feet and leaned against the car.

'Normally I can tell when this sort of things is going to happen to me,' he said. 'But this time it just crept up on me.'

'I didn't know you had epilepsy,' I said.

'Is that what it is, do you think? I am too scared to want to know.'

He got into the car. 'Come on, get in,' he said.

'Shall I drive you to hospital?'

'No,' he said sharply. Then, more softly, 'I am fine now.'

I didn't start the car. Instead, we sat there for quite a time as he told me about his greatest fear – the fear of 'something wrong in my head', as he put it. 'I fear that I may go mad.'

I asked him if there was a history of mental illness in his family; he said there wasn't. But he had realised when he was in his late teens and early twenties that something was wrong in his head.

He told me it first happened when he was doing one of his early plays. He had been standing in the wings waiting to go on when he started to shake uncontrollably. He was given a couple of brandies and almost pushed on to the stage.

'Alcohol was a cure of sorts,' he said. 'It's just one reason why I have lived the life of a drunk.'

He said that the attacks got worse as he got older. He learned to recognise early signs and would occasionally get himself to hospital. He also had medication that helped. But mostly, he said, alcohol was the best cure and he believed that if he maintained a high level of alcohol in his blood it might block the seizures. He admitted that he also drank out of fear of seizures.

It seemed Rich drank out of fear of a number of things – of having a fit, of being a homosexual, of being boring.

He said he avoided undergoing whatever tests might confirm epilepsy because he distrusted doctors. I think he simply wanted not to know for sure. He seemed to equate epilepsy with madness; mental illness was a prospect that terrified him. His youngest daughter, Jessica, was autistic and schizophrenic, and he was convinced she had inherited her illness from him. He believed that if he was to have what he thought of as a kind of madness – the seizures – it only confirmed that Jessica's illness was all his fault. And I think that was more than he could have coped with.

'Promise me you won't tell anyone what happened today,' he said.

'I promise.'

'You're a good boy, Mick. You looked after me, and I shan't forget it.'

His fits remained a secret except to those closest to him. He later told me that his fourth wife, Susan, was always prepared for one of his attacks by carrying a small stick in her purse to release his tongue after an attack as it could get stuck in his throat. Rich and I must both have been lucky that day in 1974 because his tongue didn't get stuck in his throat; I wouldn't have had a clue how to have dealt with it.

He'd been kind enough to me before that, but after that episode there remained what I felt was a stronger bond between us. We were Dick and Mick.

He had another fear. As his seizures became more frequent as he got older, so too did his moments of depression. It seems that even though he was to find fame and wealth and critical acclaim, he found himself falling helplessly into deep despair. 'I am enveloped in a black cloud,' he said, 'and can't find my way out.'

He felt he should have been able to rationalise why he had such deep, dark moods but he couldn't, and it occurred to him that this was all part of his madness – this thing in his head. And it may well be that he was bipolar. Back then it was called manic depression. It's a condition that, without medication, sends the sufferer from uncontrollable highs into the depths of despair. But Richard didn't seem to have uncontrollable highs. On the other hand, he often drank so heavily that perhaps such highs couldn't be detected.

If he was bipolar, and had he known that, he would have undoubtedly been certain, without any evidence to the contrary, that he was the cause of Jessica's illness, and that would only have driven him further into long and deeper depths of depression.

There are other possibilities, none of them to do with mental illness. He was an alcoholic, although he never used that word and preferred to describe himself as 'a drunk', but overuse of alcohol must surely cause irrational moments of melancholy.

But I think there is a more likely cause, based on what I knew of him and observed first hand. He was never entirely free of the Welsh valleys, and he both loved and hated them. They gave him his identity, but they also represented the very thing he fought to escape from – poverty and his mother's death. He sought to earn wealth, not just so he would never be poor again, but so he could provide necessities and luxuries for his family, who would otherwise have probably continued to live as all other Welsh mining families did.

At the height of his fame and wealth, he kept his family close to him, even providing some of them with employment. As far as wealth was concerned, he earned in a lifetime as much as he could have hoped for, and I think there were times when he must have stopped and asked himself, 'Is there nothing more? Is this the sum total of my life?' because although he had aspirations of being one of the greatest actors in the world, he cared little for the art itself; it was just something he happened to be good at. And so, I think, he found himself at certain times in his life feeling a sense of great dissatisfaction.

I think it was something that was at its worst when and after he was with Elizabeth Taylor. 'She fascinated me endlessly,' he said, 'and she bored me far too often.' When Richard was bored, he was at his worst. And when he was at his worst, he could lose his temper in an instant, and when he did, it was scary as hell.

There is one more thing that most certainly was the cause of much of his depressive nature: his guilt. It was immense. When he gave up his first wife Sybil and, more especially, his two daughters to be with Elizabeth Taylor, he was never able to forgive himself. On the last day that I saw him in 1984, he said, 'Nothing in life has wrenched the guts out of me more than the knowledge that I gave up those I loved most for a woman,' and I knew what he meant. 'If there is any good that came out of it,' he added, 'it was that I tried to be as much of a father as I could be. But I knew it was never enough. I'll never forgive myself.'

And so there were many possible causes for his depression, and many causes for his heavy drinking. He drank to numb the guilt, to kill the fear of mental illness, to try and cure his epilepsy, to not be boring. Richard was never boring, drunk or sober. The real reason he drank – the initial reason – was because he was the son of a drunken miner who lived in a place where all the men drank heavily. It's just that Rich made a career out of it. And as the fear of mental illness and epilepsy and guilt and depression gathered momentum into a vicious circle that couldn't be broken, his life became one huge Catch 22.

Chapter Seven

THE RELUCTANT HUSBAND

Emlyn Williams related a story to me: 'Rich and I were sitting on the grass between scenes [on location for *The Last Days of Dolwyn* in North Wales], and I pointed out a young woman who was one of the extras and I told Richard, "It's time you settled down. Now she's a very sweet girl." So Richard introduced himself to her.'

The extra was Sybil Williams, a very pretty 18-year-old Welsh girl who aspired to be an actress. 'I knew she was right for him. I just knew,' said Williams. 'She came from a mining village in South Wales. What girl could have been more perfect?'

Williams had smuggled her into the filming. The budget had called for five extras but he wanted to give her work, so she became a sixth extra. Perhaps that was partly why Richard Burton felt he could smuggle me on to his sets as an extra in several of his films. If Emlyn Williams could do it, so could he.

Welsh actor Hugh Griffith, perhaps best remembered for his Oscar-winning performance as Sheik Ilderim in *Ben-Hur*, was among the cast. Rich became immediately fond of Griffith and they worked several times together.

Alexander Korda was so impressed with Burton that he signed him to a long-term contract and, with his partner Anatole de Grunwald cast Rich in *Now Barabbas Was a Robber*. It intercut various stories of men in prison; Rich played one such prisoner, curiously an Irishman called Paddy. It was still just a supporting role while the leading characters were played by Richard Greene, Cedric Hardwicke, William Hartnell, Kathleen Harrison and Leslie Dwyer. Billed just below Richard was Kenneth More.

'Richard Burton was young and inexperienced,' Kenny More told me, 'but he seemed to stand out even with all those bigger actors around him.'

Writing in the *Observer*, C.A. Lejeunne said, 'To my mind, he has all the qualities of a leading man that the British film industry badly needs at this juncture: youth, good looks, a photogenic face, obviously alert intelligence and a trick of getting the maximum effect with the minimum of fuss.'

Then he landed a part in a new Terence Rattigan play, *Adventure Story* about Alexander the Great. It was a tremendous break for Burton, arranged by the ever diligent Daphne Rye. Paul Scofield played Alexander, and Rich had the role of Hephaestion, Alexander's slightly older friend. The director was Peter Glenville.

But Richard was fired, for reasons never entirely made clear, partly because he loved to fudge the situation with varying versions of the unhappy experience. Peter Glenville told me that casting Richard had been 'a mistake. I had cast him as a favour to Daphne Rye. Alexander called his friend "My rock on which I lean," and Burton was so short that when Scofield leaned on him, he dipped down a foot or two. Burton was fine in his performance, but not the right actor physically for that part.'

I pointed out to Glenville that Scofield was no taller than Richard. Glenville agreed and said, 'It was just the image they created side by side. Alexander needed a friend who was much taller.'

Rich had fun giving his various explanations as to why he was sacked. He would ask people, 'How could I play Scofield's older friend when Scofield looked a hundred and eight years old?'

But being fired was a huge blow to Rich and he went into despair, even though he would make light of it. He also went into despair over his impending marriage to Sybil.

When I interviewed Emlyn Williams in 1975, he said of Sybil, 'She has elegance, and she always appears to be on the point of laughing, whatever her mood.'

'I know her well,' said Stanley Baker (speaking to me in 1970 when I was with him for publicity on the film *The Last Grenade*). 'We came from the same village. We were close friends. When I heard that Rich and Sybil had got together, I thought, *the lucky bastard.* She was the best thing that ever happened to him. She was someone you just wanted to be around. Rich was like that too, so they were a wonderful couple.'

Everyone who knew Sybil had the same kind of fondness for her. 'Marvellous girl!' said Robert Hardy.

'She's simply a marvellous warm woman,' said John Gielgud.

But the great mystery is, why did Richard marry her? 'I was not,' he admitted, 'a monogamous man in those early days. Not till I met Elizabeth [Taylor].'

He and Sybil were quickly engaged. Perhaps too quickly.

Baker may have thought she was the best thing that ever happened to him, but he knew Richard wasn't really enthusiastic about marrying her. 'The night before the wedding he slipped into a terrible mood. Really dark despair,' said Baker (this time in 1975 when I formally interviewed him). 'He said he wasn't really ready for marriage, so I asked him why he was marrying her. He said, "She expects it. She expects the ring on her finger." I told him, "Don't do it if it isn't what you want." And he said, "But I have to. Maybe it will save me." And I said, "Save you from what?" And he said, "Myself!" I had never seen Rich so depressed, so full of despair. He had been slipping into some dark area inside himself, and I think he hoped that Sybil would dig him out of it.'

Rich had little explanation as to why he married Sybil. He told me, 'It was the romantic thing to do. I believed in romance. But I wasn't finding it for myself. I thought being married would give it to me.'

The wedding took place within five months of meeting, on 5 February 1949, at the Kensington Register Office. There was a small reception at Daphne Rye's house where the new Mr. and Mrs. Burton were to live. Legend has it that Richard abandoned the celebration to listen to the Scotland versus Wales Rugby International on the radio. Actually, Sybil had to go to work; she was assistant stage manager at a West End theatre where *Harvey* with Sid Field was running. So Richard took the opportunity to listen to the match. There was a rumour that after the match, he drunkenly fooled around with Daphne's maid.

After falling into a well of gloom over being fired from *Adventure Story*, his life was brightened when he was given the title role of Shakespeare's *Henry V* in a Saturday Night Theatre radio production which was broadcast on 23 April 1949, Shakespeare's birthday. Robert Hardy had recommended him to the director, Frank Houser. Rich arrived for the audition nervous and drunk. He was on the edge and, he told me, 'ready to give the whole damn thing up'.

His confidence had been shattered by the *Adventure Story* episode, and he may have been having difficulty trying to play the role of married man. His audition for *Henry V* was a disaster. Nevertheless, he won the part, although how and why is another mystery. No doubt, people worked quietly behind the scenes to ensure he got the role. And in the event, he was, I have been told, magnificent as King Hal.

He was now a jobbing actor in films, which to him was just a way to earn better money than he got in the theatre. The roles were undemanding but he did his best. In fact, he had learned how to behave professionally from the start, always arriving on time and always knowing his lines.

Waterfront, starring Robert Newton, gave Richard second billing as an out-of-work ship's engineer; the film, released in 1950, was a melodrama about unemployment in Merseyside. Then he was in *The Woman with No Name* as a Norwegian airman who marries a woman suffering from amnesia, played by Phyllis Calvert. He wasn't a film star, but he was getting regular work in films. The pay was good even if the parts were uninteresting. What he really wanted to do was prove that he could be a great theatrical actor.

Daphne Rye didn't give up on him. She was got him an audition for *The Lady's Not for Burning,* a verse play by Christopher Fry. But despite his triumph as Henry V on radio, he was in a terrible state for his audition. 'I have never known such a gifted actor who was so lacking in confidence,' Sir John Gielgud, who directed the play, said. 'He shook, I suppose with nerves or maybe because he needed a drink. I told him he should come back the next day and try again.'

Rich told me that he never knew if he shook because of nerves or because he needed a drink or because it was the onset of a mild seizure. The only thing he knew for sure, he said, was that 'the best cure for a fit *or* nerves is alcohol'.

So he had a drink or two to steady himself for the second audition. 'It was Christopher Fry who persuaded Gielgud to give me the part,' he said. He always admired writers more than almost anybody and he liked to give someone like Fry credit for any success he had. It was odd that he rarely liked to credit John Gielgud with being the one who really mentored him. Gielgud told me that he made the decision himself to cast Richard, 'because he was so striking, and his voice so very beautiful. And it was only a small part, so we could afford to take a chance.'

It may be that it was at this time, or close to it, that Gielgud made a pass at Richard, and Rich thereafter preferred not to credit Gielgud with giving him the role, even though he and Gielgud worked together again a number of times and he considered Gielgud to be his mentor. 'I like John,' Rich told me. 'He's the most gifted actor and he isn't full of himself. He is also a good director. I was in awe of him. He was my idol.'

There had been another newcomer at that audition. Her name was Claire Bloom.

Richard would tell me, 'I only ever loved two women before Elizabeth.' Sybil was one, Claire Bloom the other. The affair that he would have with Claire Bloom would be far more than a romp in the hay and lasted a considerable time. It was generally agreed, by people like Brook Williams and Stanley Baker, that before Elizabeth Taylor, the one woman who Richard might conceivably have left Sybil for was Claire Bloom.

I met her only once, when she was filming *Clash of the Titans* at Pinewood Studios in 1979. I was there as the guest of Laurence Olivier, so I took my chance to talk a little to her. Of course, I already knew that she and Rich had been passionately in love, but not quite daring to ask her outright about it, I did mention that Richard spoke well of her as an actress and as a friend.

She told me, 'I met Rich for the first time when we both auditioned for *The Lady's Not for Burning*. I thought how beautiful he was with those green eyes. We read a scene and he was very nervous. At the end of it he made some joke to cover his nervousness. John Gielgud and Hugh Beaumont [the play's producer] thanked us both.

'You often expect to wait forever to hear if you've got a job, but I heard that evening from my agent, and Rich had also got the part. So it was a lucky day for us both.'

Richard went straight to see Emlyn Williams to tell him his news. 'Binkie Beaumont offered Rich a standard £10 a week fee,' Williams told me. 'Rich demanded £20. Beaumont agreed on £17. 10s. When Rich got home and told me this, I told him to go straight back and demand £30. He did, and he got it.'

Rich told me, 'I learned quickly that I shouldn't settle for what I was told I could get because I can always get more.'

In rehearsals, Gielgud found Richard had 'a real instinct for theatre. You hardly had to indicate what you wanted, and he got it and never changed it.' However, rehearsals didn't get off to a good start. 'Richard kept yawning and checking his watch to see if it was time for a break so he could go to the pub. That was very careless of him. I told him, "Richard, you really must stop thinking about beer and think about what we're trying to do here." I think he had a real respect for me because he quickly pulled himself together and after that he worked hard.'

It was during rehearsals that Richard and Claire fell in love. Rod Steiger, who later married Claire Bloom, talked to me in London in 1984, shortly after the news had broken that Richard Burton had died.

'During the tour she and Richard lived in cheap rooms, and he'd recite poetry to her,' Steiger said. 'That voice of his – well, that would seduce any woman. But Claire didn't just jump into bed with him. They didn't touch. She looked forward to being on stage with him every night when they were able to share a little kiss. She was so young. So was he. And he was only just married. I don't know what he was looking for. But they fell in love during that tour.'

They played to near-empty houses on tour, but the play was a surprise success in London, where it opened in May 1949 and ran for a year. 'I spent a year sharing the same stage as John Gielgud,' said Richard. 'It was the best drama education I could get.' Richard Burton never attended RADA or any of the other formal drama schools. He had a natural talent, and he learned to act on the job. One time, Gielgud said to me, 'Richard Burton was, perhaps, my best star pupil.'

Although Rich had only a small role, he was often given praise in reviews, which delighted him. It was the turning point in his career, and he felt like he had really, finally made it. In fact, he had not been acting for very long; many actors who achieve greatness have much longer apprenticeships, but he was in a hurry to either become a success or give it up altogether.

Gielgud learned from other actors that Richard was stealing every scene he was in without meaning to. 'Alec Guinness said to me, "You know that scene where you and Pamela [Brown] were deep in discussion and Burton was simply scrubbing the floor." I said, "Yes, an important scene." He said, "I couldn't take my eyes of Burton." Then I heard the same from other people. That's a rare gift, a presence. It's also dangerous because it's something neither he nor anyone else has any control over.'

Claire Bloom recalled that 'when Richard was on the stage, he was hypnotic. It's his eyes, but also a quality that you can't define which I suppose is star quality. And he was very natural. He'd learned no techniques. If I made a mistake, John Gieglud would say to me, "Watch Richard, my dear. Just be as simple and as natural as he." '

Claire, according to Steiger, was besotted with Richard, although nothing sexual occurred between them during their first year together. Keeping a considerable amount of discretion in 1979, Claire told me, 'Everyone in the company thought we were having an affair.'

Gielgud remarked to me, 'Oh, yes, Richard and Claire – I have no idea what they got up to.'

They got up to nothing at all, according to Rod Steiger. Not at that time, anyway. When *The Lady's Not for Burning* came to an end, Richard and Claire parted as friends. The surprise, I suppose, is that it took Rich took so long to getting around to having a full-blown affair with Claire. He did, after all, pioneer the trend of sleeping with all his leading ladies – or most of them; there were, apparently, a few who resisted him.

He certainly had no intention of ever leaving Sybil, but he was a very reluctant husband. The only thing that everyone knew was that, generally speaking, no matter who Richard was sleeping with, he would always go back to Sybil.

The play was such a success that Fry's verse plays suddenly became a vogue, and in 1950 Richard was in another, *A Phoenix Too Frequent*. In fact, Rich had to leave *The Lady's Not for Burning* so he could do the new Fry play, which was just a two-week engagement in Brighton. Then there was another Fry play, *The Boy with a Cart*, in January 1950, again directed by John Gielgud. It was a one-act play in which he pushed an old woman about the stage in a wheelbarrow in search of a sign from God.

'It was a play with no set,' Gielgud recalled. 'Everything was constructed out of Burton's great talent for miming. He mimed building a cathedral, and it was spell-binding to watch him.'

Stewart Granger, who was then an established leading man in British films, saw *The Boy with a Cart* and wanted to meet Burton.

'I'd seen Richard Burton in a small part in a West End play [presumably *The Lady's Not for Burning*], so when I saw that he was appearing in a play in Hammersmith, I went to see him. He was breathtakingly good. Afterwards I went to see him to pay my respects. I knocked on his dressing room door and he said, "Come in", and I walked in and he stood there in just a jockstrap and clutching a glass of beer.

'He looked at me and said, "Oh my God, a bloody film star."

'I said, "Do excuse me but I just wanted to tell you that I think you're the most brilliant young actor I've ever seen, and I just wanted to tell you. That's all."

'I was about to go but he grabbed my arm and said, "Damnit, I've only got beer, I'm afraid, but if you'd like one . . ."

'I said, "No thanks. I've got someone waiting for me, but listen, when you get to Hollywood, come and look me up. I'll be over there in a few weeks."

'He said, "No thank you. I'm not going to Hollywood."

'I said, "Oh yes you are. You can be sure of that. So when you do, promise to look me up." So he promised that in the unlikely event that he ever went to Hollywood he'd look me up, and we shook hands. That was the first time I met him.'

Granger's prediction that Richard would go to Hollywood proved right, but before that he took his first trip to America, in November 1950, to appear in *The Lady's Not for Burning* at the Royale Theatre in New York, appearing again with John Gielgud.

There was another film, *Green Grow the Rushes*, an amiable comedy (released in 1951) about a Kentish village involved in smuggling. Richard co-starred with Roger Livesey and Honor Blackman.

Then came the highlight of Richard's career – his life, even – up to that point. He was picked by Anthony Quayle to play Prince Hal at Stratford as part of the 1951 Festival of Britain.

He suddenly had his chance to be a great Shakespearean actor.

Chapter Eight

THE WATCHFUL CELT

A NTHONY QUAYLE HAD a reputation as a fine director and actor of the stage before establishing himself as a good character actor in films.

'The first time I saw Richard Burton was in *The Boy With a Cart* and he was simply magical,' Sir Anthony Quayle recalled in 1977. 'I was looking for a Prince Hal for *Henry IV Parts I and II* to perform during the festival of Britain of 1951 at Stratford. I saw Burton and I knew he was Prince Hal.

'But I didn't approach Richard directly. I wanted both him and Sybil; he for Hal and she for Lady Mortimer in *Part I* which is a Welsh-speaking role. So I decided to ask her first, and told her I really wanted her to play Lady Mortimer, and she seemed delighted. So then I said, "And now try to get your husband to play Prince Hal," and I think Richard rather enjoyed that sly approach.'

While curiously denying John Gielgud credit, Rich always said that it was Quayle, who played Falstaff as well as directing, who was the one who gave him his big break. Well, in a way that was true because playing Prince Hal was a dream come true for Rich; he and Robert Hardy had often talked about those plays.

'I can't claim that I discovered Richard Burton,' Sir Anthony told me. 'He'd already attracted a lot of attention in *The Lady's Not for Burning* and the film *The Last Days of Dolwyn.*'

I was puzzled why Quayle seemed so eager to virtually pass over that episode; he had directed a number of very successful plays and was happy to be able to boast that he had discovered Robert Hardy and Robert Shaw – but not Richard Burton. John Gielgud gave me the clue; 'Oh, I think you'll find that Tony [Quayle] discovered what a difficult task it can be to direct Richard.'

When I saw Quayle next, in 1983, I told him what Gielgud had said, and he conceded rather wearily, 'When Richard did Shakespeare, the director never directed him. Philip Burton directed him.'

If anyone had thought that Philip Burton had finished mentoring Richard, they were very much mistaken. When it came to Shakespeare, Rich always turned to Philip, regardless of who the director was. Phil came up from Cardiff to go over every scene and every line of the play with Richard.

'It was Philip Burton's dream that his adopted son should play that part in Stratford above any other place,' said Quayle, 'and he had virtually taught Richard how to do the play years earlier. So when I cast Burton, he sent for his guardian, and they worked on the play together.'

This was, indeed, a slap in the face for Quayle. Philip's interpretation of Prince Hal was not Quayle's. Falstaff is one of the great comic characters of Shakespeare, and Richard arrived at rehearsals word perfect, playing the prince with a serious tone to it that didn't play well with the comedy of Falstaff.

Rich once told me – and often repeated it to emphasise the fact –

'When I play a part – *any* part – I don't try to become that character. I am not like Laurence Olivier who can bend himself to be whoever he is playing. Rather I bend the character to become more like me. I had no formal training as an actor. I never learned those tricks. I am superstitious about my acting. I don't know how it happens, and if I try to discover its source, I might lose it. So playing Prince Hal was Hal becoming like me, and when I played the part, there was no way for me to change it. I can prove very unsettling for directors, I know. Tony Quayle was very unhappy with me when I was Hal to his Falstaff. But I couldn't play Hal any differently, you see.

'Maybe it's the weakness in me as an actor. I don't mean to be difficult. But when I'm cast, I *will* play it my way, or I can't play it at all. When you're on stage, you're alone, no matter how many people are also on stage. You're fighting for your life. I can't see it any other way.'

I asked Rich if he felt that acting was a competition with other actors. 'It's always a competition with *myself*,' he said. 'And when I have bettered myself and can do no better, I become bored. But in competing with myself, I naturally compete with everybody else. They are playing against me, and it must be difficult for them. I can't help them, I can only help myself.'

This, then, was Richard Burton, not only in his earlier, rough and untrained years, but as he would always be, fighting to make every part he played his. He couldn't help but undercut Quayle's attempts to bring the humour out of Falstaff. Little wonder, then, that Quayle showed no delight in recalling the time he and Richard shared the stage, although they were very good friends in later years. But Quayle did make mention of what he called Richard's 'mystical talent'. Sir Anthony said, 'It's quite uncanny and even superstitious. He has a mystical relationship with his talent which I am sure has a lot to do with his Welshness. But I don't know where that talent or that mysticism comes from. It's what makes him utterly watchable. It's not a talent learned or that can be taught. It's simply summoned up by him, and nobody else can do what he does. And when you share the stage with him, you have to expect to fight or go under.'

Not all critics appreciated Burton's style of Shakespeare. Or even his style of acting in anything. He was criticised for being 'wooden', and too 'overt'. But he had a champion in Kenneth Tynan, one of the most respected and outspoken theatre critics who wrote for the London *Evening Standard* and the *Observer*; he said that Richard's performance of Hal 'turned interested speculation to awe as soon as he started to speak; in the first intermission the local critics stood agape in the lobbies. Burton is still a brimming pool, running disturbingly deep; at twenty-five he commands a repose and can make silence garrulous . . . Fluent and sparing of gesture, compact and spruce of build, Burton smiles where other Hals have guffawed, relaxes where they have strained, and Falstaff must work hard to divert him. In battle, Burton's voice cuts urgent and keen – always likeable, always amiable.'

That review made the people of theatreland sit up and take notice of what Tynan called 'the watchful Celt'.

Stratford proved to be a place of unquestionable and delirious happiness for Rich. 'It was one of the happiest times of his life,' recalled Robert Hardy, there to play Archbishop Scrope in *Henry IV Part I*. 'He bought his first car in Stratford. It was a Flying Standard, and I taught him to drive.' It was the beginning of Richard's love of posh cars; he would later own a Mark 10 Jaguar, a Cadillac and a red MG which he loved and kept for years.

He enjoyed having Sybil in the play – for once he was able to legitimately sleep with his leading lady – and there were friends and family from Wales coming up to visit. 'The Welsh are here,' Richard was heard to declare, 'and the English are afraid of us.' The Dirty Duck, the favourite pub of actors in Stratford, rocked to the Welsh tales told by Rich and his friends, and also to the Welsh songs he led his Welsh contingent in.

Richard had a favourite anecdote he often recounted about his time rehearsing as Prince Hal. This is how he told it to me:

'We were doing a dress rehearsal well into the early hours of the morning. I was in full armour. I knew we were in for a long night so my dresser brought 18 bottles of India Pale Ale in for me. All half-pint bottles. I got through them all and just as we reached the Battle of Shrewsbury, which went on interminably, I had reached that point where I was pretty desperate to relieve myself of all those pale ales. So I asked Tony Quayle if we could stop for the night, and he said, "Oh, no, no, Rich, not now."

'I said, "But, Tony, I really need a break."

'He said, "We'll take a break in half an hour."

'I said, "Really, Tony . . ."

'He said, "Please, Richard, just keep going."

'And I said, "Very well," and I released nine pints of India Pale Ale into my costume and it leaked out and formed a rather large pool on the stage.

'And Tony called, "Okay, take a break!"'

During the run of the play Sybil decided to give up acting. 'She wanted to dedicate herself to Richard's career,' Stanley Baker recalled, 'and to give him children. That's what they wanted so very badly – a family of their own.'

Michael Redgrave directed Rich in *Henry IV Part II* and then it was Quayle's turn again, this time *Henry V* with Richard in the title role. Playing the Archbishop was Hugh Griffith. Richard always took great delight in recounting the funny stories about his career, especially when they involved characters like Hugh Griffith. He recalled:

'I had a hidden springboard so I could leap on to it and straight on to my horse and go into "Once more unto the breach . . ." It looked like I had been riding a horse all my life and could vault on to the back of a horse like the cowboy stars. Except that one night Hugh Griffith, under heavy disguise as a soldier, slipped on to the stage unnoticed and moved the bloody horse. I hit that springboard, got one leg over the horse but ended up upside almost down, my balls crushed and my eyes stinging with tears, but I managed to deliver, "Once more unto the breach . . ." while I could hear Griffith chuckling away in the wings.'

Richard laughed at the indignity Griffith had caused him.

Henry V was followed by *The Tempest* with Richard playing Ferdinand; it was directed by Michael Benthall. Not all the critics admired Richard's rendering of the Bard, but nobody could deny that he hadn't made an impact.

In December 1951, Richard returned to New York, to play in *Legend of Lovers* by Jean Anouilh. Directed by Peter Ashmore, it also featured Hugh Griffith. It was probably too wordy and thoughtful to be a grand success, but Richard had the time of his life with Hugh Griffith to work alongside.

It was about then that he got a call from Noël Coward asking him to take part in a recording of his operetta *Conversation Piece*. At London's Claridges in 1972, I met Noël Coward, and we talked about two of our favourite people – Laurence Olivier was one and Richard Burton the other. Sir Noël recalled, 'When I decided to record *Conversation Piece*, I thought I'd give this new chap Richard Burton a chance to take part. He had such a wonderful voice. He was in New York and I gave him a call on the telephone, and I said, "I would like you to take part in this recording," and he said, "Yes, I would be delighted to." So I got my agent to call him and offer him 200 dollars for the recording. Richard said, "Oh no, I don't work for 200 dollars, even if it is for Noël Coward." So I telephoned him again and said, "Listen to me. You *will* do *Conversation Piece* for 200 dollars, and you will like it," and he damn well did it.'

Richard was back on the London stage in April 1952 in *Montserrat*, thanks again to Daphne Rye who landed him the role in this prestigious production adapted by Lillian Hellman and produced by Binkie Beaumont. It had a limited run of six weeks, during which Richard excelled as a young captain in Venezuela's fight for independence in 1812.

Next, Anthony Quayle asked him to come back to Stratford. 'He turned it down,' said Quayle. 'He felt he needed to have some time before doing any more Shakespeare, which I thought was a mistake.'

Richard defended his decision. 'It was wonderful of Tony to ask me back again, but I had a gut feeling that I needed a bit of an interval. I'd had some success in '51, and I felt that I might not do so well. It wasn't fear. It was just a hunch. I have always tried to follow my hunches. Not always with much success. In this case, I was right to step back because if I hadn't, I wouldn't have gone to Hollywood which, despite the material I had to work with there, was a major step in my career.'

Hollywood had indeed beckoned, thanks to Alexander Korda who loaned Richard to 20th Century Fox for three films. Richard was glad to go. 'I knew there had to be more money to be made in Hollywood even if the work could sometimes be execrable. And it wasn't greed. I needed the money not just for me, but for my family – my brothers and sisters. It was time to give them something in return.'

Korda threw a lavish party to send Richard off. He staggered on to the plane floating on alcohol and could barely remember the 13-hour flight to New York. Then he flew another 11 hours to Los Angeles, helped along by more alcohol. He was met by a studio executive who wondered what his studio were paying for when he saw Rich in crumpled clothing, unshaven and drunk, getting, or rather stumbling, off the plane and into the studio car that swept him to his Beverly Hills hotel where a complimentary bottle of Scotch awaited him.

Shaved, showered and dressed, he was taken to a Hollywood party where, plied with yet more booze, he recited Dylan Thomas, talked of Shakespeare, sang and told stories. He rather loudly captivated the other guests with his voice, his energy and outgoing personality.

But what they were seeing was Richard Burton egged on by copious amounts of alcohol. They had no idea how terrified he would have been without plenty of Dutch courage.

'When I knew I was first going to Hollywood I was shit scared,' he told me. 'I didn't know what to expect, and they didn't know me. I didn't much care for flying, so I flew best drunk. Coming from Wales I knew I could always take on the English reserve, but Americans could be brash and these weren't ordinary Americans – they were Hollywood! The worst of the lot. I had to be *more* brash, *more* loud than any of them. And I could do that drunk. It's funny because I was never out of control when drunk. Just . . . *bigger*!'

Richard was habitually drinking now to control the fits. 'There were times when I would shake. I never knew for sure if it was the beginning of a seizure. The only thing that steadied me and kept the fit at bay was alcohol. So I drank far too much for far too long.'

The Americans started calling him 'Dick Burton'. He recalled, 'They were just being friendly and as soon as I met them, they were calling me Dick. I asked them if they would kindly call me Richard.'

He recalled a party, one of his first, in Hollywood, at a swanky Bel Air house:

'I was very nervous but I drank and talked and tried to make myself acceptable, and people were mostly very kind, and they laughed at my stories; that to me is people being kind!

'I spotted an extraordinarily beautiful girl sitting on the opposite side of the pool, reading a book. She lowered the book, took off her sunglasses and looked at me. Then she went back to reading her book. I continued telling my stories of being a poor miner's son to those who would listen, but all the time I was watching her. She was so beautiful she took my breath away. I would not be exaggerating when I say that she was the most astonishing girl I had ever seen, and I was annoyed that she was ignoring me. So I gave my best story; about my grandfather rolling down the hill in his wheelchair to his death which always got big laughs the way I tell it. But when I had finished, I looked over at her. She was turned away and in deep conversation with another woman. I was so frustrated that I had made no impression on this girl, and I had to ask someone who she was. They said, "Oh, her; that's Elizabeth Taylor."

'And that's how much impact I made upon her the first time I saw her!'

When I did a little work on *The Mirror Crack'd* in 1979, I asked Elizabeth if she recalled that particular party and seeing Richard for the first time. 'Oh my God, yes! He was just so full of himself and didn't stop talking about himself, so I gave him the cold shoulder.' And at that, she let out a loud laugh.

During those first weeks in Hollywood, Rich established himself as quite a hellraiser. Some of the regular hellraisers of Hollywood decided that they would not accept him into their own little society, but one did. He was Errol Flynn. Richard Burton was about to get a taste of raising hell Flynn-style, and it nearly destroyed his Hollywood career before it started as Errol led him down a path that he would never have trod back in the UK.

Chapter Nine

HOLLYWOOD HELLRAISING

'I T WAS AN education, but a distasteful one,' Rich said when telling me about one particular Hollywood hellraising event he always regretted. He would never have told me this tale if it hadn't been for Ava Gardner, who was a friend of mine and who insisted, when she knew I was spending time with Rich, that I should press him about tales he had told her when they worked together on *Night of the Iguana* in 1963.

John Huston was another who gave me the tip-off; he had directed *Night of the Iguana* and I worked for him for a while in 1974. When I got together with Huston at Ava's house in London that year, the stories were flying.

One of these tales was about one of Huston's favourite people, Errol Flynn. Ava didn't really know Flynn, but she had heard Richard talk about him. It wasn't one of those tales that Rich repeated *ad nauseam* like most of his pub tales. This was a reserved-ticket-only story, much of which I heard from Ava and Huston, and a little from Richard.

It probably helped that I knew Ava and Huston so well; Rich responded to friends of his friends, and as I had become a friend of Richard's anyway, I needed only to give him the right cue to get his response.

It was the early 1950s and Richard was still new in Hollywood. Already word had spread about his marathon drinking sessions and also his sexual dalliances with any willing female participants. But despite all that, he still maintained a certain moral code. 'I always went back to Sybil,' he said. That seemed to be the one unbreakable rule.

It may not have seemed much of a moral code considering that he

64

was having affairs behind her back – or maybe even with her knowledge; the jury has long been out on that one – but there was, as contrary as it sounds, a line of morality that Richard would not cross. Unless pushed.

Errol Flynn pushed him. 'Flynn got sex wherever he could,' John Huston told me. 'His sexual appetite was insatiable; no wonder he got himself into so much trouble all the time.' Flynn, charged but acquitted of statutory rape – acquitted but not innocent – and given to crossing the border into Mexico for sex with boys, thought nothing of paying for sex with prostitutes. 'I don't know what drove him,' said Huston. 'Maybe it was the season, or a full moon, or just a sudden whim.'

Whatever his motivation, he decided he would take Richard to a favourite brothel of his.

'Rich didn't want to go,' said Ava. 'He made all sorts of excuses to get out of going with Flynn.'

'Ah, yes, but Flynn could be very persuasive,' said Huston.

Richard was delighted when he first met Flynn. 'Errol was as dashing in real life as he was on the screen,' he said. 'It wasn't just his looks, which were fading by then although he was still remarkably handsome. It was his personality. Warm, friendly and just slightly dangerous. I don't mean he would knock you on your arse. It was more to do with his complete lack of discipline and his aptitude for being impulsive without a thought for the consequences. He turned up and said, "Hello, sport. Just came to say welcome to Babylon and wish you well with whatever pleasure takes your fancy." That's pretty much his opening remark to me.'

Flynn, despite his reputation, had a certain culture. He was a great admirer of John Barrymore, and he could recite great chunks of Shakespeare. 'He just didn't try to do it in public,' said Huston. 'Errol was a really fine actor; he just didn't want the world to know it. "It would ruin my reputation," he said. So he enjoyed mixing with those with whom he could discuss the arts and poetry and plays, but with whom he could also have a good time. He thought Richard Burton, the newcomer to Hollywood, would be such a person.'

But Flynn hadn't counted on Richard's moral line in the sand. 'He wanted to show me a good time,' Rich recalled, 'and that sounded just fine with me.' For Richard, a good time was being with friends, having a drink and telling stories. His womanising tended to be basically a one-on-one private arrangement, although, curiously, he rarely tried to make a secret of it. He told me:

'Flynn had this idea that he would pay a prostitute – his *Welcome To Hollywood* gift for me. "I know the best whorehouse in town," he said, "and the best whore in the whorehouse. She's yours, and it's all on my tab." My God, this man had a tab at a brothel!

'So I said, not wishing to be rude, "That's very decent of you, Errol, but I don't go with prostitutes."

'"But my dear Richard, this girl will do things for you no woman has ever done for you before." I'm not easily embarrassed, but I was at that moment. I said, "Errol, when I'm with a woman, I love her for that period of time. It isn't just a quickie," and he said, "I promise you, you will *love* her, and it won't be quick at all." He had an answer for everything.

'And, of course, he was plying me with plenty of booze, so I was relaxing quite nicely. I was really very anxious when I got to Hollywood. The cool exterior people see can often be a lot less cool on the inside.

'He just wouldn't take no for an answer. And I was very stupid. I decided that if I was going to experience life to the full, then why not follow Flynn? What is it they say? In like Flynn! So I was in like Flynn. Not like me at all. I always go my own way. But that night I went his.'

And so he did, all the way to the brothel. Richard told Huston something he didn't tell me – but Huston told me anyway. 'Richard admitted he was swept along with the whole Hollywood thing, and really, he was very vulnerable. He was going to raise hell the Hollywood way, he decided. Well, we've all done a little of that. He was going to test the water, so to speak. And he dipped his toe in.'

When I asked Richard why he decided to go along with Flynn, he shrugged and said:

'It seemed like a good bad idea at the time.

'I thought it's what everyone did in Hollywood. Well, damnit, they *did*. Well, a good many of them did. They just didn't go to brothels. When they wanted a call girl, they *called* the girl. She came to them. But Flynn liked the whole kind of debauched thing of going to what he called the "house of well-repute".

'Actually it was a very nice house. Tidy, clean, welcoming, and the girls were lovely. As beautiful as any Hollywood actress. Of course, that's what they were – actresses. They just never got the work, so they did the work they could get.

'They had girls who sort of looked like famous film stars. They had a Susan Hayward and a Lana Turner. Even the Madam was a fine-looking woman.'

Huston told me that the Madam had been a starlet from the silent screen days who just hadn't been lucky enough to get a break. 'I knew her pretty well,' Huston said. 'Like a lot of pretty girls, she had come to Hollywood hoping to become a star, got told that she could get into the picture business by making stag movies, and the next thing she knew she was entertaining studio heads in person. But she never complained. She said, "I have a good life, make good money, and when I got older I didn't have to fuck anyone I didn't want to fuck 'cos the men all want the younger girls and not some old broad like me." She went into business, running her whorehouse and retired a pretty rich lady.'

David Niven was also familiar with this whorehouse although he insisted he never used it himself. So it seems to have been a well-known establishment with rich and famous clients; Richard Burton was reluctant to become one of them. He told me, 'The Madam said, "What can we do for you this evening, sir?" And I said, "I'm just looking, thank you." I'd got very cold feet – *freezing* cold feet – and I thought I'd be just as happy to sit and wait while Flynn had his fun. But he said, "Come on, sport, this is on me. Have a good time."'

Richard was reluctant to go any further. 'I just didn't see the point. I never had trouble finding a woman, and I never had to pay. So it was all really rather distasteful.'

Flynn got offended and said that if Richard wouldn't pick a woman, he'd pick one for him. And so he did. 'I'd lost all interest,' said Richard. 'But there I was with a woman for the next few hours or so.'

'What did you do?' I asked him.

'I recited Dylan Thomas and David Jones. At first she said, "I see, the kinky type." I said, "No, my dear, it's called culture. Let me share some with you." And that's all we did.'

So there was Richard Burton, in a brothel, with a prostitute, with his mind not on sex but on poetry. 'She loved it,' said Richard. 'It made her cry.'

Flynn was off in some other room with the prostitute of his choice, and Rich thought the evening would end sedately enough and without his morals – such as they were – being sullied. But no one was to know that on that very night the place would be busted by the police.

'I heard a great commotion downstairs and the girl I was with groaned and said, "Oh no, it's the cops."

'I nearly had a heart attack. The cops! I saw my Hollywood career coming to an abrupt end. My *whole* career! I would never be able to show my face in public again. Especially not in Wales.'

Everyone in the place was herded into the downstairs lounge. The Madam was deep in conversation with the officer in charge. Richard recalled:

'She seemed to be trying to come to an arrangement with him, but he didn't seem to want to know. I couldn't understand how this could be happening. I thought those places had some kind of arrangement with the police – at least, that's what Flynn had told me.

'The Madam was getting mad and the cops were about to herd us all out. The last thing I wanted was to be taken down to the cop shop and have my mug shot taken. But Flynn laughed; it was all a big game to him. That's when the police officer saw Flynn. "Hey, Errol, how are you doing?" "I'm doing just grand, Benny." They were like old friends.

'Flynn put his arm around Benny's shoulder and they talked and laughed, and the next thing I knew, Flynn was paying for all the cops to have a girl each, and the whole thing was settled. Then Flynn slapped me on the back and said, "There you go, sport, problem solved."

'I said, "Glad to hear it, Errol. I'll leave you to pay my bill." He said, "Are you going so soon?" I said, "Nothing would keep me here another minute. I have just lost ten years off my life."

'And he said, "That's what life is all about. You live it – every minute of it – because you never know when it will all end."'

Rich looked back on Flynn's eventual fate, dying at the age of 50 from a heart attack, with the body of a man 20 years older. Richard very nearly went the same way, but that was still in the future. His main concern was to get right away from the brothel and hope nobody would give away his secret.

'It didn't matter a damn if anyone said, "Errol was with a prostitute again," because that was Errol,' said John Huston. 'But Richard was mortified that he had actually gone there in the first place, and as far as I know he has never set foot in such a place again.'

It might have seemed like the nightmare was over. But it wasn't. Despite Flynn's generosity in providing sexual entertainment for the cops, one of them, it seemed, had taken notice of the Brit in the brothel. And this cop was an Irishman who hated the English. 'The damned idiot didn't know Richard was Welsh,' said Huston. 'So the next morning, poor Richard was suddenly arrested and taken down to the local precinct where this Irish cop was trying to decide what to charge him with.

'Richard was rather hung over and didn't have the wherewithal to deal with it all. He was thrown into a cell and he must have figured that was it for him.'

Rich might have hoped that Errol Flynn would have turned up to square everything, but David Niven summed up Flynn best when he said of his old friend Errol, 'You always knew where you stood with Flynn because he'd always let you down.'

He didn't disappoint. Flynn was nowhere to be seen.

The Irish cop finally came to Richard's cell. Rich demanded to know what he was charged with. 'For being an English bastard faggot actor,' said the cop.

'I'm Welsh, you stupid pig,' roared Richard. 'I'm a Celt. Like you.'

The cop apparently didn't have a clue what being a 'Celt' meant, but he understood the 'pig' connotation, and he apparently tried to club Richard over the head, presumably with a truncheon, according to Huston. But Rich, even hungover, could duck and dive from his boxing days, and he stepped aside and delivered a hefty punch. 'Right in the solar plexus,' said John Huston.

Down went the cop. The cell door was open and Rich ambled out, found his way to the front desk and told the sergeant on duty, 'You have a man down in the cell I was occupying.'

Officers rushed to their fallen comrade's aid, and Richard, who had made no attempt to escape, was suddenly grabbed and hauled off to a room where, he said, 'they appeared not to know what to do with me. I'd not run away, I'd explained what had happened, and half of them had been at that brothel the night before, so none of them knew what to do.'

Richard suggested they call Darryl F. Zanuck, the head of 20th Century Fox.

Before long, Richard was a free man but was now up before the great Zanuck in his office.

'He was very good about it all,' Richard told me. 'As soon as I mentioned Errol Flynn, he raised his eyes and said, "That explains everything." Then he did his studio head thing, telling me how he looked after his stars and what a wonderful future I had with him if I stayed on at Fox, and it was all over.'

Huston, who knew Zanuck well, said, 'Darryl was a good man. He understood things about life, sex, making money and motion pictures. He knew how to deal with people. So the first thing he did was invite the desk sergeant on duty that day to the studio for lunch, and by the end of lunch the whole matter was made to vanish. If there were any mug shots or fingerprints of Richard, they ceased to exist. Someone like Darryl could do that.

'He also gave Richard some good advice; stay away from Errol Flynn.'

It was advice Richard didn't need. 'Flynn never called on me again. I think I was a disappointment to him. When I did meet him, a few years later, I was cordial and so was he, and not a word about that night at the whorehouse was mentioned.

'It had been a great mistake, for many reasons. And as one always does, I decided never to make the same mistake again. There were plenty of other mistakes I still had to make, but never that one.'

Richard's Hollywood career was saved. For now.

Chapter Ten

LUST AND LIFE AT 20TH CENTURY FOX

A PART FROM RICHARD'S secret and rather failed attempt to be a Hollywood hellraiser, there was still the work itself to do. And there was also Sybil to consider. Remembering Stewart Granger's invitation, Richard and Sybil moved in with Granger and his lovely young wife, actress Jean Simmons. Granger and Jean were themselves still newcomers to Hollywood. 'We bought a lovely house on the top of a hill overlooking the whole of Hollywood on one side and the entire San Fernando Valley on the other,' Granger said. 'And our first guests from Britain were Richard and Sybil Burton.'

Granger insisted that Richard and Sybil remained with them indefinitely, but Rich had a different version of events. 'We found a large duplex apartment on Charleville Boulevard,' he said. Perhaps the Burtons did stay with the Grangers for a short while, but not for long, if at all. There was a particular problem that Granger always preferred to overlook, or ignore, or try to forget. Richard told me, 'I was waiting to start my first Hollywood film but there was a seven week delay, and so during those seven weeks I started the hunt for Jean [Simmons].'

When Rich told me this in a very offhand way in 1978 (on the set of *Absolution*), reminiscing to me and Brook Williams about his first weeks in Hollywood, I was immediately intrigued by his 'hunt for Jean', and I asked him, 'You were *after* Jean Simmons?'

'Of course. Who wouldn't be?'

So I had to ask, 'And did you catch her?'

'It didn't take long,' was his response.

So it seems very unlikely that the Burtons lived with the Grangers for too long, if at all.

That first Hollywood film on which there was a seven week delay was

My Cousin Rachel, based on the book by Daphne du Maurier. Olivia de Havilland had the title role, the mysterious widow of a Cornish gentleman whose foster son, played by Richard, falls for her. Rich recalled:

'I only agreed to do the film because it was George Cukor who had insisted he wanted me, and he was, after all, one of the finest screen directors. He came to see me in *Montserrat* and persuaded me and told me that my leading lady would be either Garbo, who would come out of retirement apparently, or Vivien Leigh. But by the time we arrived in New York on the *Queen Mary*, Cukor had been fired or he'd resigned and my leading lady was to be Olivia de Havilland who was very "hot", as they say, and had recently won two Oscars in three years.

'I was merely a second class citizen as far as Miss de Havilland was concerned. She refused to allow me to have co-starring billing with her, but I didn't care about that. I later discovered that she hoped that I would do a Rex Harrison and storm out after throwing a tantrum about billing. I think Miss de Havilland wanted Gregory Peck for the part. Zanuck had a hatchet man called Lew Schrieber who gave me the news about the billing. I told him that I had worked with the greatest living actors and actresses and that none of them had ever made a fuss about billing. So they were stuck with me, but I never warmed to Miss de Havilland.'

He did, however, make an attempt to engage her upon their first meeting; making a pass at his current leading lady was simply a game to him. It was a game he had started before his arrival in Hollywood but which intensified once he arrived there.

'I was a terrible sub-Don Juan,' he told me. 'I would make a remark or two to my leading lady of the moment, and if she replied with good humour, I knew we were going to work well together. And if she showed real interest, then I was going to make my move sooner or later. Usually sooner.'

There were girls who were not his leading ladies he made his move on. 'I have no explanation of my insatiable sexual appetite,' he told me. 'I assume it is the same for all men. Some are able to control it. I didn't want to control mine. I wanted to pursue it and satisfy it.'

There was a new star on the Fox lot, and when Richard saw her, he was unable to resist. She was Marilyn Monroe.

Rich had always been honest and open about his extramarital activities, but he had always kept his affair with Monroe a secret. He would probably never have told me about it if it wasn't for the fact that Ava Gardner had tipped me off about it, and so I asked him about Monroe in 1978 when I was with him and Brookie.

'How the bloody hell do you know about that?' he said.

I told him how I knew and he laughed. 'Bloody Ava Gardner! She always knows too much.'

There was, he believed, a very good reason to keep his affair with Monroe a secret: 'I didn't know it then, but everybody had her. So when I had her, I didn't want everyone knowing I'd had the girl who'd been had by everyone else.'

It's no secret that Monroe's early success in films was in part due to the sexual favours she gave to studio heads, executives, producers, directors and actors. 'Those bastards in Hollywood were predators,' said Richard. 'They saw Monroe as an easy lay because she was so eager to be laid in return for stardom.'

I asked him, 'What did she get from you?' which rather made Brook chuckle. Rich replied:

'Ah, my boy, that's where I was different. I could offer her nothing although perhaps she thought I could. I was supposed to be this wonderful actor from England, although they couldn't get it out of their heads that I was not English.

'Monroe was still vulnerable back then. Still not in control. I doubt she was ever in control, but she was a studio plaything at that time. I simply saw her and it was impossible for me not to be affected. She was incredibly pretty and very sexual. That is, she was sexual when she wanted to be. She could turn it on. If she wanted something from a man, even if it was a chance to move ahead in the queue at the studio commissary, she turned it on, and the men were falling over themselves to let her move up the queue.

'And yet she was about the loneliest person I ever saw. Lost little girl in the big studio. We were at a studio function. She was in a crowded room, surrounded by admiring men – and admiring women too – but she was alone; like she was apart from it all. I said hello to her, and she loved my voice; she told me that. I loved her body; I told her that. I thought my voice and her body would make a fine combination. So we slipped away and found somewhere quiet. We wound up in some kind of storeroom.

'I had a tried and tested system; I gave her poetry. I didn't think she would really appreciate it, but she cried. Tears were running down her cheeks. She said, "That is the most beautiful thing I ever heard." She was kissing me while I was delivering all this wonderful poetry. She hardly allowed me to breathe but she insisted I continued with the poetry. I call that kind of seduction, "Poetic Love".'

Brook Williams, hearing this, said, 'I've never heard you call it that before.' Richard laughed and said, 'I only just thought of it.' Then he continued his story:

'My hands were all over her by then. And what a body! I was hard and ready. She was opening up for me; ah, Mick, Brookie, there we were in the storeroom and it was blinding hot passion.

'At first I thought I could fall in love with her. But it was an animal passion only. She had nothing much more than her body to offer me – and she knew how to use it. We sneaked around together for maybe a week, and then I started to hear stories about how she'd been used by the men who ran the studios – and I don't mean just at Fox. She had done the rounds. So at first I began to feel sorry for her. And then I began to realise that she was actually very smart because she was exploiting those men – not the other way round. And then I just started to feel like I really didn't want to go where all those bastards who ran Hollywood had been, and I felt a little sickened.

'Maybe I was the only man who was ever sickened by the thought of fucking Marilyn Monroe, but that's how I felt and so I stopped, and not long after that she married Joe DeMaggio. He must not have minded.'

Later, when I was alone with Brook, I asked him if he believed the Monroe story.

'The story is true, all right,' he replied. 'I've heard it before. But what you learn with Rich is that he'll add a little colour here and there – like the "Poetic Love" thing. But he had a fling with Monroe, definitely.

And he was put off by her promiscuity. He told me she was not much better than a prostitute. I said to him, "That's a bit harsh, Rich," and he replied, "What else do you call someone who gives sex in return for something other than the sex itself?"'

I once asked Rich how Sybil had coped with his many affairs. He said, 'She just did . . . back then, anyway. Or rather, she made a show of coping. At first I thought she was simply turning a bind eye. But a smack round the face for kissing Jean [Simmons] out of work hours was her way of telling me she wasn't going to stand for public humiliation. And I can't blame her. I was a rogue.'

The kiss with Jean Simmons apparently happened during a New Year's Eve party, when 1952 turned into 1953.

Back on the set of *My Cousin Rachel*, Richard was failing to endear himself to Olivia de Havilland who described him as 'a course-grained man with a coarse-grained charm and a talent not completely developed'.

Rich didn't disagree with her criticism of his talent. 'I didn't know what I was doing in front of a camera when I started in films,' he said. 'I have always felt that the camera hasn't liked me. I'm a stage animal. I have to be big and loud, and the camera needs you to be small and naturalistic and subtle; much more naturalistic. I'm as subtle as a buffalo stampede.'

He said that during the filming in one scene he got so impatient and frustrated with himself over his inability to make his performance more 'naturalistic' that he banged his head against the studio wall.

Richard's perception of himself as a film actor is accurate as far as those early films were concerned. He wasn't a natural screen actor and any histrionics tended to be very theatrical. However, this style suited *My Cousin Rachel* perfectly since it was a Victorian melodrama, and as *Variety* reported, 'Richard Burton, debuting in Hollywood pictures . . . creates a strong impression in the role of a love-torn, suspicious man.'

There were other critics who also liked him in the film; 'I would say he is the most exciting thing in movies since the advent of Gregory Peck,' wrote Jympson Harman in the London *Evening News*.

The Academy of Motion Pictures Arts and Sciences was enthusiastic too; he was nominated for an Oscar as Best Actor of 1952 which wasn't bad going for a first American film.

His next film was *The Desert Rats* which, curiously, was a Hollywood-made film about the British at war in the North African

Campaign; Hollywood has never been known for producing war films in which the Americans were not actively engaged in winning. It was filmed on location – in Palm Springs to be exact. Richard enjoyed this experience far more. There were no leading ladies to distract him, and as the English captain of a detachment of Australian soldiers at the siege of Tobruk, he enjoyed the company of the all-male cast, particular that of Robert Newton whom he admired greatly as Bill Sykes in David Lean's *Oliver Twist* and as Long John Silver in Walt Disney's *Treasure Island*. He also liked Newton because he was a heavy drinker.

He particularly enjoyed a single scene with James Mason who was reprising his role of Field Marshal Rommel which he'd played in Fox's highly successful *The Desert Fox* in 1951.

'James Mason was a true screen actor,' Richard said. 'He had conquered the camera, and I envied him. I also like him enormously.'

James Mason told me that apart from insisting that he and only he play the role he had cast in his own mould, that of Rommel, he was keen to work with 'the exciting new discovery called Richard Burton'.

I asked Mason if Burton had lived up to his expectations. 'Oh, definitely. He had a strength that didn't come across on screen at the time. But it was there on the set. He was also very amiable. Easy to be with. I was aware that he had a reputation with the women and that he liked to drink. I was half expecting someone who would turn up an hour late on the set, heavily hung over. If he was hung over, it didn't show, and he was never late. He was highly professional.

'I was never a heavy drinker so it seemed we might not ever have a rapport, but the thing we both had was a love of books. He read avidly, and so did I.'

Being with Mason actually had a calming effect on Rich, according to the film's director Robert Wise. I interviewed Wise by telephone in 1979, and he told me:

'In between takes Burton and Mason would discuss the books they had read. I think Burton envied Mason's grasp of screen acting, and I know that Mason gave him some tips; not like one actor giving another unsolicited advice. Mason would never do that. But Burton would tell him how he was having trouble working to the camera, and Mason would tell him, "Well, if it was me, I'd do this and that," or sometimes Burton would simply say that he felt he was overstating something, and Mason would say, "Well, if it was me saying that I would say it like this," and, of course, Mason had a wonderful soothing kind of voice, and Burton would . . . not do an impression of Mason, but he would kind of copy his manner. Before Mason began work on the film, Burton was anxious and nervous and eager to do well, but just so intense. Then he worked with James Mason and he began to calm down.

'The other thing about Richard Burton was that he was easy to work with from my point of view. I was very glad we had no women in the film because I'm sure that would have distracted him. He really liked the company of the men that we had, particularly Robert Newton, who did get very drunk at times and then Burton took care of him.

'I'd expected Burton to be resistant to the kind of role he had, that of an army officer. I thought he would have preferred a script with some lovely language. But he said to me, "You know, I am really enjoying being an action star. It's tremendous fun." So he was having a good time, and he was perfect for that kind of role because you really can believe that he is a leader of men.'

Being an action hero was a long-held ambition for Richard. When I was with him as an extra on *The Wild Geese*, he told me, 'I loved to see action films when I was a small boy at the Cach – the Shithouse. When I got the chance to do some action stuff [in *The Desert Rats*] I absolutely loved it. Some of my happiest times have been on war pictures, and I think some of my best screen work has been in those films. I was better in *Where Eagles Dare* than I was in those 1950s epics they put me in.'

His big regret from the 1950s was being unable to accept an offer to play Mark Antony in the 1953 MGM production of *Julius Caesar*. 'Mark Antony is one of the great roles because it combines some of the best dialogue Shakespeare ever wrote and action; Antony was a man of action,' he said.

We would talk long and often about Mark Antony, whom he played most famously in the infamous 20th Century Fox *Cleopatra*, a film and a performance he was to loathe for many years. In 1953 he had hoped to play the role as written by Shakespeare; we shared a great love of that play and the role of Antony (I was lucky to play the part on stage in *Antony and Cleopatra*). But he couldn't do it because in 1952 he had been cast by Fox in the leading role of the Roman Tribune Marcellus in the biblical epic *The Robe*. Ironically, Marlon Brando had turned down *The Robe* and instead played Antony in *Julius Caesar*, giving one of his finest screen performances, while Richard took a role that had at first been intended for Tyrone Power, who had been dropped because he cost too much, then offered to Brando and then to Laurence Olivier, who also declined. Being fourth choice did little to boost Richard's ego or his insecurity about acting for the camera.

The Robe was supposed to be Fox's answer to MGM's *Quo Vadis?* but the original budget of 16 million dollars that Fox had set aside for *The Robe* was slashed to $6 million.

Richard learned a valuable lesson with *The Robe*; 'A screenplay can look good on paper. But getting it on to film is another thing.' The screenplay was by Philip Dunne, and not at all bad of its type. But the film had major flaws; after filming began, 20th Century Fox decided to start over again and film it in CinemaScope, the new anamorphic widescreen process that made the image more than half as wide again as a conventional film. It therefore became famous for being the first film in CinemaScope. That in itself wasn't a bad thing and no doubt added to its commercial success. The opportunity was there for grand vistas and sweeping scenes of spectacle. Unfortunately, the film had little of that. Even the opening shot of gladiators in the arena was actually lifted from the film's sequel, *Demetrius and the Gladiators*, which went into filming as soon as *The Robe* was completed. The scenes of grand spectacle just weren't there.

However, director Henry Koster made good use of the new wide screen; his reputation for filming actors standing in a line for the CinemaScope image is ill deserved. Koster, like many directors of the time, did little coverage on a scene – often a master shot and some cut-aways – but he nevertheless made use of some good dolly shots and created some fine compositions.

Jean Simmons was very good as Diana, the Roman girl who falls for Marcellus despite the fact that he appears to be driven mad after overseeing the crucifixion of Jesus. For Victor Mature, playing beefy slave Demetrius was a walk in the park. And there is an extravagant performance by Jay Robinson as the mad Caligula.

Rich felt his performance was poor. 'I tried,' he told me. 'I tried so hard, and the harder I tried, the worse I got.'

And yet, his performance isn't bad at all. Just very uncinematic. It is, essentially, a theatrical performance. And that, in a way, makes his performance exciting to watch. Unused to the subtleties of acting for the camera where the most minor of expressions can sum up so much, he gave the film an extra dimension, particularly in the scenes where he displays madness and paranoia by doing it the way he would have done it on stage. It isn't true film acting, and it can at times look too stagey, but it nevertheless remains, after more than 54 years, a mesmerising performance; a preview, if you like, of a great stage performance caught on camera. It also demonstrated his special charisma when in costume, and I often told him all this.

But nothing I could say ever made him feel better about his work in *The Robe*, and indeed there were better screen performances to come. 'Nobody showed me how to do it,' he said. 'I didn't know how to do all the histrionics and make them believable for a wide screen.'

He also hated how he appeared on screen. 'I don't have the body for it. I'm like a small barrel on legs. Even my neck is short which makes my head look too big. And I have no grace when I walk. I'm better when I stand still.' He also hated wearing historical costumes. 'I'd rather be in casual modern clothing. I hate wearing tights and skirts.'

The one aspect of his performance he did enjoy was when he became a man of action. He had a scene in which he and Jeff Morrow, as a subordinate officer, have a sword fight, and even compared to more recent cinematic offerings such as *Gladiator*, it remains a fierce, fast moving and highly dangerous scene in which doubles were only used sparingly. For the most part Rich and Morrow did all the actual sword fighting themselves, at some risk. 'They were real swords,' Richard said. 'Real steel blades.

'The big fight scene certainly was different to anything I had done before. We had to hack our way through that in deadly earnest from beginning to end without a break – and no spoofing. I suffered not a split skull, as it happened, but split skin on my skull, and a gashed hand.'

Because Richard was to play one of the first Roman converts to Christianity, he was told not to smoke on the set. 'Very bad for the image, they said,' Richard told me. 'I smoked anyway. I couldn't do anything about the image.'

One of the pleasures of making *The Robe* for Rich was working with Victor Mature. 'I've never known an actor so happily aware of his limitations. He rejoiced in them. He liked to joke that he was no actor and he said he had 60 films to prove it. But against him I looked like an amateur. We had a scene where the robe falls on to me and I scream like a girl before becoming overcome with religious fervour. And all the time Victor just stands there gazing into heaven with great conviction. I asked him, "How do you do it? What are you thinking?" He said, "I'm thinking of the money they're paying me." What a wonderful man. He taught me to play craps. So there we were, the first Christians smoking and playing craps.'

Filming wasn't made easier by the conditions CinemaScope imposed on the cast. Jean Simmons told me, 'We had no idea at first how difficult it was going to be filming in CinemaScope. They had to use more lights, and it got so *hot*! I've never known heat like that in any scene of any other film. We would have to stand there for hours, just so they could focus on all of us.'

Her memory of working with Richard was 'a marvellous experience because he is such an exciting actor. But he was new to films and he wanted to learn how to do it well for the camera, and he didn't have a director who could help him. It all had to be shot as quickly as possible.'

'Jean was exquisitely beautiful,' said Richard. 'I was quite envious of Jimmy [Stewart Granger].'

When I asked Stewart Granger about the rumours of an affair between Jean and Richard, all he said was, 'When Jean was doing *The Robe* I was in Jamaica filming *All the Brothers Were Valiant*.'

Another beautiful young actress caught Richard's eye. She was Dawn Addams, who played a Roman girl jilted by Burton. I met Dawn in 1974 when I was running the stills department for both Warner Bros. and Columbia and she came looking for photographs from a film she was in. She took me to lunch and naturally I brought up the subject of *The Robe* and Richard Burton; she told me, 'I was in my early twenties and still new in films, and Rich swept me off my feet and into bed.'

The Robe was a huge success when released in 1953, probably because of the novelty of being the first film in CinemaScope. It was nominated as Best Picture and Richard earned an Oscar nomination as Best Actor. Neither the movie nor the nomination made a major film star of Richard, but he was established as a leading man in films. Darryl F. Zanuck had plans for him and offered him a million dollars to make seven films over seven years. Rich had a commitment to return to

England to perform *Hamlet* at the Old Vic and follow it with *Coriolanus*, *Twelfth Night* and *The Tempest*, all for £45 a week.

Zanuck wasn't impressed with Burton's decision to decline his offer and it led to a showdown in Zanuck's office. Richard recalled:

'There he was on one side of the room with his band of corporate boys and lawyers in suits, and me on the other side, standing alone.

'One of the lawyers shook a fist at me and said, "You shook hands with Mr. Zanuck on an agreement in this very office."

'I said, "I don't believe Mr. Zanuck told you that happened, and if he did, then he's a fucking liar."

'Nobody had ever said that before, and the lawyers virtually fainted on the spot.

'It was true that Zanuck had offered me a seven-year contract. I'd turned it down. He knew that and I knew that, and he kept very quiet about it while the lawyers ran around making plans to sue me, which they didn't, of course, because there was no agreement.'

Exhausted from filming *The Robe*, Richard and Sybil took a few weeks' holiday. Doubts about his ability to go back to *Hamlet* had begun to set in and he woke up at night sweating and shaking. He had something to prove, if only to himself, and the thought scared him to death.

Chapter Eleven

TO BE OR NOT TO BE
IN LOVE WITH CLAIRE

W HEN RICHARD AND Sybil returned to the UK in June
1953, they went back to Wales and moved in for a few days
with Cis, who was still at 73 Caradoc Street. He was like a
returning hero who delighted everyone with his tales of Hollywood
over several beers at the pub, although no doubt he omitted one or two
of his escapades and probably invented a couple to take their place.

He had presents for all his family and closest friends. For Cis he
brought a Russian squirrel coat. 'When he was a boy,' Brook Williams
told me, 'Cis would sing to him about she would buy a Russian squirrel
coat if she had the money. He now had the money and so he bought it
for her. He had more money than he needed and he began setting up
his siblings in homes of their own.'

'He wasn't showing off,' said Stanley Baker. 'He was repaying his
family. And he was giving them what they would otherwise be unable
to afford. They were gifts of love. He wanted to earn money not just for
himself but for his family.

'His father, though . . .! Well, he disappointed Richard. He hardly
seemed to care about what his son had achieved. Rich told me that
depressed him. Rich loved his father, but he really didn't like him.'

In the summer of 1953, Richard began work on *Hamlet*. It was
directed by Michael Benthall, but Rich came to the first rehearsal ready
to play the part as coached by Philip Burton. To Richard, Philip knew
more about Shakespeare than anyone else and, as before, he had turned
to his 'adopted' father for the direction he needed in the part.

Under Philip's coaching, Rich approached *Hamlet* as a revenge play.
Philip also told Rich that Hamlet is never sure if his father was
murdered because he can't be confident that the ghost of his father is

for real. It was an interesting concept. It was further enhanced by Richard's – or Philip's – concept that Hamlet was fearful of committing regicide, which was considered the worst of crimes in Shakespeare's day.

Out for vengeance, Richard's Hamlet was very different to the poetic Hamlets of the past, and he was criticised for taking the poetry out of the dialogue and replacing it with something approaching realism. What Richard was also doing was moulding the role as much as he could to his own personality, to make Hamlet live through him rather than become another character the way Laurence Olivier could do it.

Robert Hardy, who played Laertes in that production, recalled, 'Rich was good, but not great in that production of *Hamlet*. He was too strong, I thought. He was playing the Prince of Vengeance and I think it was too much for the audiences at that time.'

Sir Michael Horden, who played Polonius, thought that *Hamlet* of 1953 'a staggering performance. But then, Richard only has to walk out on the stage, open his mouth, and the rest of us can go home. He has such charisma. But he didn't hog the stage. He didn't mean to take it away from you – unless you tried to take it from him; then he put you down and you couldn't defeat him.'

Robert Hardy's favourite memory of that production was of the sword duel at the end. 'I was something of a swordsman,' he said. 'I had taken proper fencing lessons. Richard had never taken a fencing lesson in his life, but he never lost his way, never forgot a pass – and I'll tell you, by God, I had to fight for my life every night on stage. He was staggering.'

Giving so much of himself on stage didn't prevent Rich from carrying on an affair with his leading lady; Claire Bloom had been cast as Ophelia.

Rich and Claire had not seen each other since *The Lady's Not for Burning*. On their first day of rehearsal for *Hamlet*, Claire heard someone mention what a large head Richard had. She recalled, 'I laughed and said that maybe he was growing it to play Caliban [in *The Tempest*, which would close the season]. That's when he caught sight of me and came over, and we kissed hello.'

According to actor William Squire, who was also in the production, Claire Bloom asked him to make sure Richard stayed away from her. In an interview I did with Squire in 1984, shortly after Richard's death, he said, 'Richard was mad about her and wanted her, but I told him, "It's no good, Rich, she won't have you. She won't have anybody." He said, "I bet I'll have her." I said, "You won't, you know." He asked, "What do you bet?" This was a matter of his honour now. A challenge! So I said, "A pint."

'It didn't take Claire long to become attracted to Richard without him doing anything. She was sitting with me in the stalls watching him rehearse on stage, and she said to me, "He is really rather marvellous, isn't he?" I knew then I'd soon be owing Rich a pint.'

After the first time they made love, 'In the morning,' said Steiger, 'Burton left to go home to his wife. Claire was deeply in love with him. It took her a long time – many years – to realise what a mistake it was to fall in love with Richard Burton. So she didn't feel guilty at the time. Their dressing rooms were right next door to each other, with an adjoining door.'

'I truly loved Claire,' Richard told me in 1977, not for the first or last time. 'We used to lie on the grass in Regent's Park in between rehearsals.' I told Richard I knew Regent's Park well because in my youth I lived right around the corner from it. 'You must know what it's like then,' he said, 'being with a girl you love in that wonderful park, just lying there, touching, talking, kissing.' I did know. I'd experienced that with a lovely actress too. That was something else that impressed Richard about me.

But I didn't have a wife when I was smooching in Regent's Park and Richard did, and I still find it difficult to understand how he could have justified what he did – and justify it he did, often. But there was the rare occasion when he admitted he couldn't justify it at all, such as the time in 1974 when he said to me, 'The thing is, Mick, you can justify anything, and today I can't justify what I did.' He was talking generally then about the many affairs he had.

Claire would go to Richard's dressing room. He enlisted the stage manager to assist him in case Sybil suddenly turned up. 'If Sybil came into the theatre,' said Squire, 'the stage manager let him know and Claire slipped back to her own dressing room.'

What I wanted to know was, did Sybil know about Claire? 'She must have,' said Squire. 'She was incredibly tolerant.'

That is an understatement! Richard's rule was that no matter who the woman of the moment was, Sybil was the woman for ever. Nobody has ever been able to fully explain what was in Sybil's mind because nobody ever understood her – and she preferred to keep it that way. It simply seems that she knew he would come back to her, and that was what mattered most. Richard said, 'If I knew I could get away with something, I didn't think twice. I was alive and I was living – and I was a fool. But better to be a living fool than a dead wise man'; that's what he said to me while he lay in a hospital bed on the set of *The Medusa Touch* in 1977 at Pinewood Studios, and the simple corn of his spontaneous wisdom made him laugh. 'But it's true, you know. I didn't know what I wanted when I was young. I just wanted . . . it all.'

Steiger had a good theory: 'Sybil was the mother Burton never had. Claire was the woman he needed physically, emotionally, maybe even spiritually.' Steiger joked, 'To be or not to be . . . in love with Claire. That is the question.'

The answer was, Burton loved Claire so much that Stanley Baker thought that this might be the time when Rich actually left Sybil.

Hamlet moved from Edinburgh down to London and into the Old Vic. There is a myth that John Gielgud didn't like his performance and it led to a famous anecdote that Richard himself loved to recount. 'After the performance, John came to my dressing room to take me to dinner, but I had so many visitors that he said, "Shall I go ahead or wait until you're better – I mean, ready?"'

Gielgud said that wasn't quite the case. 'When he played the part at the Old Vic, I went to see his performance and enjoyed it very much. We had arranged to have supper afterwards and he took rather a long time getting changed, so I said, "I'll go ahead. You come along when you're better . . . I mean, when you're ready." It was just a gaffe, but one of my favourite gaffes.'

Another of Richard's favourite stories was the one when Winston Churchill came to see the play. 'He sat in the front of the stalls and he knew the play as well as I. I looked down and saw him muttering the lines along with me throughout the whole play.' It's a funny story, and possibly partly true. Churchill may have known the play, or some of it, but he couldn't have known the cuts which had been introduced for this production.

Richard's Churchill story continued: 'After the final curtain he came backstage, came into my dressing room and said, "My Lord Hamlet, may I use your facilities?" He was desperate for a pee and didn't want to use the public toilets.'

After each evening's performance, Richard lived a double life.

Sometimes he went home with Claire, sometimes he would go home to Sybil. Some nights he just stayed up drinking with friends.

Steiger told me, 'He would turn up at Claire's before dawn. He had a key and would let himself in. Then after they'd made love, he'd go back to his wife before it got light.

'Claire became very tense and anxious with the secrecy of it all. She was quite lonely because her mother had moved out, and she never knew if Burton would come to her or not. That was no way to treat a lady.'

Richard, surprisingly not coy about his escapades, told me, 'We'd make love in our dressing rooms between the matinee and the evening performance.'

They also checked into a hotel in Norfolk during a period when they had a free weekend – as Mr. and Mrs. Boothby.

'I couldn't have left Sybil,' Rich told me. 'I loved Claire more than I deserved to, but it was real love.'

After *Hamlet* he was in *King John*, with Michael Horden taking the burden of the title role while Richard played Philip the Bastard. The play's director decided to leave Richard on stage throughout as a sort of Chorus, but when it became evident that all eyes in the audience were on him and not on Horden or anybody else, this idea was abandoned.

His lack of theatrical training showed up in *Twelfth Night* in which he was Sir Toby Belch. 'They put me in a stupid wig,' he said, 'and I should have known better and should have told them to take it off.'

He didn't know how to use theatrical make-up, and despite his rich voice he didn't know how to project in the quieter moments. Boredom was setting in. 'I wanted to conquer each and every role,' he said, 'but having done so, even if only for one night, I was already bored. I had a long season of plays for the Old Vic in 1953 and I couldn't see how I was going to get through it.'

He nearly didn't. He decided he didn't want to do *Coriolanus*. Philip Burton was called in to persuade him to play the part. The play and Burton's performance were triumphs, but it was also a hit and miss affair. Robert Hardy said, 'His Coriolanus is easily the best I've ever seen. But when he was at his best one night, you couldn't count on him to do the same the next.'

Something else disturbed Richard: Dylan Thomas died on

9 November 1953. There was more than a sense of great loss that caused Richard enormous distress. It was, he thought, a prophecy come true, and it brought with it a belief that his own death would come early, at precisely the age of 33. It's curious because generally he wasn't superstitious, but this was an exception. He explained the situation to me:

'Years ago I was in London one rainy Sunday afternoon where I was with Dylan Thomas, Constant Lambert [the composer], Esme Percy [actor] and Louis MacNiece [the poet]. We were reading Thomas Love Peacock's *Nightmare Abbey* for the BBC Third Programme. My father [Dic] was there too because he was up from Wales for the week and I took him to have a look at the BBC. Then we went to a drinking club, a filthy hole-in-the-wall kind of place but we loved it there.

'There was this fellow from Cardiff at the club – a Welshman who was a writer, he said, who was never published, and he was an actor, he told us, although he never acted. He said he could read our palms, so we let him. He told my father he would die when he was 81. Dylan would die when he was 39, and Lambert when he was 55. I was going to die when I was 33. He told Esme when he would die but I can't recall what age he would be.

'I didn't take it too seriously at first, but then Dylan died when he was 39. That was rather frightening, and I began to think that I would actually die when I was 33. Lambert had died a few years earlier, [in 1951] and Esme was 70 [in 1957]. My father died when he was 81. Esme died and I'm the only one left.

'I was still so young and thought I was invincible but when Dylan died, I suddenly thought that maybe the predictions were true and I would die at 33, even though Constant Lambert wasn't 55 when he died. I told myself that anyone can make a mistake. I also told myself I was stupid to believe in such nonsense. But there it was, lurking in the back of my mind for years.

'I was 33 when John Huston offered me a role in *The Unforgiven*. It meant flying to Durango, and I decided not to risk unnecessary aeroplane journeys, so I turned it down. I was earning good money then and I said to myself, "Why should I risk my life for a mere $150,000 when I have a million in the bank? Why don't I just stay at home until the year is up and it's safe to go out again?" When I turned 34 I celebrated with a tremendous booze-up.'

Rich always celebrated just about anything with a tremendous booze-up, but it seems that his thirty-fourth birthday was one he was particularly happy to see.

But that wasn't the greatest cause of grief to Richard when Dylan died. He felt enormous guilt because, shortly before, Thomas had telephoned him in a drunken state and asked to borrow £200 for what he described as 'the education of my children'.

Two hundred pounds was a lot of money in 1953, and Richard simply didn't have that much cash on him. Then Thomas told Rich that he had written a play, *Under Milk Wood*, which he would sell to him for £200, but Rich still had to explain he didn't have the money. Shortly after, Thomas went to America and there died.

Rich blamed himself, unnecessarily, but he felt that Dylan Thomas had died 'for the sake of £200', he said. After that, Rich always made sure he had plenty of spare cash with him and would often ask those he knew well, 'Are you okay for cash?' He asked it of me every time I saw him. 'Here,' he would say, stuffing often around £50 into my jacket pocket, 'you might need this.'

He even asked John Gielgud, when they appeared together in the 1983 TV movie *Wagner*, 'You okay for cash, John?' Gielgud, of course, was flush. But Rich always considered that his great poet friend and hero Dylan Thomas had died for the lack of £200, and he never wanted anyone to die for lack of cash ever again.

His Old Vic season finished in early 1954 with *The Tempest*; his Caliban won good reviews. But Robert Hardy's Ariel was panned. 'Richard saved me,' Hardy told me. 'I was shaken by the critics, but Rich said, "Ignore them, they don't understand. Do what you want to do and don't back down." It was the best advice I ever had. I am entirely and eternally grateful to him.'

Claire Bloom was back on stage with Richard, as Viola. The affair was still going strong.

By the last night of the Old Vic season, Richard's legion of fans, which had become considerable, became like a frenzied mob waiting at the stage door, so he had to be smuggled out of another door and straight into a taxi.

He had become a star of the stage, but he still had not reached the heights set by Gielgud or Olivier. He decided he would aim that high by taking *Hamlet* to Elsinore in Denmark where both Olivier and then Gielgud had been with their interpretations of the Danish Prince. A check-up by a doctor revealed that Richard was suffering from exhaustion and he was advised not to go. But he ignored the advice and went, believing that he wouldn't die before he was 33.

'I became convinced that I was invincible for the time I had left,' he told me. 'I could drink as much as I wanted, work my balls off, make love as often as I wanted, and I thought nothing could kill me before my time was up.'

Most nights after the performance, which usually ended just before midnight, Rich and his male companions stayed up all night drinking. But there were times when he spent a few hours with Claire Bloom who, according to Rod Steiger, was growing increasingly anxious and desperate as the end of the tour grew closer because she was afraid that would mark the end of their love affair.

After Elsinore, the company went to Zurich by train. Rich and Sybil had a compartment, and Claire had the one right next to it. Rich dared to leave his wife's bed and go to Claire's.

Then came the end of the tour, and Richard and Sybil returned to London while Claire went to stay with Charlie and Oona Chaplin in Vevey for a short holiday.

Rich did *Under Milk Wood* on BBC radio – the play's first ever performance. Philip was also in it. So was Sybil. They all donated their fees to Dylan's widow Caitlin and their children.

Sybil and Richard began to consider adopting. Despite his affairs, he was still devoted, in his own way, to her, and she to him. 'They were a beautiful couple,' said Emlyn Williams. Sybil actually had a life independent of Richard, with a close circle of friends including actress Rachel Roberts and Stanley Baker's wife Ellen. It became important to both Richard and Sybil that they have children and the fact that they were considering adoption may have meant they had been trying for some time without success; they were never publicly frank about their reasons for considering adoption.

There were still three more films Richard had to make under his contract to Korda. Richard had pre-planned a special farewell with Claire in London before he flew off to America. On his last night in London, he went to her house, but she was so exhausted while waiting for him that she fell asleep. He had forgotten his key; though he tried knocking quietly, he couldn't get it.

The next morning he telephoned her, furious that she hadn't heard him knocking. Then he left for America, and Claire waited for the day he would come back home.

Chapter Twelve

A RICH SOCIALIST

ACK IN HOLLYWOOD in 1954, Richard made *Prince of Players* as actor Edwin Booth, the brother of John Wilkes Booth, who had assassinated President Lincoln. Written by Moss Hart and directed by Philip Dunne, who had written the screenplay of *The Robe*, it gave Rich the opportunity to recite great chunks of Shakespeare on screen. But he hated the screenplay and called it 'a disgrace'.

He drowned his sorrows in booze and sex. He seems to have almost callously gone after his leading lady, Maggie McNamara, the 26-year-old starlet probably best remembered for playing one of the American girls seeking love in *Three Coins in the Fountain* which she made just before *Prince of Players*. She had appeared on Broadway and had scored a fine film debut in Otto Preminger's controversial *The Moon is Blue*, for which she was nominated for an Oscar.

Richard displayed a rare sense of regret about his affair with Maggie McNamara. 'She was too vulnerable,' he told me in 1974. 'I was too cocksure. There was something about her that made her seem lost, while I was confident and could never understand why any girl would resist me. I was not the best of men back then.

'Maybe I gave her some sense of confidence in herself. Maybe I didn't do the wrong thing. But why did she die so young?'

She killed herself in 1978. Her career went nowhere after *Prince of Players*. 'She is one of Hollywood's forgotten victims,' said Richard. 'There have been too many of them. Monroe was another. Elizabeth [Taylor] in a sense is one, but she always fought back. You could argue that she won, you could argue that she lost. But Hollywood turned her into who she is, and she has survived. At her best she is the most wonderful woman in the world; at worst, she *is* the worst.'

Over time, I found that Richard compared most women with whom he was intimate with either Elizabeth or Sybil – they were

91

each in their own way the yardstick by which all other women were measured.

'Sybil was constant. I knew where I was with her. Maybe I needed that sense of danger I found with other women. But I'll tell you, Mick – most of them didn't complain. So I have nothing to feel guilty about. But Maggie [McNamara] was different, and I can't be sure I was good for her.'

Sybil had joined Richard in Hollywood while he filmed *Prince of Players*, and as usual she never let on whether she knew about the affair.

By now the hard work, the drinking – though never while he worked, only after – and the lusting was taking its toll on him. He lost weight quickly and was constantly tired. Then he was struck down with a flu virus and was confined to bed for a week. Despite his illness and his dislike of the script, Rich was always the consummate professional and gave his best. 'My best wasn't always good enough,' he said. 'My best was on the stage. But I did what I could. At least I could enjoy some Shakespeare on film. I was envious that Larry [Olivier] had made such a success of filmed Shakespeare. I wanted to do the same. But I wasn't a star – not in Hollywood. It wasn't going to be easy.'

It was never going to be easy if, as in the case of *Prince of Players*, he was going to be compared to Olivier. It was bad enough that the film was as poor as it was, but it rubbed salt in the wound when *Time* said, 'Burton shows a pretty talent though not exactly for Shakespeare. In almost every scene, this one-time junior colleague of Laurence Olivier does more a parody of his senior than an imitation of life.'

But Rich had higher hopes for his next film, *Alexander the Great*. It was written and directed by Robert Rossen who had come close to being blacklisted as a former Communist during the witch hunts of the late 1940s and early 1950s. In fact, he was subpoenaed to testify before the House Un-American Activities Committee but the hearings were suspended after the conviction of the Hollywood Ten – the alleged Communist writers and directors who refused to testify in Washington and were subsequently imprisoned and blacklisted.

Rossen had made a number of hard-hitting, gusty dramas including *All the King's Men* which centred on political corruption and won the Oscar as Best Picture of 1949. Richard felt that he was finally in the presence of Hollywood class, and being of the opinion that all Hollywood epics were generally crass, he hoped that *Alexander the*

Great would be the historical epic that finally broke the mould and displayed respectability.

He sounded off at a Hollywood party about how badly Rossen had been treated by the right-wing politicians who ruined a number of fine careers in the Communist witch hunts led by Senator McCarthy.

'I am a socialist,' he told me, 'and I always will be. I can be a rich socialist, but it's there, in my life, in my background – it's what I came from. I don't care for Communism, but McCarthy went for the people who had the real talent in Hollywood which appalled me . . . and I'm afraid I couldn't keep my mouth shut about it. It got me into some trouble.'

Politics was something best never discussed at Hollywood gatherings in the 1950s. Among those who disliked what Richard was saying was Ronald Reagan. 'He thought all Communists were the Devil's disciples,' said Richard in 1978 to me and to Brook Williams (as we sat around in priests' cassocks for the film *Absolution*). He continued:

'I had drunk too much and my tongue was too loose, but nevertheless, I felt I was free to speak my mind. I just spoke it more freely after a few drinks.

'Reagan started calling me a "Red" and a "Commie", and there were a number of others who agreed with him. My opinion of Hollywood was not particularly high but it plummeted when I found myself in the centre of an argument about politics. I told them they knew nothing of real poverty, which may have been unfair as I didn't know what their real backgrounds were – but there they were, all living as millionaires but with very little talent. I'm afraid I told Mr. Reagan that his talent was only second to his big mouth and small brain. That was unkind of me, but I was up for a fight, and as far as his talent was concerned, I wasn't completely dishonest.

'I can't be sure, but I think that fixed it for me and my so-called career in Hollywood. I was, in a way, blacklisted. I had *Alexander* to make and another picture [*The Rains of Ranchipur*] but I knew that was it for me as far as a career in Hollywood was concerned.

'A lot of people got upset with me. I came in for a berating from Frank Sinatra. He was no right winger, but he didn't like Hollywood being trashed. I bumped into him when I was back at

Fox for *Ranchipur,* and he made it clear that he didn't want to hear another word against Hollywood spoken by me. That, of course, made me say it.

'He went crazy. He almost tore off his jacket and came swinging at me with his fists. But he was no boxer, and I am. I think he landed one or two punches on me but after that I side-stepped every blow. I kept saying to him, "Frankie, if you don't stop trying to hit me, I'm going to have to hurt you." And he kept saying, "Hurt me! Hit me! See if you can!"

'So I let loose a volley of punches – left and right, left and right – and he went sprawling on the floor.

'We were in some nightclub, and someone said to me, "Be careful. The guys who own this place are the Mob and they're Frank's friends. They'll break your legs."

'Sinatra was getting up off the floor, and I said, "I hear you have friends who'll break my legs. Well, let me tell you, I've heard all about you and your Mafia pals, and I don't give a shit because I've got a bigger mob than you'll ever have and they'll come over here from Wales and they'll make mince meat of you and your Mob friends."

'He looked like he would kill me, and he said, "Oh yeah? And who are these men you're going to bring all the way from Wales? Bring them on and let's see what they can do. Who are they? Tell me?"

'And I said, "They're the *Tafia!*"

'There were several moments of silence. And then Sinatra began to laugh. He got hysterical and kept saying, "The Tafia! Oh Jesus God, that's the funniest thing I ever heard. The Tafia!"

'Then he told me to sit down, he ordered Jack Daniels, we drank ourselves into oblivion and we became friends. Even when I see him now, he says, "You got the Tafia with you? Where are they?" '

Alexander the Great was filmed in Spain from February to July in 1955. That was a long schedule to keep Richard interested. Sybil came out to be with him and many of his friends had roles, including Stanley Baker, Michael Horden and Claire Bloom; Rich had by then learned to ensure that he had a small community of close friends around him, especially since the filming was going to last six long months.

Claire spent most of her time alone in her hotel suite. 'It wasn't much of a part for me,' she said. 'Most of the film was about the men conquering Greece and Persia.'

She waited endlessly for the moments when she would have a chance to spend time alone with Richard. But it wasn't easy. 'Sybil was keeping an eye on Rich,' said Stanley Baker. 'Rich wanted some time with Claire, but he wasn't able to find much time, what with being in virtually every scene of the film and with Sybil keeping an eagle eye on him.

'I think perhaps that Sybil had some inkling that Rich had more than a passing fancy for Claire, who is incredibly beautiful and very, very serene but also gutsy, which was a wonderful combination to find in a woman – certainly for Rich, anyway. He told me he loved Claire very much in a way that was different to the way he loved Sybil. I hoped that Claire wouldn't succeed in taking Rich away from Sybil, and I don't believe she intended to.'

Rich and Claire managed to find some time alone. Rod Steiger told me, 'Claire made no secret that Richard Burton was her first love. Maybe her greatest love. But it was a love that was wasted because he wasn't leaving Sybil for her. It took Elizabeth Taylor to make him do that. I guess Elizabeth Taylor is like no other woman. Claire wasn't the right kind of woman to make Burton leave his wife. And I think it was during the making of *Alexander* that she finally realised that. They decided to call it a day.'

Well, it wasn't quite that cut and dried. Rich told me that he said his final goodbye to Claire but then find himself compelled to meet her for another final farewell. 'Our life was suddenly full of farewells,' he said. 'I found it almost impossible and unbearable to leave her. But she needed much more than I could give her, I do believe. I think she would have married me if she could. But it wasn't written, and other destinies awaited us. [Rod] Steiger for her and Elizabeth for me. We had our final *final* farewell in Hyde Park. We walked among the trees that dripped with the heavy rain that had fallen, and we said goodbye one last time.'

It wasn't to be an eternal goodbye as their paths would cross again when they came to make the film version of *Look Back in Anger*, and that would bring a new twist to their unresolved love affair.

Alexander the Great proved not to be what Richard had hoped for. He had read all he could on the subject and sat discussing it over with Rossen as often as time allowed. The script seemed literate. But it was dull. Despite all the battles scenes, the film had no heart. It was like a lavish docudrama. Sir Michael Horden recalled, 'I had the job of narrating the story, but not as an off-screen voice. I did it on screen, striding around ancient Greek columns and statues like a Chorus from Shakespeare throughout the film. I think Robert Rossen thought he *was* Shakespeare.'

Richard expressed his disappointment to me; 'It looked like it was going to be a superior epic. Rossen was a very talented man; I loved his picture *The Hustler*. But he should never have written *and* directed *Alexander*. I knew very little about films in those days. Now I can see it needed a co-writer to take Rossen's often very fine dialogue and work it into a filmable scenario. And then another director should have taken over. I hoped so much for *Alexander* and it delivered nothing but bad reviews and a conviction in Hollywood that it was somehow all my fault.'

Richard left Spain unaware that he had made a disaster, but he had no doubts about the poor quality of his next picture, another 20th Century Fox 'epic', *The Rains of Ranchipur*. It was a remake of a 1939 successful Fox picture, *The Rains Came*, but this time in Eastmancolor and CinemaScope.

Richard played a Hindu doctor who falls for Lana Turner as a temptress; he fell for her off the set too. 'She was not someone I loved,' he told me frankly. 'She was just incredibly attractive and remarkably good in bed.'

Ava Gardner, who was my friend as well as Richard's, was no friend of Turner's. 'That tramp fucked everyone,' said Ava. 'She fucked Frank [Sinatra] when he was married to *me*. Of course, she fucked Burton. I bet it was one time he didn't have to chase. She would have gone after him.'

I suggested to her that it took two to tango. 'Well, of course, but, baby, she saw Richard as a bit of a trophy. She felt she could have anyone she wanted, and she wanted Rich because he was the one who had the reputation for fucking every one of his leading ladies.'

Richard laughed when I told him what Ava had said. 'I was never so happy being a trophy in my life,' he said. 'The film bored me to death, although I did my best with it. I liked to joke, "It never rains but it Ranchipurs."

'In between takes there was only one thing to do to make the time pass more agreeably. Lana and I passed that time together.'

So it wasn't always necessary for Richard to fall in love with his latest conquest?

'Not at all,' he said. 'Sex is one of life's great pleasures. It's there to be enjoyed. It's like drink, or reading, or rugby.'

I told him I never saw sex as being on a par with rugby, to which he replied, 'It is when you are Welsh, boyo!'

Was he telling me that sex was sometimes just a pastime for him?

'It's more than that. It's a pleasure that's one of a kind. There's nothing else like it, and we are made to enjoy and express it. I expressed it whenever I could.'

I wondered if he expressed it to Lana while also reciting poetry or Shakespeare as he so often did when seeking a conquest.

'Not in Lana's case, because I didn't set out to catch her. She set out to get me, and I let myself get caught. Why not? Who's going to turn down Lana Turner?'

Their affair was brief and uncomplicated. It began while filming *The Rains of Ranchipur* and ended when the filming was over. 'Besides,' said Richard, 'who knows who else she was bedding? I didn't care and I didn't ask.'

He hated the film, not surprisingly, and few people went to see it. 'Like my other films, it did me no good whatsoever.' It virtually brought Richard's Hollywood career to a dead stop; that and his unpopular attacks upon the right-wing element of America.

At least he left America a rich socialist.

Chapter Thirteen

LOOK BACK IN JOY

H E RETURNED TO England and the Old Vic to play *Henry V* in December 1955. *The Times*, which had not been impressed with his earlier efforts at the Old Vic, now said, 'Mr. Burton's progress as an actor is such that already he is able to make good all the lacks of a few short years ago. What was gratingly metallic has been transformed into a steely strength which becomes the martial ring and hard brilliance of the patriotic verse.'

Kenneth Tynan even called Richard, 'the natural successor to Olivier'. He added, 'Within this actor there is always something reserved, a rooted solitude which his Welsh blood tinges with mystery. Inside those limits he is master.'

Richard's Henry V won him an *Evening Standard* Drama Award in January 1956 for best performance of the year.

Just about the time he was going into his next Shakespeare at the Old Vic, in *Othello* in February 1956, *Alexander the Great* and *The Rains of Ranchipur* were bombing in America; the word in Hollywood was that Richard Burton was box office poison. Yet there he was on the London stage winning plaudits and being hailed as the new Olivier.

For *Othello*, Richard and John Neville alternated the roles of Iago and Othello. For his Othello, Richard was criticised for losing the poetry of the verse, but his Iago was a big success. He told me, 'I tried to play the Moor. Or I tried to make the Moor more like me, and that didn't work. But I could find Iago within me. It suited my traits much better than Othello. I always wanted to be a great Shakespearean actor. And I was good, I admit it, in some of the parts. I was better than Olivier could have been as Iago. You don't have to be perfect in all Shakespeare, you know. You just have to make your mark on some of them, and people will remember you. Then, when you have achieved that, you – or at least, I – have to find something else to conquer.'

While not a star in Hollywood, he was a star of Shakespeare. People who have accused Richard of squandering his talent forget that he was, for a time, exercising his talent to its fullest, and both Gielgud and Olivier conceded that of all the younger actors who sought to make their name in Shakespeare, Burton was the one they both admired the most.

He had another film offer, this time from respected director Roberto Rossellini, who specifically asked for him to star in *Sea Wife* as an RAF officer who finds himself shipwrecked on a desert island with a nun. Rich was excited at the prospect of working with this fine director, and he looked forward to the Jamaican locations. But before shooting began the studio replaced Rossellini with Bob McNaught.

'I don't know if *Sea Wife* could have been a better film with Rossellini,' Rich told me,' but it couldn't have been worse. I'm sure it would have been much better.'

Joan Collins played the nun, and Rich typically attempted to make a move on her. She rejected him, and perhaps in a moment of sardonic humour he told her that women always gave in to him. She told him, 'I believe you would screw a snake,' and he replied, 'Only if it was wearing a skirt.'

Suffering from insomnia, he drank to make him sleep for just a few hours and be up at 5am with a hangover but still ready to do a full day's work on *Sea Wife*. In the end, the only worthwhile thing to come out of that film was the money he earned.

He didn't know what he was going to do next. With the exception of one more *Hamlet* to come, he was suddenly virtually through with Shakespeare on stage. What did he think he was doing with his talent? 'I was using it to climb mountains and once I'd climbed it, I had to find something else. You know, Mick, I have never felt that acting was the noblest vocation. But it's what I found I could do, so I wanted to do it well. Even on the worst films, I do my best. But more important than acting is *living*. More important than acting is *writing*. I have always wanted to be a great writer. But I'm a better actor than I am a writer, so that's what I do. And I want to be the best. You can't be considered the best unless you have done your best in Shakespeare. So I did the best I could and sometimes I succeeded and sometimes I didn't. But those successes . . . oh, boyo, they are treasures to me.'

Towards the end of the 1950s he was no longer wanted by Hollywood. He was disappointed because, despite the disparaging remarks he tended to make in interviews about films, he really wanted to see if he could be a fine screen actor. He told me, 'I wanted to be good in movies. I honest to God did. I did those films with the same attitude I did Shakespeare. But it didn't work for me. I can blame the directors, the screenwriters, the studio for putting me into films that were basically shit. But I tried to rise above the material; some good film actors can. I didn't.'

Still, he had made good money, earning £82,000 from his last three films. But he had to pay 92 per cent of his earnings from his first year in Hollywood in taxes, and the rest he spent on a house, presents, a car and, of course, alcohol. In 1954, after tax, he earned only £6000.

That was still a lot of money to Rich who didn't squander it but used it to help his siblings. He even put Ifor and Gwen on his payroll. In 1956 he decided that in order to keep more of his money in the future, he needed to escape living full time in the UK, and so, in January 1957, he bought a modest house in the quiet village of Céligny in Switzerland.

Philip Burton disapproved of the move, believing that it took Richard away from the London theatre where he was at his happiest. There was a renaissance in British films and theatre featuring working-class outsiders which would ideally suit Richard.

But the move to Switzerland wasn't just for the tax-breaks. It was a place he felt he could finally stop and reflect on his life which, since he left the RAF in 1948, had moved so fast he felt he was unable to get a proper perspective on where he was and what he should do next.

Brook Williams said:

'He named his house *Le Pays de Galles*. It was about half a mile from Lake Geneva. A beautiful place, and very quiet. Ifor and Gwen moved with them. Gwen was company for Sybil while Ifor's job was to build a guest chalet and turn the upper part of a barn into a library because Rich loved books, and he had always wanted a massive library. It was a place where his life slowed down considerably.

'I would visit there a lot. I had just come out of the RAF and didn't know quite what to do with myself. Rich made me extremely welcome and I looked up to him like an older brother. Maybe even a father. He was certainly a hero. He and my father were friends up to the time Richard died. I virtually moved in with them and lived with them for rather long periods of time.

'He would lunch at the Café de la Gare in the village, and each Sunday morning he drove to Geneva Airport, just 20 minutes away, in his much-loved red MG to pick up his Sunday newspapers. That was the perfect life for Rich . . . for a while.'

In early 1957, Sybil became pregnant and plans to adopt were abandoned. For the next nine months, Richard was 'profoundly happy in a way I had never seen him before', said Sir Stanley Baker. 'He seemed to be at peace with himself.'

Back home at Céligny, Rich wondered if there was more to life than acting. 'I never understood where this so-called talent for "acting" came from,' he told me. 'I was sure that it would disappear as mysteriously as it appeared. I sometimes felt I had to work just to see if it was still there.'

In 1957 his father died. When he received the news he reputedly asked, 'Which one?' It was Dic Bach, aged 81, just as predicted by the Welsh fortune-teller some years before. It only served to alarm Richard even more that his time would come when he was 33 the following year.

Neither Rich nor Ifor attended the funeral of the father who had neglected them all his life. 'For too many years I made my father sound the lovable rogue with my stories,' he said. 'But he was a useless drunk. I might be a drunk at times, but I hope I am not useless.'

Richard himself had become something of a figurehead for the Jenkins family. His main contribution to them all may have been financial, but it was more than their father had ever done for them.

Stanley Baker had a particular theory about Richard's attitude towards his father. 'Rich saw his father as being the cause of his mother's early death. Too many children because of too much sex and not nearly enough work to provide for the growing family or a thought for the woman who sacrificed her very life to keep hearth and home together.'

Rich went back to work in films for director Nicholas Ray in *Bitter Victory*, playing a British Army captain leading a patrol in the desert to capture German documents. Curt Jurgens played the Allied major who had had an affair with the captain's wife, so amid the action there was personal conflict between the two officers. It was a bold attempt at a different kind of Second World War picture, but as *Variety* noted, 'the script is basically flawed by the unclearly delineated key character of the major,' but it noted the 'fine thesping by Richard Burton'.

The film was not a success. Richard had still not cracked the film market and it seemed he never would – at least, not in Hollywood.

Sybil and Richard's daughter Kate was born on 10 September 1957. 'Kate was the child they had wanted for so long,' said Stanley Baker. 'Sybil was particularly happy because she had what she wanted: a child, a life she enjoyed with wonderful friends, and a husband she was sure would never leave her, despite his games.'

In late 1957 Richard was offered a play in America, *Time Remembered*, a comedy adapted from Jean Anouilh's *Léocadia*, at the Morosco Theatre in New York. Needing to discover if his stage talent was there still there, he accepted the play. He had the leading role of Prince Albert, Helen Hayes was a duchess and Susan Strasberg a ballerina the prince falls for. He fell for the ballerina off stage and on.

Susan Strasberg was the 19-year-old daughter of Lee Strasberg who ran The Actors Studio which taught 'The Method' style of acting. Marlon Brando was perhaps his most legendary student. Susan's mother, Paula, coached Marilyn Monroe.

As was the way with Rich, he decided to have Susan the instant he saw her. In 1974 he told me, 'I was obsessed and possessed by her. Obsessive and possessive. Does that constitute love? If so, then I was in love. But it feels now like it was more of a sexual compulsion. If anything, I love *love*. I am in love with being in love. And I love to make love.'

In the play he had to pour a glass of champagne. He never went on stage drunk, but his hand noticeably shook in this scene. Susan Strasberg wrote in her memoir that he told her that he was afraid he would die of drink. He never lost that fear; 'It's my destiny to die drunk,' he told me in 1974. He still feared, in 1957, that it was his destiny to die when he was 33.

While most considered the shakes to be nothing more than the need for alcohol, Richard often feared he was in danger of suffering a fit. 'I know that booze helps to keep the fits away,' he said. 'That's what I tell myself, and I believe it.'

Whether the alcohol really kept the seizures at bay is questionable; that Richard believed it did was enough – perhaps even a placebo effect. Or maybe it was just a good excuse to drink, although he disputed that theory when I put it to him. He said, 'I hate alcohol. I'd rather do without it. It's a tool for me. I have gone for periods in my life without it and been happier. I can stop. I *have* stopped. And I'm better without it. But, really, I do fear the fits.'

He would prove he could go without alcohol when he really had to. But at the age of just 32, as he was when performing *Time Remembered* in New York in 1957, he felt he had no real need to go on the wagon. And yet, as he confided to Susan Strasberg, he nevertheless felt the booze tugging at his mortality.

His affair with Susan appears to have been quite unconventional. They went to bed but, according to Strasberg, they never actually consummated their love, if love is what it was. They certainly made no secret of their relationship, attending nightclubs together, having lunch with the Strasbergs where he would discuss acting at great length with Lee, being entertained by Laurence Olivier and Vivien Leigh. 'Richard seemed not to care who noticed or knew,' Olivier once told me.

And yet it was almost an innocent kind of relationship. He was an older actor simply engaging with a younger actress for professional reasons, such as throwing her a surprise party at the Morosco Theatre attended by the cast and the toast of Broadway.

But his presents to her may have proven a touch extravagant for anything so innocent – a diamond pin, a white mink muff and scarf, and a satin lounge suit. She hated the suit because it made her feel like a mistress; she loved the white mink muff and scarf until she found out that he had bought Sybil a white mink coat and suspected they were all part of a set, but she loved the diamond pin and always wore it.

For the most part, Richard carried on his affair with Susan at the theatre; Sybil and Kate had come to New York and they lived with Richard in an apartment where he spent most of his nights.

While the play was still running, Richard found time to record a television version of *Wuthering Heights*, playing Heathcliff. It was, apparently, well thought of, as was his performance and it re-awakened interest in him in Hollywood.

He had already had the foresight to start thinking in terms of films as a business from which he could earn good money, much of which he could keep while living in Switzerland. He had even started to employ some respected business advisers and started to think of himself as a business *and* a businessman. His advisers began working with Warner Bros. on a three-picture deal which would earn him around $450,000.

By the end of the 1950s, he had a million dollars in his Swiss bank account. But Hollywood was going to have to wait a little longer because something of far greater interest captured his imagination. At a party thrown by the Oliviers in New York, he met playwright John Osborne whose latest stage hit, *Look Back in Anger*, had brought about a watershed in British theatre: plays with a social conscience. Olivier had become so impressed with Osborne's work that he was able to get him to write *The Entertainer* for him.

Osborne had a proposition for Richard; would he play Jimmy Porter in the film version of *Look Back in Anger*? Richard didn't hesitate to say yes. His advisers advised him to say no. His fee for *Look Back in Anger* would be less than $100,000. Richard was adamant.

He was also trying to set up a film of *Coriolanus* and was attempting to raise the money while Philip worked on adapting Shakespeare's huge play into a screenplay. Olivier had enjoyed success with Shakespeare on screen, but it had lasted only a season. Olivier's third Shakespearean film, *Richard III*, was considered a commercial failure.

When *Time Remembered* ended, Rich took Susan on a late-night horse and carriage ride through Central Park, and having said his farewells, he and his family took a cruise back to Switzerland. He continued to write to Susan, and when he went to England in 1959 to film *Look Back in Anger*, she turned up too. So did Claire Bloom, but she had a legitimate reason; she was co-starring in the film. Suddenly, Claire Bloom was back in his life.

'When we made *Look Back in Anger*, I hadn't seen Richard for about four years,' said Claire in 1979. 'Our first rehearsal was in a pub. He was very nervous.'

Also in the film was Mary Ure, John Osborne's wife – she later married Robert Shaw. It was during that later marriage that I got to know Mary well. Rich was delighted to find out that Mary and I were friends, and he told me, 'She's a lovely lady and Shaw doesn't deserve her.'

She was obviously somebody Rich was particularly fond of, and neither he nor she made any secret – to me, at least – that they had shared some pleasurable sexual time together when making *Look Back in Anger*.

'Claire [Bloom] came into the film expecting to find Rich wanting her as he had done before,' said Mary. He gave Claire no indication that things had changed between and at first they carried on pretty much where they had left off.

'But she was in for a shock,' said Mary. 'Rich was very cleverly juggling his time between me and Susan Strasberg. I made sure I kept a low profile and have no idea if Claire knew that Richard was fucking me.' (Mary had a very frank and colourful vocabulary.) 'But she soon discovered he was fucking Susan because she walked in on them; Rich told me that. Poor Claire. She'd had no idea. She told them, "Fuck off, the both of you," and slammed the door on her way out.'

The day I was with Richard in Winchester in 1974, I saw him actually look vaguely embarrassed when I related Mary's version of events. 'It's true,' he said. 'But I was hopelessly in love with Susan by then, and I hadn't expected Claire to come back into my life. I'd thought that was all over. Actors never know when they are suddenly going to be thrown together in a piece of work. But as soon as I saw Claire, I knew I still had strong feelings for her.'

I asked him what his relationship with Mary was. 'She was just so fuckable and such a wonderful friend,' he said. No love between them, then? 'Not from me.'

He said this in 1974, by which time Mary was in a bad way physiologically, drinking heavily and taking drugs. I did see her again but didn't talk to her about Richard; she died a year later, aged just 42 – a beautiful woman whose talent had long been ignored by theatre, films and even her husband. But she had told me a few years earlier, 'I love to be fucked, and Rich loved to fuck me.' And that, it seems, was all there was to it.

How he found the energy, let alone the time to frolic with two women on the same film set was beyond me, and when I asked him how he managed, he said, 'You find the time for anything that's worth the while.' He also had the possibility of his premature death tugging at him from time to time. In November of 1958 he turned 33 – the age at which he was told he would die. There obviously seemed little point in trying to conserve energy if the end was inevitably close.

Claire was left feeling humiliated, according to Rod Steiger. 'She was more mad at herself for thinking she could ignite those passions again. But he was being ignited enough by so many other women. Poor Claire!'

That was the end of her affair with Richard. If she felt humiliated at all, it never came across on screen; in Look Back in Anger Claire Bloom gives one of her finest performances. As, indeed, did Mary Ure and also the underestimated Gary Raymond who had a major role as Jimmy's best friend.

Claire never spoke of her affair with Richard to me, but she talked a bit about their working relationship:

'Richard gave one of his finest screen performances [in *Look Back in Anger*], and it was one of the finest films I ever made, so I am proud of it, and proud to have worked in it with Richard.

'There was a great deal of his real self in the film. He had the same kind of emotions, some of it anger, as Jimmy Porter. Rich had known poverty and social injustice, and I think he felt a certain kind of inadequacy because he had the rather cushy life of an actor while his family and the people he knew had endured so much. He brought all those emotions to the surface to play Jimmy Porter.

'Tony Richardson, our director, was wonderful. He didn't want performances. He wanted us all to be natural. He'd not directed a film before, although he directed on stage and this was from his own stage production, and if you asked him what he wanted you to do in a scene, he'd say, "Do what you like. I have no idea." I loved working like that. I was allowed to give what I think was my first really adult performance in a film.'

Rich also enjoyed Richardson's style of directing. 'We filmed in a real house. No phoney sound stage. And we rehearsed in that house too, and I lived in it for a while, to make it *my* home. Tony never told me how to play the part. He said, "You're Jimmy Porter now, Rich. You know him better than I do. I'll set the camera up and you play him how you want." I've never known a film director to do that before. But then, Tony hadn't directed a film before. He gave me the freedom to become Porter and not just *act* the part.'

It was the first time Richard had really enjoyed making a film. It was also the first time he looked forward to seeing one of his own films. Today the movie is considered a classic and Burton's performance one of his finest. Ironically, at the time of its release in 1959 it was not well received and was a box office flop. But he always remained proud of his work in it. 'I didn't care what the critics thought. *I* liked the film, and I liked me in it,' he said. He could look back, not in anger, but in joy.

During filming, he managed to find time to return to Wales to do a radio play, *Brad*, by Saunders Lewis who was a contemporary and friend of poet and painter David Jones who was one of Richard's idols. When Rich arrived in his old village of Pontrhydyfen in his Rolls-Royce, he went straight to the Miner's Arms and bought drinks for everyone. He was greeted as a hero and he enjoyed the adulation. 'There was no point in pretending I was still one of them,' he said to me once. 'I could have arrived in a cab, but I drove up in my Rolls. I wasn't showing off; I was just saying, *this is what a Welshman from the valleys can achieve.* I think my friends and family back in Wales have always celebrated *with* me that fact. I wasn't better than any of them. I was just someone who had done well. But my heart was – *is* – always back there.'

Chapter Fourteen

I WONDER WHO THE KING IS SCREWING TONIGHT

RICH WAS KEEPING more of the money he earned now that he was living in Switzerland, and he made sure there was more money for his family. He bought houses for them, cars for some, and paid for holidays for older family members.

But back home in Céligny, he lived relatively modestly. 'There was nothing very grand about his house,' said Brook Williams. 'Much of his considerable library was made up of paperbacks, and he didn't fill his house with the usual trappings. There were no expensive pieces of artwork, no antiques. He wasn't really rich but he thought he was. Not nearly half as rich as he would become. But he was more than comfortable. The only thing he threw money at were cars – his red MG, his Rolls-Royce and a Cadillac.'

His 34th birthday came and went on 10 November 1959, and was celebrated in more robust style than usual. He hadn't died at the age of 33 after all. 'I seem to have spent my 33rd year relatively peacefully,' he recalled in 1974. 'I think I must have reached a point where I was trying to avoid going too far from home or working too much in the hope that my life might be saved from whatever calamity destiny thought it had in store for me.'

He had turned his back on the Warner Bros. deal to do work he thought worthwhile, but he still recognised that films earned him the money he needed to keep himself and his entire family in comfort. So in 1959 and 1960 he made two films for producer Milton Sperling, *The Bramble Bush* and then *Ice Palace*, receiving a fee of $125,000 plus overtime for each. *Ice Palace* went so far over schedule that his fee doubled.

In *The Bramble Bush*, Richard played a doctor standing trial in Massachusetts accused of blackmail, adultery and a mercy killing. It ran into censorship problems and in America its final scene was cut. 'It was one of those films that looked good on paper, but a lot less so on film,' Richard said. 'I'm not sure I've ever learned that lesson. I don't believe any actor does.'

Ice Palace was a saga about the development of Alaska from 1918 to 1958 when it became a state. There were a few weeks of filming on location in Alaska in temperatures often below freezing. Always professional in his work, Rich was up each morning at five, but he had little sleep. To fend off the cold he drank after work into the early hours – probably more an excuse than a reason. He told co-star Jim Backus, 'Here we are, drinking at three o'clock in the morning, sitting on top of the world and making this piece of shit.'

He was even more despondent when he was unable to get home for the birth of his second daughter, Jessica.

Neither of the two films did well. But he returned better off financially to Céligny where he practised writing; 'I would have preferred to have been a writer than an actor,' he said, 'and I was pretty much convinced my film career was over. I could make little money from the stage, so I thought it was time to become a writer. But the truth is, writing is harder than acting, and I grew more lazy as I grew older, and acting was the easy option.'

He continued to act, he said, 'because they kept asking me to.' Tony Richardson and John Osborne collaborated on a play for BBC Television, *A Subject of Scandal and Concern*, and asked Rich to play the real-life 19th-century schoolteacher George Jacob Holyoacke who stood trial for saying he didn't believe in God. Richard was paid £1000.

Then there was a film for American television, *The Fifth Column*, with Maximilian Schell. Rich became more convinced that having gone from playing Shakespeare to making bad Hollywood films in Hollywood to making telemovies in America meant his acting career was approaching an inevitable end. 'I'd reached a stage where the only thing that could keep me acting was a real challenge – and lots of money!' he said.

The challenge and the money came when, out of the blue, he was offered the role of King Arthur on Broadway in a new musical by Lerner and Loewe. It was called *Camelot*.

'I was thinking along the lines of someone like Howard Keel to play King Arthur,' Alan Jay Lerner told me when I was at his house in 1984 (I was there to interview his wife, Liz Robertson). 'Then, at a party, Moss Hart [who had written the screenplay of *Prince of Players*] said, "You know, Dick Burton and his wife Sybil sang at a Hollywood party, and Dick wasn't bad." I said, "Is he a baritone?" He said, "Not exactly. He doesn't sing sweetly, but he can put over a song. You should try him." So we did. His voice was so rich that he didn't need to be a great singer. He had a great voice. He was the perfect king.'

Rich told me, 'It never occurred to me to try a musical. I talked to Larry [Olivier] about it and he thought it was an excellent idea. But I thought that a musical about knights in armour was also very daring. At first I thought it was ludicrous. But then I realised that it was so outrageous that I couldn't resist the challenge.' He felt that *Camelot* was a gamble that could backfire, and that was anything but boring.

I am sure his decision to rise to the challenge was encouraged by the fee; he was to be paid $4000 a week plus a percentage.

Despite his seemingly failed film career, there was still money to be made; he was paid $100,000 to provide a voice-over for an American 26-part TV series, *The Valiant Years*, which was based on Winston Churchill's account of the Second World War. Although Richard didn't do an outright impersonation of Churchill, he provided a voice-over that was based on Churchill.

He started rehearsing *Camelot* in September 1960, and before long the whole enterprise looked doomed to disaster. Alan Jay Lerner told me:

'The advances [for tickets] were astounding. This was our follow-up to *My Fair Lady* and we had Julie Andrews from that show in this one as Guinevere, and people were expecting something wonderful. But we were all falling apart. I was going through a divorce and then had a nervous breakdown and had to spend a fortnight in hospital, Fred [Loewe] was hospitalised after suffering a haemorrhage, and our director Moss Hart had a heart attack, and we found the show was running far too long. When we opened in Toronto it ran four and a half hours. The curtain didn't come down until twenty minutes to one in the morning.

'It was Dick Burton who held the whole thing together. I tell you, *Camelot* would never have been the success it was if it hadn't been for Burton. And that isn't to take anything away from Julie Andrews or anyone else. I mean, this man was really like a king, and you could believe he might have been one for real. He was English aristocracy.'

When I pointed out that Burton was Welsh, Lerner said, 'It was that mixture of his Welsh boldness and voice and his command of the English language that fooled you into believing he could have been part of the English aristocracy. It was commanding, and when we played to the public, they were mesmerised by him. He cast a spell.'

Roddy McDowall played Mordred in *Camelot*. When I interviewed him in 1978 (on the set of *The Thief of Baghdad* at Shepperton Studios), we talked of Richard Burton – and most everyone else; McDowall knew *everyone* in movies, and everyone liked him. 'Did you ever see Rich on stage?' he asked me. I said I hadn't but had watched him at work on a few films. McDowall said, 'The stage is where the magic really happens with him. Film isn't able to capture his true power, only the essence of it.' That is true of many actors. Laurence Olivier was at his greatest on stage, despite many great film performances. It's the same with Peter O'Toole.

McDowall said:

'Richard had two not-so-secret weapons that gave his King Arthur the power and brilliance which turned *Camelot* into a massive hit. One was his voice. He could have stood on stage and read the obituaries in the newspaper and he would have made it sound like an epic poem.

'The other not-so-secret weapon was Philip Burton, who was living and working in New York at that time. He came to Richard's apartment and coached him through the script and the score before rehearsals had even begun. By the time Richard began rehearsing with our director Moss Hart, he knew his lines and lyrics, and he knew how he was going to deliver them. If he hadn't, it might have been a disaster when Hart fell ill after rehearsals began. Then Richard suggested – well, *insisted* – that Philip take over the direction of *Camelot*.'

Richard's King Arthur, then, was the result of loving labour by Philip Burton who was, it seemed, the one person in the world who knew how to bring out the best in Richard on stage, even when there were songs involved.

'Phil saved *Camelot*,' said Richard. 'He cut the running time to a more manageable three hours and yet managed to add three new songs.'

Rich didn't object when his own part was cut; everything Philip Burton did was for the good of the show, and also for the good of Richard. Rich had complete faith in everything Philip did. And all this happened while the show was in its pre-Broadway tour.

McDowall said, 'Philip's contribution cannot be underestimated, and he was very generous in agreeing to allow Moss Hart full credit as director.'

Philip's presence ensured that Richard behaved on and off stage; he didn't drink until after the final curtain, and then only in moderation, except for one day, which Roddy McDowall told me about: 'He made a bet that he could drink a bottle of vodka during the matinee and another during the evening performance with no effect.

'At the end of the day he asked Julie Andrews, who knew nothing about the bet, what he she thought of his performance that day, and she told him, "I think you were a little better than usual."

'After that, he never went on stage drunk again and he hardly ever drank off stage as well. He really made an effort to stay dry.'

Rich was loved by the whole company, according to Lerner. 'He got the show to New York. He was a star who really behaved like a star and not a prima donna.'

Richard brought Sybil and the children out to New York. Once the production had settled into its run in New York at the Majestic Theatre in December 1960, he and Sybil refurbished his dressing room with their own money and renamed it 'Burton's Bar'. He continued to refrain, by and large, from drinking during the day, but often, Lerner observed, he arrived at the theatre 'sleepless, shaking, his voice a mere croak, and he'd say, "Don't worry, luv", and he would literally take control of the shakes before going on stage, then begin with a few whispered words and finally will that amazing voice to its full strength. He was always word perfect, sometimes good and often magnificent. He was remarkable.'

He was also, as would be expected, involved with another woman, in this case Pat Tunder, a dancer from the Copacabana Club. Lerner said, 'When he sang, "I wonder what the King is doing tonight", I would swear that it often sounded like, "I wonder who the King is screwing tonight." '

Curiously, despite the advance bookings, sales of tickets were beginning to slow down and it was feared the production would not last long. It was saved by a 20-minute performance by the cast on the ever-popular *Ed Sullivan Show* on TV. Ticket sales suddenly soared, success was assured, and Richard won the Tony Award for Best Actor in a Musical.

The original cast recording album topped the charts, and Rich was invited to the White House shortly after John F. Kennedy became President of the United States. The Kennedys chose to call their official home *Camelot*.

Richard loved working with Julie Andrews and felt it was a crime that, following the success of the stage production of *My Fair Lady*, she wasn't allowed to play the part in the film version. 'She is a real pro and a wonderful lady,' he told me. I asked him if she was one of his numerable conquests. He said, 'Let me put it this way. Our Lancelot, Robert Goulet, had quite a passion for Julie and tried it on with her but was given the brush off. So he came to me and asked my advice. I said, "Why come to me? I couldn't get anywhere with her either."'

Through 1961 Richard pushed himself to go on night after night and give the same performance, more or less. He became bored with it. It had made him an undisputed star of Broadway, and earned him good money, but he started to feel desperate to escape.

The way out came when director Joseph L. Mankiewicz convinced 20th Century Fox to offer Burton the role of Mark Antony in the most opulent of all historical epics, *Cleopatra*.

Richard's life was to change forever.

Chapter Fifteen

LIZ AND DICK

THE EXECUTIVES AT 20th Century Fox were horrified when director Joseph L. Mankiewicz told them he wanted Richard Burton to play Mark Antony. He was, they argued, box office poison. But Mankiewicz was, at that time, in total control of *Cleopatra*, and what he wanted he got. He got Richard Burton.

Stephen Boyd, who had been so brilliant as a Roman tribune in *Ben-Hur*, had originally been cast as Antony when filming on *Cleopatra* began in 1960 at Pinewood Studios in England. Rouben Mamoulian was then directing the film which had grown from a modest sound remake of Fox's 1917 Theda Bara *Cleopatra* into a considerable epic starring Elizabeth Taylor as the Queen of the Nile.

When the film's producer Walter Wanger had offered Taylor the role, she said that she would do it for a million dollars plus profits, thinking he would turn her down. He accepted her terms and she became the highest paid film star in history. But filming in the English climate made Elizabeth continually ill, delaying production. Mamoulian had repeatedly threatened to quit the film and when he did so again in January 1961, his resignation was accepted. Elizabeth wanted Joseph L. Mankiewicz, who had directed her in *Suddenly Last Summer*, to take the helm, and she got her wish.

Mankiewicz, a fine screenwriter, began rewriting the screenplay. In March, Taylor was rushed to hospital with pneumonia where an emergency tracheotomy saved her life. While she recovered, Mankiewicz decided to film *Cleopatra* in Rome. By then Boyd had left the film for other commitments, as had Peter Finch who was to have played Julius Caesar.

Rex Harrison replaced Finch, and Burton replaced Boyd. (There is a sad irony here in that Stephen Boyd was to have played the leading role in the 1979 adventure *The Wild Geese* but died before filming began, and so Boyd was again replaced by Richard Burton.)

Mankiewicz told me that when he was recasting Antony, Burton wasn't actually his first choice. 'I wanted Brando. He had been so good as Antony in the *Julius Caesar* we did in 1951. But he was making *Mutiny on the Bounty* so he wasn't available. Richard was my second choice. There's no shame in being second choice to Brando. But Fox was very unhappy because they'd tried to make a star out of Burton in the fifties but he didn't catch on. My only concern was that he was a very fine actor. A great actor. And when we met it was love at first sight. We liked each other. No pretensions. No false flattery. We said what we thought.'

'I can't tell you what a relief it was to see a sudden end to playing King Arthur,' Richard told me. 'I had become so unbearably bored playing it night after night. And the money they [20th Century Fox] were offering was too good to say no.'

His fee was $250,000 plus overage. But what exactly, I wondered, persuaded Richard to accept the role of Antony without ever seeing a screenplay? He said, 'It was because Joe [Mankiewicz] was a good writer, and he knew about Shakespeare – he had directed *Julius Caesar* and when I heard he was rewriting the screenplay of *Cleopatra*, I thought it had a chance of being a superior epic screenplay.'

'We hated to lose Burton,' said Alan Jay Lerner, 'but we owed him so much that we felt we couldn't hold him back, so we let him go.' But not without a good financial return from Fox.

'I told them that they should ask for a nice fat amount in compensation from Fox,' Richard said, 'and they were able to get $50,000.'

Richard persuaded Mankiewicz and Walter Wanger to cast Roddy McDowall as Octavian, and so they had to compensate the *Camelot* producers a little more. *Cleopatra* was proving to be extremely costly, the budget having risen from $10 million to $14 million with only seven minutes of film shot, none of it usable.

Rich arrived in Rome with Sybil in October 1961. Roddy McDowall arrived shortly after; he was now a close friend of Richard and had been friends with Elizabeth Taylor for many years; both Taylor and McDowall had left their native England as children to become actors in Hollywood. 'When I arrived in Rome Richard insisted I moved in with him, the children and Sybil in Rome,' said McDowall. 'And then we all waited to work.'

Mankiewicz was concentrating on filming the scenes between Caesar and Cleopatra which didn't involve Antony, so Rich and Sybil enjoyed a holiday. 'It was taking forever to film,' said McDowall, 'because Mankiewicz was writing the script at night and shooting the scenes the next day. Most films are shot out of order, with a schedule based on what sets and actors are available to keep costs down, but Mankiewicz was writing the screenplay from scratch, and he was shooting every scene in order. That isn't the most efficient way to make a movie.'

When I asked Joe Mankiewicz about that, he said, 'It may not have been efficient, but it was the *only* way I could make that movie. The dialogue was not good and I needed to rework it all, and I could only do that starting from the beginning.'

Richard's fee grew while he waited to work; he finally did his first shot on 2 January 1962. It was a scene in which Caesar reveals to Cleopatra and Antony his plans to become emperor.

Roddy McDowall recalled:

'Richard arrived on the set on his first day terribly hungover. He shook as he often did after a night of drinking. Elizabeth helped him to raise a cup of coffee to his lips. She found him very childlike and that appealed to the mothering instinct in her. If you are ever sick, Elizabeth will always take good care of you. Rich kept giggling like a small boy and forgetting his lines and she found that very endearing. She saw this highly intellectual actor was just like a needy child, and she became his mother. I think that struck a chord in Rich because he had lost his mother when he was still a baby, and here he was with a mother who was not only warm and soothing but was extremely sensual. I knew before we ever arrived in Rome that Richard was never going to be able to resist her. I told him so. He said, "Perhaps I'll play hard to get." He thought that would be a great game. He was on a losing streak the moment they began filming.'

Elizabeth's husband, singer Eddie Fisher, was also in Rome and the couple were seemingly very much in love. Just exactly when Richard and Elizabeth fell in love with each other is a matter of conjecture; everyone seems to have a different opinion. But each recalls the moment they realised something had happened.

Roddy McDowall said, 'They were shooting a love scene and were in

116

a passionate embrace, and Joe yelled, "Cut!" And then "Cut!" Finally he yelled "CUT!" and they stopped kissing. Well, everyone laughed, but we all knew what was happening.'

Martin Landau, who played Antony's loyal general Rufio, recalled, 'I got to work one morning early and Liz was in the make-up department, and I sat down in a make-up chair. Richard came in and gave her a big kiss which I saw in the mirror, and I thought, "Oh my God!"'

I asked Richard how and when it happened. He said, 'It was not one thing but many. I don't recall it being sudden, but in a way I was suddenly in love with her. But I can't tell you when that happened.'

I told him I had heard it had happened when he saw her naked in the bath scene. 'Oh, her *body*,' he said, as if talking about one of the great wonders of the world. 'It was . . . intoxicating. You could not look at Elizabeth nude and not want her. So, yes, of course, as soon as I saw her nude, I wanted her. But that isn't love. That's just lust, and I have always had plenty of *that*.'

Obviously, Rich was intensely attracted to – and intoxicated by – Elizabeth, and he was certainly capable of carrying on an affair with her, as he had done so often in the past with his leading ladies. But there was a different dynamic to this affair that became a serious threat to his marriage. It was a fusion of many things. Joe Mankiewicz thought:

'Richard Burton was overawed by her sheer power in Hollywood. Her power and her wealth. She was virtually brought up in Hollywood, and she knew how to get what she wanted, and people fell over themselves to give it to her. That is incredible power, and Richard loved that about her. She had a great contract [for *Cleopatra*] because she had a great head for business, and he was mesmerised just by her contract.

'You put all that together as well as her staggering beauty and you have a very potent combination of sexual and economic power which Richard clearly found unable to resist.

'And there was the drinking. Burton had fun drinking and she loved that sense of fun because she liked to drink too. I recall that at the time Eddie [Fisher] was trying to control her drinking, but it was hopeless, of course.'

Rich had one very simple, although hardly definitive, explanation as to why he fell for her: 'She has the best pair of tits in the world!' He was only partially joking. He said, 'There was nothing better in life, apart from a good book, to wake up in the morning and the first thing I see is the most fabulous pair of tits.' He affectionately called her 'Miss Tits' on the set.

There was another aspect of Elizabeth which intrigued him. 'She really knew how to act for the camera, and I didn't. I would go into all kinds of contortions to display a range of emotions, but all she had to do was to have a single thought and it showed on camera. She was my film acting teacher. I began to learn from her on *Cleopatra*. That was something I loved about her, and it must be one reason for loving her.'

Roddy McDowall believed that what turned a sexual affair into something much more was Elizabeth's own peculiar moral code:

'She wasn't one to have casual affairs. She always had to marry her men. And when she and Rich were having an affair, she decided that she would have to have him for good. I think she loved him before he loved her.

'It was very difficult for me because I loved Sybil and was living with them, but I love Elizabeth also. The oddest thing was that both Eddie [Fisher] and Sybil were often on the set, and it was as if they were the only two people who didn't know what was going on.

'But I think that was what Sybil wanted people to think. Eddie, however, couldn't believe Elizabeth would ever fall for anyone but him. He had been married to Debbie Reynolds and frankly I was appalled at the way he dumped her for Liz and maybe his ego was such that he couldn't begin to consider that she might be falling in love with Rich.'

Richard's sex life was nothing if not complicated. Pat Tunder was in Rome to carry on her affair with Richard even while he was involved with Elizabeth. He still had no intention of leaving Sybil. 'It was amazing that he managed to remember who was who,' said McDowall.

Richard's contract stipulated that he had St David's Day – 1 March – off, and to celebrate in 1962 he embarked on a mammoth tour of the Roman bars. The next day he arrived late on the set with Pat Tunder. 'Elizabeth was furious,' said McDowall. 'I doubt that it was because he was late because *she* was always late. It was because he was with this other woman, and she berated him for keeping everyone waiting, and he yelled back at her that it was good for *her* to be kept waiting for a change.'

Pat Tunder left Rome a few days after the St David's Day incident. With her gone, that only gave more space for the chemistry between Dick and Liz to intensify. She went after him and he made only feeble efforts to resist.

'The thing is, I was attracted to all the beautiful leading ladies I was lucky to have. But Elizabeth was simply intoxicating.' The word 'intoxicating' was the one he frequently used to describe her. He found alcohol intoxicating and hard, though not impossible, to resist, and he was finding that she had the same effect upon him. 'But, you know,' he told me, 'I was still with Sybil and I had two daughters, one of whom [Jessica] was ill. I had no intention of giving them up.'

The problem with Jessica was not at first obvious. 'She couldn't speak,' said Roddy McDowall, 'except to call out "Rich! Rich!" That plaintive call came when her daddy finally left her and sister Kate and their mummy.'

Richard only spoke to me once of Jessica, in 1974, saying, 'I fear I gave my daughter a mental illness that is part of my own.'

She has spent all her life in care, her family unable to reach her emotionally through the terrible mental barriers which Richard thought was all his fault. 'I am a basket case – in real terms,' he told me. 'I have terrible days of being unfathomably depressed and I have no idea why, and then there are these blackouts.' He never stopped blaming himself for Jessica's condition.

His depression was something that seemed to manifest ever more strongly with age; or maybe he just didn't notice it so much when he was younger and invariably inebriated. He despised doctors and rarely saw one. The idea of seeing a doctor for his self-confessed mental illness must have been unthinkable, but had he done so, he may well have been diagnosed, possibly with bipolar disorder – once better known as manic-depression – as well as epilepsy. Not that he would have wanted the prehistoric treatment that was available back then. 'Nobody is putting electricity through my brain,' he told me. 'I heard from Larry [Olivier] what they did to poor Vivien [Leigh] for her illness. I'm sure they only made her worse, not better.'

I talked a little about this to Roddy McDowall who commented,

'Jessica's illness is not Richard's fault. But he believes it was, and he suffers tremendous guilt because of that. But you can't tell him. He knows better.'

I asked Roddy if he thought Rich enjoyed wallowing in self-pity and guilt. 'Not at all. But he has a sense of duty to those who he is responsible for and he cares for every single member of his *huge* family, and that includes all of Elizabeth's children. His own children are more special than all other people, and for him to even think for an instant that he had caused one of his daughters to be ill in the mind is only a mark of his incredible sense of responsibility. But it's also a mark of his fear for his own sanity, I think. He has a tremendously dark side when that dark side takes hold of him.'

Richard had experienced many moments of depression, but as he became increasingly caught up with Elizabeth, his somewhat manic-depressive state manifested itself more acutely. He was never more happy then when with her, and he was never more depressed either because he knew he was making his family suffer, such as when the paparazzi surrounded his house and terrified Jessica so much that all she could do was scream.

Back in the UK, many of his friends were stunned by the rumours of a passionate romance between Richard and Elizabeth. 'Even by Richard's standards, it was unbelievable,' said Stanley Baker. 'We, their friends, all loved Sybil and frankly we came down on her side.' He was talking about people like Emlyn Williams, Philip Burton and Richard's own family, especially Ifor and Gwen.

Brook Williams recalled, 'My father flew out to Rome to try to get him to come to his senses. He told him, "Look, Rich, you're just being Mark Antony to her Cleopatra. It's just you becoming the part again." And Richard said to him, *"Dwi am broidi'r eneth ma."* He was saying, "I'm going to marry this girl." That's when we knew he'd really lost his head. Ifor was furious. He and Rich had a fight – I mean, they exchanged real blows. He and Ifor agreed it would be better if Sybil left Rome until the film was finished and then they would be one family again. By now Sybil knew about Elizabeth and seeing a real threat to her marriage she let Richard know that she knew, and then left with Ifor and Gwen and the children.'

Sir Stanley Baker recalled hearing the news that Sybil had left for London in March and would be waiting for Rich when the filming was over; he said, 'When I heard that, I felt better. I thought, "Yes, Rich has gone a little further than usual, but he's going to be his old self again before long." Oh, what a fool he made of us. Well, not really us. Only himself.'

Richard was quite bemused by the strong reaction to his affair with Elizabeth and later tried to make light of it. 'I couldn't understand all the fuss,' he said. 'I *always* slept with my leading ladies . . . except Julie Andrews!'

When Sybil went back to London, Richard rushed to tell Elizabeth that Sybil knew about them and that 'the game was up', as he put it. Their affair had to end.

'That sent Elizabeth into a panic and over the edge,' said Brook Williams. 'She took an overdose of pills and was rushed to hospital. Of course, the studio couldn't admit to what had happened so the news was put out that she had food poisoning. But she had wanted to show Rich in the most dramatic way possible how much she loved him.'

Eddie Fisher rushed to her hospital bedside and there was the strong impression of a reconciliation between them. He then left Rome also that March, returning to New York from where he called her on the telephone to ask for her reassurance that she still loved him. She was unable to lie to him and couldn't tell him what he wanted to hear. What she didn't know was that he had invited reporters to record the telephone call. The scandal hit the headlines.

Rich made an effort to stay away from Elizabeth, but the suicide attempt had worked, according to Brook Williams who went over to Rome 'just to try and support him', he said; he even ended up as an extra in the film. 'How could he resist a woman prepared to kill herself for his love? He was quite out of his mind. He told me, "Brookie, I don't want this woman for my wife. What am I going to do?" And the next minute he was saying, "Oh my God, Brookie, I have got to marry Elizabeth. I've simply got to. What do I do?" He was asking *me*. I was only 24, but I had become his confidant and maybe even his closest friend when all his other friends turned their backs on him.'

Richard and Elizabeth tried to escape the scandal by slipping away for a day on their own, but the paparazzi found them, photos were taken, they made headlines around the world, and Elizabeth was condemned by the Vatican for what they described as her 'erotic vagrancy'.

Richard's emotions were all over the place. 'I knew it was a choice, not between Sybil and Elizabeth, but between Kate and Elizabeth,' he told me. 'I was fighting it, but I was telling all my friends, all my family, everyone who wanted to save me, to stay away from me. I was finally alone in Rome. Nobody deserted me. I sent them away. I was guilty and ashamed because I could feel I was turning my back on Kate.'

Brook said, 'Kate was the daughter he knew he could care for in what he thought of as a practical way. He loved Jessica, but she was in need of professional care. Kate was the only one of his children he could lavish love on, and he knew that by choosing Elizabeth, he would be refusing Kate all the love he could give her. But he really was not in control of himself although he thought he was.'

Rich bought Elizabeth a diamond she had seen in Bulgari's in Rome. It cost him $150,000.

'I bought her a diamond and then felt I was walking into my own trap, so I decided that this *would* be just another affair and no more than that,' he said. 'Elizabeth understood. She was willing to give me up for the sake of my family and her own children. I told myself that when the filming came to an end, so would the affair.'

It is easy to forget that there was a major motion picture being made while all this was going on. Filming continued at a slow pace as Mankiewicz wrote new scenes for the next day's filming. 'The writing was good – very good,' said Richard. There were other delays, often due to Elizabeth's constant lateness on the set.

'The work was slow,' said Rich, 'and it wasn't all because of Joe or because Elizabeth was late. The lighting cameraman, Leon Shamroy, was shooting in Todd-AO and he was creating exquisite shots. The quality of the photography is simply exquisite, but it took too much time to light each shot. *That's* what took up almost all the time.'

Back in Hollywood, the studio executives were getting nervous about the amount of coverage the Dick and Liz scandal was making, and they were convinced at first that it could damage any chance the film had of making back the increasing amount of money being spent on it.

Joe Mankiewicz was adamant, when I spoke to him in 1972, that the film's exorbitant costs were not all due to the actual production. 'There were executives and studio people who were having a good time and writing off their expenses to *Cleopatra*. They had nothing to do with the picture, but it was something anyone's lavish expenses could be lost in. The film was expensive, sure, but it never cost the 40 million they claimed it did.'

Mankiewicz tried to concentrate on making the film rather than worrying too much about the scandal that was getting all the attention. 'Joe was having to listen to Richard telling him all his problems,' said Roddy McDowall in 1978, 'and then Elizabeth would come to Joe and he would have to listen to her. He was too kind to them. I can understand that. Elizabeth has her way of making men do what she wants them to do, and as for Rich . . . well, Joe was in awe of his incredible talent and so he indulged him. He indulged them both.

'They were both really hard on Joe because he was getting hardly any sleep. He was shooting the film by day and at night he'd sit up for hours to write the next day's dialogue. He'd have shots to make him sleep, and then shots to keep him awake in the day. He was in a rough way and it eventually made him very ill.'

Mankiewicz recalled, 'I got so tired of the press, I said, "I'll tell you the truth. Richard and I are in love." Richard heard about this and the next time he came on the set he kissed me on the lips!'

Mankiewicz wasn't too bothered about the Liz and Dick affair; he was only concerned with the way it interfered with the work. He told me, 'The studio was sure the scandal would hurt the film. I was sure it would help sell the film. Burton and Taylor really *were* Antony and Cleopatra.'

When the film unit moved to Ischia for the sea battle, Richard and Elizabeth arrived together in a helicopter and took adjacent suites in their hotel. Still believing they would end the affair when filming was over, Elizabeth finished her contribution to the scene and reaffirmed that she would not see Rich again.

But she returned to him just a few weeks later. 'Richard and Liz came to stay with us at Portofino,' Rex Harrison told me; by 'us', he meant he and his wife Rachel Roberts. 'They were souls being torn apart. I knew they couldn't be without each other but they were trying to convince themselves that they *would* be without each other. I knew then that their fate was written.'

Mankiewicz was convinced he was making a superior epic film, but as he came to the end of principal photography in July 1962, he had little money left to film the battle scenes. What he managed to shoot looked cheap, especially compared to the rest of the film. Nevertheless, he edited his film and turned it into two three-hour long films, *Caesar and Cleopatra* and *Antony and Cleopatra*. It was, in essence, a film and a sequel shot back to back, which had not been what Fox had wanted.

Back in Hollywood, Darryl F. Zanuck, who had left 20th Century Fox in 1956, managed to take control of the studio once more. Fox was close to bankruptcy because of the escalating costs of *Cleopatra* and Zanuck had to do something to save it. He had been making his labour of love, *The Longest Day*, for Fox in which Richard Burton and Roddy McDowall had appeared briefly along with just about every other major star in America, Britain, France and Germany. Zanuck had been very shrewd and had shot the film in black and white which kept the costs down considerably. He felt that *The Longest Day* could save the studio, but it was necessary to get *Cleopatra* salvaged and into cinemas as a single film. He fired Walter Wanger and Joe Mankiewicz, and had his own editor, Elmo Williams, cut the film. It was too much for Williams to accomplish and Zanuck rehired Mankiewicz who reluctantly but carefully edited the film to four hours. He even succeeded in getting Zanuck to allocate money so he could reshoot some of the battle scenes.

On 5 March 1963 the last scene was shot – or rather re-shot. It was the opening scene which should have involved Richard Burton but he had left for Céligny, and so his lines were given to Martin Landau.

But even that wasn't the end. According to Martin Landau, 'The four-hour version still had great holes in it. Zanuck agreed to give Mankiewicz more money so he could shoot additional scenes six months after the filming had actually finished. There were 39 pages of script that Joe wrote to fill in the blanks. So I was sent to London where I shot a number of vital scenes with Richard Burton at Pinewood Studios. So we did some pick-up shots, some close-ups and even some crowd scenes.'

The four-hour version premiered in America to mixed reviews. Judith Crist of the *New York Herald Tribune* called the film 'a monumental mouse'. *Newsweek* said, 'At six hours, *Cleopatra* might have been a movie. At four hours, it is the longest coming attraction for something that will never come.'

But *Variety* called it, 'a remarkable literate cinematic recreation of an historic epoch.' It went on, 'The result is a giant panorama, unequalled in the splendour of its spectacle scenes and, at the same time, surprisingly acute in its more personal story. This is due not only to the quality and focus of the screenplay, but to the talents of the three leading players.' But it conceded that 'some of the weaker moments in the film are the love scenes between Liz and Dickie'.

The film was cut further by another hour for its premiere in London. I once had the chance to ask Elizabeth about her work in *Cleopatra*. 'I gave that part everything, but it is unplayable, really,' she said. 'Shakespeare's version of Cleopatra [in *Antony and Cleopatra*] is the most difficult female role he ever wrote, and Joe was writing the second half of the film based very much on the play. I bared my soul for that role. Richard gave everything he had. Half of it ended up on the cutting room floor. I refused to see the film but was persuaded to go to the London premiere. They had cut the film down to three hours, and I only just managed to get back to the Dorchester where I threw up.'

In 1963, *Cleopatra* was considered by many critics as just another Roman epic which had come on the heels of *Ben-Hur* and *Spartacus*. Roman epics were everywhere, it seemed, and the critics had become jaded about them. A year later, in 1964, came one of the biggest, *The Fall of the Roman Empire*. But it was considered a commercial failure.

But the success of those great epics was never cut and dried. They cost so much that the studios relied heavily on reissues of those films and eventual sales to television to recoup their cost and make a profit. *Cleopatra* has the reputation of being a box office flop. It wasn't. It had certainly cost more than it should have, and nobody actually knows how much it really cost to make, but it did as well as it possibly could have on its first run by filling theatres. But it couldn't recoup its cost quickly enough; over the years, with reissues, television rights and video and DVD sales, the film went into profit. It took a long time, far longer than it should have, but it made a profit.

The word was out that Roman epics were no longer in vogue. In America, Paramount cut *The Fall of the Roman Empire* and it did poorly, while in Europe the film was handled with great care and did well, but not enough to recoup its costs. The film was never reissued and no further true Roman epics were made until *Gladiator* in 2000.

But time can be kind to many films. For instance, *It's a Wonderful Life* with James Stewart was a resounding flop but is now considered the quintessential Christmas movie. Both *Cleopatra* and *The Fall of the Roman Empire* today really do look far better than they did when first released, especially in comparison to the heavily computer-generated *Gladiator*. The screenplays are superior, the sets were real three-dimensional structures, the extras actually were there in their thousands, the performances are still generally good to excellent, and the camerawork remains often breathtaking.

Rich always said to me, 'You haven't seen *Cleopatra* because you only get a very long trailer of it.' He was talking about the three-hour version which is all I saw until I managed to acquire a copy of the four-hour version on video. On the set of *1984*, I told Richard I'd at last seen the movie. He was then quick to point out that the complete film remained lost, with two hours still missing. But he conceded that the four-hour film 'may retain' the elements that he felt gave *Cleopatra* the 'intelligence and integrity we all gave our blood for'.

Over the years he and I discussed the film – or rather, I discussed it and he listened, barely agreeing with me on anything. But in 1984 we talked it through again, and I reminded him of the clever editing of a montage scene between Antony and Cleopatra which linked a single conversation over different scenes which was one of Mankiewicz's brilliant touches; I talked of the devastation Richard portrayed as Antony following his defeat at the Battle of Actium, and with my ability for memorising lines of dialogue, I delivered poor redactions of some of his finest moments. He was a sick man by 1984, and one who was prepared to reflect on things past. I saw a tear run down his cheek, and I believe for a few moments he was back on the set in Rome, making Antony becoming Richard Burton, and sweating blood to make him so.

'It *was* something special,' he said. 'I never saw it. But I knew, on the set, it was going to be – supposed to be – something I would actually be proud of. But everybody hates it. Elizabeth hated it.' And then he looked like he remembered something and said, 'We were sailing to Capri [on their yacht] in 1970 or 71. We used to show films on board, and one night Elizabeth and all her children sat and watched *Cleopatra*. I wandered in and could only manage about ten seconds and then went to bed. The next morning she said to me, "Richard, it wasn't bad." I said, "What wasn't bad?" She said, "*Cleopatra*." I said, "But you hate that movie." She said, "I thought I did, but it's really not at all bad. And, Richard, you were fabulous as Antony."

'So maybe you are right. If Elizabeth could sit through the picture and think it wasn't bad and that I was good, then maybe you are right, Mick.'

I said, 'I am, Dick,' and he laughed.

And then, for maybe only just ten minutes or so, he asked me to tell him about some of the scenes that I could recall, and I did, quoting single lines – Antony struggling to push his sword into his own belly saying 'I always envied Rufio his long arms'; Antony single-handedly challenging the entire army of Octavian, crying, 'Will no one grant Antony an honourable way to die?'

'Ah, yes, I remember,' he said with a half smile. 'I was good, wasn't I?'

Rex Harrison received the better notices but it is Richard who gives the film a vibrancy that neither Harrison nor Elizabeth Taylor can provide. Elizabeth, although staggeringly beautiful as the Egyptian Queen, is often ill at ease with the classical nature of Mankiewicz's dialogue. But Burton relished it, giving something that is neither a real film performance nor a purely theatrical performance but something of a hybrid performance – a bit of both. He is not afraid to go so near the top that he only just manages to keep from going over it. It's a dangerous performance, and the more exciting because of it. I get the feeling that, having never had the chance to see Burton on stage, that this is as close as I could come to experiencing something of the soaring power of one of his live performances. To capture that on film and keep it within the bounds of a cinematic drama is rare, and it should be treasured.

Today *Cleopatra* is regarded as something unique and there is a growing awareness that it was undervalued and underrated in 1963. The four-hour version has been carefully restored on to DVD, and the search for the other missing two hours continues by film restorers. Some of it has been found, and perhaps the original Mankiewicz six-hour cut, or something close to it, may materialise in due course.

While the film awaited its fate at the cinema, the affair between Richard and Elizabeth continued on and off. 'It seemed the more Rich tried to stay away from Elizabeth,' said Brook Williams, 'the more he wanted her. And she was certainly not giving up.'

When Richard finished principal photography on *Cleopatra* – not counting the scenes he shot six months later in England – he returned to Céligny where Sybil now waited for him. Elizabeth went to Gstaad to be close to her children who were at school in Switzerland. Sybil believed, or hoped, that she finally had Richard back.

But after a few weeks Richard and Elizabeth, living no more than 85 miles apart, saw each other.

I asked Rich how it happened. 'I can't recall,' he said. 'It seems so long ago.' It was actually only 11 years earlier; I was asking Richard this in 1974. But the time he spent with Liz was, he had said more than once, 'like ten or more lifetimes'.

He tried to explain how the reconciliation occurred. 'Somebody phoned,' he told me.

'You or her?'

'Maybe her. I think it was.'

'And then?'

'And then lunch.'

'Who took who to lunch?'

'I must have taken her.'

'What do you remember of it?'

'Driving through the Alps, at speed, and then . . . we were together.'

'Like Antony at Actium,' I suggested.

'My God, it was! I ran away to be with her when I should have stayed. But I couldn't stay. I couldn't stay away from *her*. And I paid the price.'

It was art imitating life. This was the way it had been, on film and in history, Mark Antony giving up everything for the women he couldn't live without. And maybe that's what, today, partly makes the film of *Cleopatra* so spellbinding – because Richard had made Antony become him, and Elizabeth Taylor was Cleopatra after all.

'Only one thing was sure,' Rich said to me. 'It would all end badly. That's the nature of a Tragedy.'

It actually began as a Tragedy. Sybil did not tolerate Richard's affair with Elizabeth as she had done with his previous mistresses, and her desperation this time culminated in a suicide attempt. It happened when Richard was in Gstaad for one his liaisons with Elizabeth. Sybil took an overdose, probably of sleeping pills. Ifor was there to deal with the situation. When Sybil was well enough she turned to Philip Burton, who not only gave her his full support but cut Richard out of his life. Rich had now lost the man he had always considered to be his father.

A lot of Richard's former friends did the same as Philip. Stanley Baker said, 'I loved Rich very much, and thank God we became friends again, but I didn't like what he did to Sybil. He lost himself when he met Elizabeth Taylor.'

Not only family and friends turned their backs on Richard but the film industry did too. He had never had an easy relationship with the movies, especially Hollywood, and while the world – or at least 20th Century Fox – waited to see if *Cleopatra* would attract the masses, nobody was knocking down his door to offer him work. He was convinced that the scandal had wrecked his film career.

And that's what executives at Fox had first feared. But Darryl Zanuck began to realise that the public were so interested in the Burton–Taylor scandal that they might well be eager to see it happening before the cameras, which was one sound reason he decided that *Cleopatra* should remain one four-hour film and not two three-hour films. He thought that if the second half, *Antony and Cleopatra*, were to follow maybe several months or a year after the first half, *Caesar and Cleopatra*, Burton and Taylor might by then have gone their separate ways, and then nobody would want to go and see the second instalment.

There was, however, one film producer who wanted Richard for a film. He was Anatole de Grunwald who had produced some of Richard's earliest films. De Grunwald was preparing *The VIPs*, from a screenplay by Terence Rattigan, for MGM. It was a multilayered story, much like the old MGM classic *Grand Hotel*, but this was set in a fog-bound London airport where passengers, all played by well-known names though not necessarily top stars, lived out a night of individual drama. The character Rich was to play was a tycoon whose wife is in love with another man. The wife was to be played by Sophia Loren, and the other man by Louis Jordan.

Somebody suggested that Taylor play the wife instead of Loren. Orson Welles, who played a European film director in the picture, told me that it was Elizabeth who came up with the suggestion. 'She and Richard were in Paris together when [de Grunwald] called. She thought she was doing de Grunwald a great favour by offering herself for a mere million dollars. And she was right. It was perfect casting for good commercial reasons at the right time.'

But the right time had to be carefully planned. De Grunwald apparently spent just one afternoon planning how he could shoot the film in only ten weeks – very fast for a major movie – and get the film into cinemas around the same time *Cleopatra* premiered. Even with Elizabeth's million dollar fee and Richard's half a million dollar payment, the film could be produced at a tenth of the cost of *Cleopatra*.

The VIPs was filmed at MGM's studio at Borehamwood, just outside of London. The other stars included Rod Taylor, Maggie Smith, Elsa Martinelli and Margaret Rutherford. Taylor was the biggest of the film's stars; Burton was still not a major star and there was still the question of whether people would go to a Richard Burton movie.

Rich and Elizabeth arrived in London by train together but put on a pretence of being apart by arriving at the Dorchester Hotel in separate limousines; they had adjoining penthouse suites. He also rented a

Hampstead house where Sybil and the two children stayed. He hadn't left Sybil, and he couldn't give up Elizabeth.

He never excused himself, telling me:

'I was torn, and it serves me right. I should have been torn apart for the way I behaved. I was unable to do the right thing by anyone, not because I wanted it all but because I didn't know what to do. I behaved very badly, even by my own standards. I was trying to resist leaving my family for Elizabeth, and yet I wasn't trying hard at all to give Elizabeth up. I was less than a man should be.

'It drove me mad. I was working by day with Elizabeth, making a film neither of us much cared for, and spending my nights with her at the Dorchester. I was mad with guilt – and just plain mad.

'I wanted to see my family [in Hampstead]. Ifor was there. They were preparing for Christmas, and he wouldn't let me see them. The worst of it all was, I couldn't see my Kate. That broke my heart more than anything. Ifor told me, and rightly, that I broke my own heart. And there was Jessica who I lost through her own sad world of illness which I may have led her into. She cried for me, you know. She wasn't entirely lost. Her one word – the only word she could speak – was my name. Not "Daddy" but "Rich". And she cried "Rich! Rich! Rich!" over and over when I wasn't there. My God . . . what kind of man was I?'

Stanley Baker recalled that sad, sorry time when *The VIPs* was in production:

'When he was in Rome Rich had told us all to mind our own bloody business. When they were making *The VIPs* at Borehamwood, he decided he should make the effort to patch things up with his friends, and he wanted us all to meet Elizabeth. I had already met her, but not all of his friends had.

'He took her to meet Robert Hardy who was delighted by her. She knew how to play her part very well. She said to him, "Tim" – Tim was his real name and we still called him that – "Tim," she said, "don't hate me." What is a man going to do when asked so plaintively by Elizabeth Taylor *that*? She has always known how to make friends with the people she wants to be her friends.

'As for myself, my wife and I decided to mend things by asking Rich over to dinner, but not with Liz Taylor. We asked him to come with Sybil. It was a difficult evening. Rich looked pretty cheerful but the strain on Sybil's face was plain to see. It didn't help that bloody Elizabeth phoned three or four times.

'They left at the end of the evening and I hoped they would be together again. But the damn fool took her home to Hampstead and then went back to the hotel.

'I call him a damn fool, and he knows he was. A man torn apart by love is the biggest kind of fool. He wanted his family even at that time; he didn't want to leave Sybil. But in my opinion, Elizabeth wasn't going to give up until she had him for her husband. She had him and wasn't giving him up.'

As hoped, *The VIPs* was filmed in ten weeks, thanks to careful planning and some unfussy direction from Anthony Asquith. Richard was allowed time off to shoot those extra scene for *Cleopatra*. Martin Landau recalled:

'I hadn't seen Richard since we were filming in Rome. I remember the morning of the first day of shooting the extra scenes at Pinewood; I was collected from my hotel by a car, and as we were going along we passed Richard standing by the roadside, his Daimler at a halt. I remember it was six o'clock in the morning. I told my driver to turn around, so we did a U-turn and Richard was standing there while his driver was changing a tyre. I told Richard to get in and we spent the last leg of the journey catching up on what we had been doing. He was doing *The VIPs* and I doing *The Greatest Story Every Told*. But we didn't talk about his private life – just the work.

'It was great to work with him on those extra scenes. There was no Elizabeth around to distract him. He took the work seriously, as he always did, but he was keen that these extra scenes would make a difference to the finished film. Richard cared about the film, about his work. He was always very professional. Even when the times were bad.'

Cleopatra was finally finished, and so too was *The VIPs* but with a lot less trouble. A week after *Cleopatra* premiered, *The VIPs* hit the cinemas and was a huge success. It, and *Cleopatra,* proved that the public wanted to see Richard Burton on the screen but they wanted to see him with Elizabeth Taylor. They had become 'Liz and Dick' to the world, and, for now, the public wanted to see Dick and Liz movies. They had become the hottest screen team since Spencer Tracy and Katharine Hepburn, another couple madly in love but not entirely together because the man in the relationship was still married and didn't intend to get a divorce. But the Tracy/Hepburn affair had been kept a closely guarded secret from the public. The Burton/Taylor affair was the juiciest story hitting every film fan magazine which outraged everybody but which everybody also loved because it was the gossip of the most glamorous kind.

Dick and Liz became, quite literally, a franchise.

Chapter Sixteen

THE BEST BAD PRIEST IN THE BUSINESS

W ITH PROFITS ON top of their salaries, Richard and
Elizabeth made around $3 million between them from *The
VIPs* alone. It was an indication of just how much money
they could expect to make, especially when they co-starred together.
'Money must have played a part in Richard's decision to finally leave
Sybil,' said Stanley Baker. 'I'm sure he loved her very much – or was
certainly obsessed with her – but he needed money, not because he
wanted to be rich but because he had people who depended on him.'

At that time, there was actually no real indication that Burton and
Taylor would find much opportunity to work together, simply because
the movie offers for Richard were still not coming in from Hollywood.
There were a few offers outside of Hollywood, and one of these in
particular he couldn't turn down because it was 'one of the few films I
felt I had to do because it was for the sake of the part and the play and
not for the money', which is how he explained it to me. There was not
even a part in it for Elizabeth.

The film was *Becket*, based on the play by Jean Anouilh which had
run on Broadway very successfully with Laurence Olivier in the role of
Becket and Anthony Quinn as King Henry II. Olivier grew bored with
the part, and when Quinn left the production, Olivier played the
King and Arthur Kennedy played Becket. Peter Glenville had directed
the play and was now directing the film for producer Hal Wallis
and Paramount.

Richard was to give one of his very finest film performances as
Thomas Becket, the close friend of King Henry II who was made,
unwillingly, Archbishop of Canterbury by the King and later murdered
by the King's barons. The film charts a strong, loving friendship which

falls apart when Becket does his job too well and chooses 'the honour of God' over his love for the King, who was played magnificently by Peter O'Toole.

Rich had often complained about the quality of the screenplays he had to work with but with this film he had a superior screenplay by Edward Anhalt adapted from a superior stage play, and it was directed intelligently by Peter Glenville. Rich had not forgotten that Peter Glenville had fired him from the play *Adventure Story*. Peter Glenville told me, 'Richard said he would only do the part if I didn't fire him again. He said it with good humour and it was wonderful to see that he held no malice.'

Olivier may have grown bored with playing Becket on stage, but Richard discovered all the virtues of the character. He told me, 'The King is great fun for any actor with his ranting and raving, and nobody could have played it better than Peter [O'Toole]. But Becket is a little man, taciturn and almost laconic despite having the most beautiful dialogue. That was my challenge, to keep the man quiet and almost small against the lion of a king, and yet he must keep the audience's interest.

'And the battle Becket fights, from temperance to spiritual, is a fascinating one, and difficult. Sometimes you want a role to be easy, and sometimes you need it to be difficult – to provide a challenge. This was my great challenge.'

Richard was sincerely pleased that I admired his performance so much; I've never been one to flatter an actor but I have always given open and honest appreciation for the roles I have admired and enjoyed. His performance is perfectly balanced and complemented by Peter O'Toole's loud, boisterous and spoiled King. But O'Toole's performance is not just all noise. He is heartbreaking in the scenes when he desperately reaches for his one-time friend but can't because their roles in life have made them opposites – the King must rule and Becket must obey God. It's the very heart of the film and the play, and the casting of Burton and O'Toole is as perfect as any casting can be.

Peter O'Toole told me, 'but we became good friends on that picture'.

Making *Becket*, with Peter O'Toole as his screen partner and also having John Gielgud to act opposite for the first time on screen, was one of Richard's happiest professional experiences. He recalled:

'O'Toole and I had a wonderful rapport. It's essential for any performance, but especially that one. If two actors playing Becket and the King didn't get on, it would be impossible to make it work for the camera. Peter and I got on superbly.

'We had a certain reputation for being a bit wild. I actually gave up drinking three days before beginning work on the film, and everyone was amazed to see Peter and I drinking only tea for the first two weeks. We were still getting to know each other, and when it was obvious that I really liked this wonderful Irishman, I put on my best Irish voice and said, "Peter, me boy, I think we deserve a little snifter." And then we drank for two nights and a day, and played the scene where Henry puts the Chancellor of England's ring on Becket's finger absolutely smashed. It didn't matter too much because for that shot we had no dialogue, but Peter had a very hard time getting that ring on my finger.

'And it was wonderful to have a few scenes with John Gielgud as the other King [Louis VII of France]. John was always the King of Theatre. I tried to be the King, I suppose, when I was in *Camelot*, but when John played the King of France in *Becket*, he really was *the* King of the Theatre – or Cinema. I have always been so in awe of him that he can make me feel somewhat ill at ease. The irony is that I always had Gielgud in mind in my early days, no matter what part I played. I thought, *how would Gielgud play this part?* and I did what I thought he would do, but it was always so different because we are such different people in our voices and our physicality and our temperaments. Nobody has ever known that because it was never obvious, but John Gielgud was in all my early performances. They just came out as *me*.'

Peter O'Toole told me, 'John Gielgud was Richard's mentor, so when Rich had a scene with him, he knew he had to be at his best.'

Elizabeth was often at Shepperton Studios where most of the film was shot. 'When you hired Richard Burton,' Peter Glenville told me, 'you also took on Elizabeth Taylor who watched him like a hawk. She just loved being with him but perhaps she was also making sure he behaved. But there were no women to fool around with. Siân Phillips was in the film but she was married to O'Toole, so Burton wasn't going there. So his fun was had with O'Toole, and they were two boys spending their nights in the pub and delighting each other with their drunken stories and quotes from Shakespeare, and

Elizabeth loved it all. But I did have to make it clear that she couldn't come to the set *every* day because he would have rather talked to her than worked.'

I was once able to ask her, in 1980, what she had loved about Richard. She said, 'He was a boy who loved to play, and when he played, he was wonderful. When he and Peter were together on *Becket*, they were two boys getting up to mischief – but only after hours. They worked hard on the film, and they loved what they were doing. I watched Richard and it was impossible not to love him for all that.'

It was while making *Becket* that Richard came to the decision that he was going to finally choose Elizabeth over Sybil – and most painfully of all, over Kate. In March 1963 he told Sybil that he wanted a separation.

Brook Williams remembered, 'She didn't make a fuss, as though she had long expected it. She simply packed and took Kate and Jessica to New York. I don't think she even truly believed it was over and although she announced their separation in New York, she said there would be no divorce.'

She told her friends, 'He's tied hand and foot, like so much lend-lease. I'm not going to cut the lease now and when I get him back he will be two million dollars richer.'

Over in America, she found many supporters. She had long been independent with her own interests and friends, and in New York she put money into a small off-Broadway play and even ran a successful nightclub called Arthur's. She became something of a celebrity and was much liked by many in the film community.

Brook said, 'There were clearly two camps: those in Sybil's and those in Richard's and Elizabeth's.'

Taylor had been a major star for years in Hollywood, but many now turned against her. As for Richard, he had never been much liked by the Hollywood crowd.

Although he had begun work on *Becket* sober, once he returned to drinking, he went at it with a passion – at least, he did when he separated from Sybil. He drank, he said, to kill the pain. And, as best as I can gather, it was never quite so much the pain of losing Sybil that hurt him but the pain of having chosen Elizabeth Taylor over his daughters.

'It was self-inflicted pain,' said Stanley Baker.

The self-inflicted pain was manifest one day in the foyer of the Dorchester Hotel where Rich and Elizabeth drank themselves into a stupor and Richard threw up. 'Rich never throws up when he drinks,' said Baker, 'but he did that day.'

The hotel waiters cleaned up his mess while he was driven to the studio and forced into his costume and then delivered unceremoniously to the set where he couldn't remember a single line of dialogue.

'He finally arrived drunker than any lord,' recalled Peter O'Toole of that occasion, 'and said something incredibly insulting to me. I forgave him.'

When I interviewed O'Toole at the Old Vic in 1980 where he was performing *Macbeth*, he was reminded of a rather famous interview Richard gave to Kenneth Tynan in which Rich had said of marriage, 'Monogamy is absolutely imperative. It's the one thing you must abide by. The minute you go against the idea of monogamy, nothing satisfies any more . . . It's fascinating to do what I do which is to move outside the idea of monogamy without physically investing the other person with anything that makes me feel guilty. So I remain inviolated, untouched.'

'I'd read that article,' said O'Toole. 'We were on the set and Rich was terribly hungover, and I said to him, "What the bloody hell does 'inviolate' mean?" Elizabeth had read the article and she was saying, "I love Richard and I'm going to marry him," and I said, "Yes, darling, but, Richard, please tell me what inviolate means." And he didn't have a clue, drunk or sober, I suspect.'

O'Toole made no secret that he was opposed to the idea of Richard marrying Elizabeth and that resulted in a falling out between O'Toole and Taylor that lasted many years.

Both O'Toole and Burton had started the film sober. 'We were good boys,' O'Toole told me. 'We got a little naughty as time went on. When we did the scene on the beach [filmed in Northumberland] we were both drunk. But I think we did that scene just as well as if we had been sober.'

The success of *Becket* put Richard tenth on the list of top box office stars in 1964, suggesting that the public could be tempted to see Burton in something without Elizabeth.

It was in June of 1963, during the filming of *Becket*, when *Cleopatra* hit London to scathing reviews that made Elizabeth increasingly paranoid about the future of her career. 'She kept phoning the set,' said Peter Glenville. 'She was in a bad way. She needed reassurance. That's when I heard Richard say, "I will marry the girl," and that was his mind made up.'

The separation from Sybil was to be permanent. When filming ended, he decided he had to take Elizabeth to Wales to meet the family. It didn't take her long to win them over, despite their initial shock and disgust at their antics during *Cleopatra*. There were other friends for Elizabeth to meet in other parts of Britain.

'There was no point in pretending to dislike him any longer,' said Stanley Baker. 'It was a relief to be on speaking terms again.'

The good news was that *Cleopatra* continued to do good business and even won Oscars for photography, costumes, art direction and special effects. Rex Harrison was nominated, as was Alex North for his astounding music score, and it also got a Best Picture nomination. Curiously, Joe Mankiewicz didn't get nominated, and neither did Burton. 'It was political,' said Roddy McDowall. 'The studios just refused to put Joe's name forward, or Richard's.' The studio had, apparently, intended to put McDowall's name forward as Best Supporting Actor, but forgot. 'I think they forgot to put a number of names forward,' said McDowall philosophically.

But there was plenty of compensation for both Rich and Elizabeth with the success of *The VIPs* which, unlike *Cleopatra*, made an instant profit. It also won Margaret Rutherford an Oscar as Best Supporting Actress.

Richard seemed to be making films that won Oscars, but none for him. It looked like he might win one at last for *Becket* which was generally considered his finest screen performance so far by critics and the public alike, as well as the American Academy of Motion Picture Arts and Sciences which nominated him for an Oscar. They also nominated Peter O'Toole as Best Actor, John Gielgud as Best Supporting Actor, Peter Glenville for his assured direction, and there was also a Best Film nomination. It only managed to win one Oscar, for its screenplay.

'I was never going to win an Oscar, no matter how wonderful I might be,' Richard told me in 1984. He wasn't bitter, but he was disappointed. 'Rex Harrison – and I love Rex – won [for *My Fair Lady*], but for God's sake, he was just playing himself. I'd have been happy if O'Toole had won [for *Becket*]. He never won an Oscar either.'

Hollywood still didn't like Richard much, and yet his best work in films had begun with *Becket* and would continue throughout the 1960s.

His next film was another fine picture, John Huston's *The Night of the Iguana*. Richard played a defrocked priest who becomes a travel courier in Mexico.

I worked for Huston in 1974, and I asked him why he cast Richard. He said, 'There's a kind of spirituality in Richard that is flawed. That's what I needed.'

Richard was fascinated by the idea of spirituality; it's what attracted him to playing *Becket*. He once told me, 'I'm the best bad priest in the business.' He was referring to his roles in *Becket*, *Night of the Iguana*, *The Sandpiper* and one or two other films in which he struggled to serve the clergy.

The Night of the Iguana was based on Tennessee Williams' play, and for it Huston had cast some wonderful actresses: Ava Gardner, Deborah Kerr and Sue Lyon who shot to fame as *Lolita* – but there was no part for Elizabeth Taylor.

'I underestimated Elizabeth,' Huston said. 'I thought she was a lousy actress and would be trouble. I was wrong, so I worked with her later [in *Reflection in a Golden Eye* in 1967].'

Elizabeth flew into Mexico with Richard; their arrival was extremely traumatic, as Huston recalled:

'When Elizabeth and Richard landed, a film director called Emilio Fernandez, who always carried guns and called himself El Indio, rushed into the cabin of their plane. He had shot his last producer – he was quite insane. He was assisting on our picture as associate director but his main function was to deal with the press. A man with a gun can be useful when the press are about.

'He grabbed Elizabeth's arm and shouted, "Follow El Indio! You will be safe with me!" Richard was naturally enraged and said, "Get this bloody maniac off the bloody plane before I bloody well kill him." The crew managed to disarm El Indio and get him off while Richard swore at them in Welsh.

'I explained to Richard, "It's okay, Richard. Emilio's only weakness is his tendency to shoot people he doesn't like. The fact that he didn't shoot you means he likes you. I'm sure you'll adjust to each other." Richard said, "I don't want to bloody adjust to that maniac. If he comes near me again, I'll kill him."

'When they got off the plane there was a huge crowd waiting for them so Richard and Elizabeth made a run for it. They could have done with Emilio and his gun because Elizabeth got grabbed and pretty badly roughed up. Richard saved her – very bravely. He punched at those who were grabbing her, and they finally made it to their car.

'After that Richard refused to attend a press conference that we'd organised, but he wrote a statement which was handed out to the press. It read, "This is my first visit to Mexico. I trust it shall be my last." What I always like about Richard is, he doesn't mince words.'

Elizabeth was often on the set with Richard throughout filming. 'She wasn't going to take her eyes off him with Ava, Deborah and Sue around,' said Huston. 'Liz was often there – maybe to make sure Richard didn't play around with Sue Lyon or Ava or Deborah. Elizabeth's ex-husband Michael Wilding was there to publicise hers and Richard's marriage which was imminent. That made for an interesting combination, I thought.'

When Richard took Elizabeth into his life – or perhaps she took him into hers – he acquired a second family. Elizabeth had three children. Michael Wilding Junior, born 6 January 1953 and Christopher, born 27 February 1955, were her two sons with Michael Wilding. Liza, born 6 August 1957, was the daughter she had with Michael Todd. Elizabeth was also in the process of adopting a little crippled girl called Maria; she was born 1 August 1961.

Only Liza went with her mother and new stepfather to Mexico; Michael Junior and Chris were at school in California, and Maria, not yet legally Elizabeth's, was undergoing hip operations in London.

Richard had made up his mind from the moment he knew he would be with Elizabeth permanently that he would not cheat on her the way he had with Sybil. 'She's the only woman I could stay faithful to at that time,' he told me. 'That says something about Elizabeth, or Sybil . . . or just me. Probably me. I'll never understand it.'

Ava Gardner was a huge temptation for him; I know of no male who was ever able to resist her. Rich said to me of Ava, 'Oh, by God, Ava was a woman who made me tingle.'

All tingling was kept under constant supervision by Elizabeth. 'When Richard and Ava had a scene, Liz was watching over them,' recalled Huston.

I once asked Elizabeth if she had trusted Richard in those early days;

she said, 'I trusted Richard completely, but I didn't trust fate because it was fate that threw us together.'

Ava admitted to me she would have easily been tempted by Richard if the opportunity had presented itself, but with Elizabeth there, and with young, bronzed Mexican men seeing to Ava's every desire, temptation with Richard was easily avoided. 'We all got along well,' Ava told me. 'I was friends with Elizabeth from our days at MGM. I'd not met Richard before but I liked him immediately. I felt like I would have liked to have had him for a brother.'

'Not a lover?'

'Oh yes. But Liz was like an eagle. I would have fucked Richard if I could have. So I'd settle for having him as a brother.'

There was little socialising between the stars after each day's work. 'Richard and Elizabeth made the daily trip to the location by yacht, and I arrived and left by speedboat, usually water-skiing behind it,' said Ava. Her boat was driven by those sun-bronzed young Mexican men I mentioned.

According to Huston, it was a very happy cast. 'Everyone got along really well,' he told me. 'There were no tantrums, no fireworks.'

Huston was something of a renowned hellraiser himself, but even he was staggered at the amount, and the quality, of alcohol that Richard was able to consume. He said, 'Richard was rather fond of spending his spare time in the local bars swigging *raicilla*, a terrifyingly potent blend of cactus brandy stronger even than tequila. Richard said, "You know, John, if you drink it straight down, you can feel it going into each individual intestine."

'I said, "Richard, I think that's because they left the needles in."'

Ava was also amazed at Richard's incredible intake of booze. 'I thought I drank a lot, and I thought John drank a lot, but Richard drank more than anyone I ever knew. He insisted that John arrange to have a bar at the top and bottom of the long stairs we had to climb to the mountain plateau. He wanted to make sure he had a drink before going up and then another when he got there, and when we came down, he could have a drink before climbing down, and there was a drink waiting for him at the bottom.'

Huston discovered that Richard was very shy about baring too much of his body. In fact, Rich always felt his body was rather unattractive and out of proportion and preferred to keep it hidden. He was especially embarrassed by the acne that often covered his back. Huston said:

'I was surprised when he refused to get into his swimming shorts. But Liz would get him to drink a few shots of cactus juice and he'd strip down to his shorts for a swim. But then she would always do her best to make sure no one could see him. Maybe she didn't want anyone else to see him almost naked!

'I must say, Richard obviously adored Liz, but he wasn't always complimentary about her. He would see her approaching and he'd say, "Look at her. She walks like a French tart." I think that was their way of communicating. When she started turning up in bikinis that got more revealing each time, he said, "Now she even *looks* like a French tart."

'She was very happy being there. She sunbathed and ate imported hamburgers. At the end of each working day she arrived to call for Richard and they would return to their house, Casa Kimberly at Puerto Vallarta, which they had rented and which they later bought.

'Richard's mood often swung from fun to depression. His varying moods usually followed a large intake of alcohol. When he was low, Liz was the only one who knew how to handle him.

'One time, he had several Mexican boilermakers and fell out of his chair on the set and cut his thigh. But he waved off any help from anyone and got on with the scene.

'Liz fussed over him. Far too much. She fussed with his hair after the hairdresser had finished with him; she wasn't happy with the way it was. He tried to hold his temper but finally he blew his top, poured a can of beer over his head and said, "How do I look now, by God?"'

Richard and Elizabeth were on the verge of getting married; they just needed their respective divorces. Huston said, 'I sometimes felt that Richard wasn't in such a hurry to get married as Elizabeth was. He would joke about their wedding. He said, "I'm going to marry Liz for her jewels and all that I offer in return is myself which should be enough for any woman." She punched him in the stomach. She liked to do that. He had worked out with a trainer and had a hard stomach, so Liz would show it off by punching it.'

Rich had been working on a settlement with Sybil and he was prepared to give her all she wanted. 'I wanted her to have it all, if she wanted it,' he said.

Stanley Baker told me, 'He would have given Sybil every penny he had, if she'd asked. He felt ashamed, you know. He knew he had treated her very badly over the years. And he felt he had betrayed his daughters. I think he was trying to ease his conscience by giving her all she wanted. But I don't believe he ever forgave himself.'

Sybil wasn't interested in breaking Richard; she didn't want the house in Céligny as she was now settled in New York. They agreed on an annual amount he would pay her, and when he discovered he still had a great deal of money left over, he decided to give much of it to charities and to his relatives. 'I was starting fresh, with a clean slate,' he said.

His divorce from Sybil came through in December 1963.

'Elizabeth made the claim that she was also broke,' said Brooke Williams. 'She had jewels and paintings, properties, and she was earning royalties from past films. But she didn't want to be seen as the rich one. So she announced, "I'm broke too." I think she saw that as being funny.'

They were still a pretty wealthy couple and despite their initial hatred of Mexico when they first arrived, they decided to buy the Casa Kimberley. They were the richest poor couple in the world.

Chapter Seventeen

NO MORE MARRIAGES

I N JANUARY 1964, Eddie Fisher finally agreed to divorce Elizabeth. By that time Rich was in Toronto rehearsing his last great piece of Shakespeare for the stage, *Hamlet.*

The idea of doing *Hamlet* came up during the filming of *Becket.* Rich had told John Gielgud that he would love another chance at that great role and that he especially wanted Gielgud to direct him. They decided it should be done on Broadway. Rich had been a huge success on Broadway in *Camelot,* but he felt he needed to be a huge success on Broadway in Shakespeare.

While the cameras were still turning on *The Night of the Iguana,* Rich got cold feet about opening *Hamlet* in New York, convinced the critics would be waiting to savage him. So he decided to play safe and open *Hamlet* in Toronto first.

Since Elizabeth had come into his life, he had discovered that being one of the two most sought-after celebrities in the world had its drawbacks and dangers. John Gielgud was sensitive to this shift in Richard's fortunes, recalling:

'The sort of celebrity Richard now had was very difficult for him to cope with. It would be difficult for anyone, but Richard was the kind of man who always liked to go to a pub and talk to anyone who would listen. But while doing *Hamlet* he and Elizabeth had to walk their dogs on the hotel roof because it was too dangerous for them to go out in public. They even had a guard with a machine gun outside of their room.

'Richard suddenly had to withdraw from the kind of life he was used to. He was, quite literally, a prisoner of his own celebrity. I wouldn't say "success" because you can have that and still be relatively free, but the kind of celebrity Richard had not only made him a target for the photographers, who were like a swarm around them wherever they went, but also from maniacs. They often had threats of kidnap. Elizabeth's children were almost constantly with them, and it was her children who were at risk.

'I got complaints from Richard's old friends that they couldn't get him on the phone any more. He wouldn't return their calls. They felt shut out.'

Rich was becoming increasingly isolated. He didn't mean to slight his friends. Often he just didn't get told they had called, so he never knew to call them back.

'I would try and call Rich,' Sir Stanley Baker told me, 'and I'd get someone telling me he wasn't available, so I'd ask them to ask him to call me. It was a puzzle why he never did. But when I finally got to speak to him and told him, he said, "Oh my God, I had no idea. These idiots are here to protect me from intruders, not my friends," and he was very apologetic. Being Richard's friend has not always been easy.'

Richard admitted was very nervous about doing *Hamlet*. 'I was out of practice,' he said. 'My whole concentration was on trying to remember the prose which is much more difficult than remembering the verse. I could recall the monologues with no trouble.'

He had asked only one thing of Gielgud in regard to the type of production this *Hamlet* should be; he didn't want to wear the customary tights. Gielgud recalled:

'Richard was most anxious not to wear a period costume with tights. He told me that he had been impressed when he saw me play Richard II in rehearsal clothes, and he asked if we could do something similar. So I conceived a production of *Hamlet* in modern dress, performed on a stage with hardly any props or any real set but just a few platforms. I thought it made for a very bleak, very unattractive production and I was frankly disappointed.

'But the play was an enormous success. I think the people came to see Richard Burton who was now the great celebrity. But they were mesmerised by his talent. And the voice, of course.

'The only help I could give to him was to show him how the more relaxed scenes were placed so he wouldn't have to tear himself to shreds in scenes, such as with the Ghost and the other scenes with highly emotional climaxes. I think he found that very helpful.

'The very odd thing was, he never wanted to work alone with just me. There always had to be someone else there.'

This was quite an unusual practice for Richard who often preferred to rehearse with nobody else there but the director.

Hamlet opened at the O'Keefe Centre in Toronto where, on the first night, Elizabeth was mobbed as she went to take her seat in the stalls. 'People actually stood on their seats to get a glimpse of her,' said Gielgud. 'The first night everyone was watching *her*, to see what her reactions were; they hardly watched the play. I felt it was too much of a celebrity event, although Richard was very good.

'As we toured, he wasn't keen to re-rehearse and it became very difficult so I was reduced to writing long notes for him which I would leave on his dressing table before the performance in the evening. He'd read them and discard what he didn't think was important but he always used three or four of my suggestions that evening without even trying to rehearse them. I must say, he had an instinct about what was right.'

But Richard felt he was failing in the part. Despite his great admiration – even awe – for Sir John Gielgud, he felt he needed more to help him deliver the role. So Elizabeth took it upon herself to call Philip Burton in New York. He had not spoken to Richard for two years.

Roddy McDowall recalled:

'Philip had really devoted his life to Sybil and the two girls. He helped her to set up home in the apartment block where I also lived, and I gave her all my support too. Rich and I didn't speak for many years. Thank God for Philip Burton because he did so much for Sybil, and he took Kate to the park every Sunday.

'And then out of the blue Philip got the call from Elizabeth. Rich needed his help. She said he was the only one who could help Richard. And to prove it Richard was there, beside Elizabeth, waiting to speak to Philip.

'Philip spoke to Sybil before committing himself, but she was so wonderful and said to him, "He needs you so you must go." Sybil never spoke ill of Richard. She said to me that he was the father of their two girls and she would never denounce their father. In fact she said, "I feel sorry for him because I can survive this better than he can."

'But she cut herself off from Rich. How could she forgive him? He and Elizabeth wanted to be friends with her, but that wasn't even reasonable of them let alone realistic. She refused to speak to them and so all communication had to go through their lawyer who also lived in the same apartment block as I and Sybil. When Rich wanted to see the children, Sybil took them to her lawyer's apartment and he collected them from there.

'Sybil made a life for herself and was very happy. She ran a nightclub and fell in love with a musician who played there. They married and had a lovely daughter, Amy.'

Brook said that Philip had been hoping for a reconciliation and so when the chance presented itself he hurried to Toronto where he was greeted by Elizabeth at their hotel. 'He then went alone to the theatre where he found Rich in quite a bad state during the interval,' said Brook. 'Phil spent the next day going over the play with Rich, giving his comments and suggestions, and he filled Rich with confidence and he really did give a better performance that night.'

When it came to Shakespeare, Richard could not do without Philip Burton. Even John Gielgud was, to Richard's mind, second best to Philip in matters of the Bard.

Most importantly, it healed the rift between the almost adopted son and father.

Gielgud admitted that he felt he had not done a good job of directing Burton. 'I think I had become too familiar with the play,' he said. 'I shouldn't have directed another actor in a part I knew so well. I felt that my work was generally ill conceived.' That was a remarkably generous comment as he might easily have accused Richard of refusing to play the part the way Gielgud had asked him to. But Gielgud insisted that Richard wasn't difficult. 'He was ill at ease with himself. He was, after all, the one who had to get out there and deliver.'

Rich told me that acting a classic part on the stage was 'a constant battle. You are out there on your own and no one will help you. It's terrifying, but when it goes well there is little to top it.'

'Except rugby?' I suggested.

'Nothing can top rugby,' he said.

It was while during the play's run in Canada that Richard and Elizabeth finally married on 15 March 1964 in Montreal where they found a Unitarian minister who was prepared to marry divorcees. Richard's best man was his dresser, Bob Wilson. Elizabeth had no one to give her away. Typically, she arrived late, decked in jewels including the $150,000 emerald brooch he had given to her when they were making *Cleopatra*.

They spent the weekend in Montreal, and on the Tuesday Rich was back on stage as Hamlet. They never did have a proper honeymoon.

By this time, Elizabeth had been banned from watching the show from the stalls because of the disruption her very presence caused. So she watched virtually every performance from the wings. On the Tuesday night following the wedding, at the end of the performance, Richard brought Elizabeth on to the stage. He took her hand and delivered a line from the play; 'I say, we will have no more marriages.'

The theatre thundered to the sound of the applause that followed. Richard was convinced that here was the woman he would spend the rest of his life with. He was not only making a public declaration from the stage that night but a promise to himself. 'I *had* to make my marriage to Liz a marriage to last a lifetime. After what I put Sybil and Kate and Jessica through, the marriage *had* to be the one I would end my days in.'

From Toronto the play went to Boston. Gielgud recalled the reception that awaited the most glamorous couple in the world: 'When we landed at Boston we were surrounded by a great surge of fans who tore Richard's hair and his clothes. It was terrifying for him and Elizabeth, but only marginally alarming for me. They had to get back on board the aeroplane which was moved to another part of the airport where they could get off in safety.'

Hamlet was a smash hit at the Lunt-Fontanne Theatre in New York. Sir John Gielgud noted, 'It played for more than a hundred performances in New York which I'm sorry to say beat my own record there in 1937.' Gielgud was, of course, delighted to have a successful play as director, but he really was disappointed that somebody had broken his record. 'If it had to happen, at least my name is still attached to it,' he said. I think he always felt some hidden sense of resentment that this *Hamlet* had been directed as much by Philip Burton as it had been by him. But he never mentioned it.

During the run, Elizabeth took it upon herself to mend more bridges between Rich and estranged friends; she called Emlyn Williams. 'She asked me to forget all that happened in Rome, and I was glad to do so,' Williams told me. 'I said to her, "You met Mr. Hyde in Rome. Now meet Dr Jekyll."'

Said Brooke Williams, 'Elizabeth really put herself out to give back to Rich so much he had lost. She flew his family over to New York and paid for everything. She made a big effort to befriend Cis, and they became very close. The family had met Elizabeth before and some of them had taken to her, but not all, and Rich had been something of an outcast. Liz saw to it that he was fully back within the family fold. That was a wonderful thing she did for him.

'And then she stepped in to help Phil when the drama school he was attempting to run [The American Musical and Dramatic Academy] got into financial trouble. So she and Rich decided they would perform on stage together to raise funds – and she had never performed on stage in her life! So she asked Phil to coach her, which he did for several weeks. That was a good move. Philip really warmed to her, and she responded well to his guidance.'

Seats sold for a hundred dollars. High society and celebrities came to the event. Richard redacted Marvell and D.H. Lawrence and then gave the St Crispin's Day speech. Elizabeth gave her first stage performance doing Thomas Hardy's *The Ruined Maid* followed by some Frost and Elizabeth Barrett Browning.

Emlyn Williams was in the audience. 'She was marvellous,' he said. 'Bea Lillie was sitting in front of me and I heard her say to the person sitting next to her, "If she doesn't get bad pretty soon people are going to start leaving." But nobody left.'

Brook said, 'Rich told me, "I didn't know she was going to be this good."'

She looked like a million dollars because everything she wore cost around that much or more. She provided glamour and culture that night, as well as spontaneous wit; when she joined Richard to close the evening with the Twenty-third Psalm, she made a tiny mistake and said, 'Sorry. Let me begin again. I sure screwed that one up.' She and Richard received a standing ovation.

Recalling the event, Rich said, 'The accolades were for Elizabeth more than they were for me because she had the guts to get out there and do it. I'd been playing Hamlet every night so nobody had to be impressed by me. But she was a true star and they loved her.'

Emlyn Williams remembered that at the party afterwards both Richard and Elizabeth got very drunk 'but they managed not to row. I think that night they may have loved each other more than any other time in their lives.'

There was a low point though during their time in New York. 'I was in the middle of *Hamlet*,' Rich told me, 'and giving everything I had to the part when suddenly I was wracked by pain. I could barely move. I had raised an arm above my head and I couldn't get it down again. I used my other arm to pull it down and then I slowly shuffled off the stage. I felt like I was a hundred years old. Fortunately Elizabeth knew all the best doctors and she found a man who fixed me up, and I only missed a couple of performances.'

'But you dislike doctors,' I reminded him.

'When you're in desperate pain like that, so intense that you just cannot move, you'd see Dr Mengele if he could fix you up.'

Rich said he was diagnosed as having arthritis. But it was more than that. His back had been something of a mess for years from the days when he played rugby. And there had been that tumble down the stairs at Oxford when some idiot had spiked his drink. Now the damage was taking its toll. Once he was able to move again, he just ignored the condition and would continue to ignore it, avoiding doctors as much as he could. Things would only get worse with time.

While in New York, Richard spent time with Kate and Jessica. 'Kate was a lovely girl and she was Richard's delight,' said Brook Williams. 'He loved Jessica just as much but he was finding it harder to reach her because of her illness and that disturbed him very deeply. She had been diagnosed as being autistic and schizophrenic. As she got older her conditioned worsened until she was simply unable to recognise him. It tore him up to see that she showed him no affection because she was locked in a world he couldn't get through to.'

Roddy McDowall recalled, 'It was a huge strain for Sybil to take care of Jessica because she became impossible to take care of. The poor child wouldn't even smile at her mother. At first Sybil tried to treat her as normally as possible, taking her out to the movies or to eat and to be with other children, but Jessica became more disruptive as she got bigger. She would scream and smash things. She became too strong to restrain. Sybil did all she could to cope with her but in the end she was told that Jessica would be better off if she were cared for in a special home.'

She was placed in a hospital run by the Devereux Foundation, and her excellent care was paid for by Richard.

The Burtons were forever surrounded by security in New York. Rich told me, 'You know, I always thought that interest would be lost in us once the illicit essence of our relationship had been legitimised by marriage, but it only got worse.'

Liz and Dick were probably the most famous married couple in the world, and their marriage was always tinged with a whiff of scandal.

It didn't help, he thought, that wherever they went, Elizabeth's children came too. 'A world like that is no place for children,' he said.

And then there was the entourage that now went everywhere with them – the agents, lawyers, publicists and personal secretaries. There was Richard's dresser Bob Wilson, who was always more of a friend than an employee, Elizabeth's personal photographer and his wife, and Liz's hairdresser and make-up people. For the children there were tutors, governesses, nurses. There was ex-boxer Bobby la Salle the bodyguard. There was Richard's faithful driver, Gaston.

Richard hated the whole entourage fiasco wherever they went. 'I need only my secretary, driver and dresser,' he said. 'Elizabeth needs someone to blow her nose. And just about everything else.' And then he said, 'But she isn't totally undomesticated. She will wash and dry the dishes.'

Marriage didn't make much difference to the way Richard and Elizabeth treated each other. They loved each other with a passion, and their arguments were often just as passionate. Very often their rows were pure screaming matches. She once said, 'I just adore fighting with Richard. I need a strong man. We have delicious fights.'

And she also claimed 'Our fights are exhilarating. They make me feel like his intellectual equal, which of course I'm not. I love him because he corresponds with the great writers and the greatest actors, and he can do the *Times* crossword every morning.'

Rich would joke about her intellect and her education. 'She was educated at Metro-Goldwyn-Mayer,' he said to me once. 'But she learned what I could never truly grasp, which is that films are a business. She knows how to make money better than I have ever done. And she is tough, which I find very sexy. She always negotiates a great financial deal *and* a present. She must always have a present from the studio or the producer. And she gets to choose the present she wants. I'm just grateful to get paid a decent fee and am invariably impressed by how much I get. Liz is never impressed, even when she's paid a million dollars.'

They always had nicknames for each other which were never meant to be flattering but were nevertheless endearing. 'I'd call her Fred or Sam,' he said. 'She'd call me Agatha.'

He treated her children as bona fide members of his own extended family, but he liked to make sure they knew exactly where they stood with him. He told me, 'Elizabeth's daughter Liza Todd referred to me once as her third daddy. I told her, "Never call me your third daddy. I am not your daddy. Your daddy was Michael Todd, a very wonderful man. Never forget that."'

Since they had been together, they were unable to be apart. 'We just couldn't bear to be apart,' said Rich. So they made as many films together as they could, of varying quality, throughout the 1960s. It was the decade that seemed to be dominated by the Beatles and the Burtons. Liz and Dick were as well known throughout the world by their first given names as was John, George, Paul and Ringo.

Chapter Eighteen

FOR THE MONEY, WE WILL DANCE

W ITH *HAMLET* OVER – Rich could have continued to perform it because the demand from the public was there but he had grown bored – the Burtons considered the options coming their way. They were offered a film together to be made in Israel which would earn them a collective two million dollars for 90 days' work. Elizabeth preferred another project called *The Sandpiper*, the story of a married church minister who has an affair with a female bohemian artist. The part of the flawed church minister was, of course, perfect for Richard, and she was perfect as the artist.

The film seemed to reflect something of their real-life situation; he is married but becomes intoxicated by the bohemian temptress. It was again Antony and Cleopatra, more or less, but played out in contemporary California. The location scenes were shot in Big Sur but because of the usual tax complications, interiors were shot in studios in Paris.

'It was a bore,' Richard said of that film. 'It wasn't a happy time. We had a once-good director [Vincente Minnelli] but he was past his best. I had an argument with him. I didn't like the part and I was bored in it, but I told Minnelli, "For the money we will dance."'

The Sandpiper was a hit when released in 1965, proving that for now the public would go and see Liz and Dick in anything. He was more impressed that a story he had written, *A Christmas Story*, was published Christmas 1964; it thrilled him more than playing *Hamlet* ever did. He aspired to becoming a writer and giving up acting.

For the most part the Burtons lived in Gstaad from where he flew to London in January 1965 to meet with director Martin Ritt to discuss a film, *The Spy Who Came in from the Cold*, to be shot in Dublin. It was different from any of the James Bond-type spy films being made around that time. This was to be a bleak thriller in black and white. At that meeting with Ritt over lunch was the film's leading lady, Claire Bloom; she played the Communist librarian in love with Burton. Of all the people from Richard's earlier life, Elizabeth hated Claire the most, or so some said. Before Elizabeth, Claire was considered to be the only other woman who might just have prised Richard away from Sybil. Now Claire might be the one who could prise Rich away from Elizabeth. But by then the affair was over and Claire had made up her mind not to become involved with Rich again. As for Richard, he said, 'Claire was quite simply perfect for the part and that's all that mattered to me.'

Rod Steiger told me:

'I am sure it was a big surprise to Claire when Richard agreed to have her in that picture because he could have had her removed from it; he was the star and had that power of veto. But he didn't. She was anxious about what I would think of her working with Burton, and I told her that she had to do it. She wanted the part and there was no reason why she should walk away from it. What had happened, had happened. It was in the past.

'But Elizabeth – oh my God – she hated Claire being with Richard. Elizabeth would be there on the set, of course, and whatever he was doing, wherever he was, when she wanted him she would cry out in a shrill voice, "*Richard!*" which would carry for miles, and he would come running every time. Claire would do a wonderful impression of Liz Taylor's cry of "*Richard!*".

'Claire said that Richard was still drinking heavily and his hands shook in the morning until around nine when he had a coffee that was not all coffee – something stronger was also in the mug.'

Rich was to give one of his finest screen performances in *The Spy Who Came in from the Cold*, but he worked throughout it in one of his deep depressions, or as he would call it 'a sense of unfathomable melancholy'. There were a number of possible reasons for this. For a start, Ritt made Richard underplay his part to keep the character very anonymous which Rich felt gave him no opportunity to exercise his acting muscles or, in particular, his voice, and he felt as though he were just walking through the part with no interest or enthusiasm. Another reason was the screenplay; Richard felt the dialogue was dull. And then there was the presence of Claire Bloom which didn't upset Rich but it did Elizabeth; she barely let Richard out of her sight because, said Rod Steiger, 'Claire was now the one woman who could have taken Richard away from Elizabeth'.

Rich disputed that. He said, 'There was a time, perhaps, when Claire might have been the one. But I was never – *could* never – be unfaithful to Elizabeth.'

Nevertheless, Elizabeth wasn't taking any chances. It hardly made for a happy marriage situation. Michael Horden, one of Richard's numerous actor friends who often turned up in his films including this one, told me, 'They did rather drink a lot and row a lot. They were staying at the Gresham Hotel, and they had intercoms between every room, so no matter where each of them happened to be in the suite, they could continue fighting. And when you visited them, you would hear them shouting over the intercom. I also heard the sound of slapping. But it wasn't Richard who was doing the slapping.'

I asked Horden if he could be sure of that. He said, 'Richard was the one who emerged with the side of his face red.'

Yet Richard still gave a great screen performance, which baffled him. 'They said I was good in it,' he told me. 'I don't see how I could have been.' But he was, and he was Oscar nominated for it.

Variety hit a number of nails on the head when it noted the 'perfectly controlled underplaying', in what was a spy film absent of all the usual 1960s spy film gimmickry. It noted how 'Burton fits neatly into the role of the apparently burned out British agent.' Rich really was weary, often drunk and bored, and that is perhaps exactly what director Martin Ritt wanted in the role. Ritt told me, 'I needed Richard Burton to be weary and sick and tired, not a man of action. The opposite of James Bond. He wanted me to let him loose but I held on to the reins. He said I pissed him off, and if I did, that worked just fine in his performance.' Richard, typically, had made no attempt to create a character but had simply made the character like him, as he was at that time.

The success of both *The Spy Who Came in from the Cold* and *The Sandpiper* put Richard tenth again on the list of the ten biggest box office star attractions. The success of *Spy* now confirmed that the public definitely would go and see Burton without Taylor.

It was while *The Spy Who Came in from the Cold* was being filmed in Dublin that Franco Zeffirelli, a noted director of Italian opera, offered Richard and Elizabeth the chance to do some filmed Shakespeare. Zeffirelli told me:

'My agent came up with the idea of making *The Taming of the Shrew* which had been done once before as a film [with Douglas Fairbanks and Mary Pickford]. I thought it could be done with [Marcello] Mastroianni and [Sophia] Loren but my agent insisted I should consider British actors. I knew I needed a couple with an international profile, and then it dawned on me that it could only be the Burtons. But I didn't expect them to be willing to work with a new film director which is what I was.

'My agent knew that Burton was longing to get back to doing Shakespeare and he managed to arrange for a meeting between the Burtons and myself in Ireland where they were filming.'

Zeffirelli saw for himself the madness that surrounded the lives of the Burtons:

'I went to their hotel in Dublin and it was complete chaos there. Liz had a bush baby which had gone on a rampage and was hiding in the bathroom where it clung on to the hot water pipes.

'Liz's maid had blood on her face where the bush baby had attacked her, and so she wasn't going near it again. I was talking to Richard who had his back to Liz who was yelling at him to come and help. He just sipped his drink and talked to me about Shakespeare. Liz came storming out of the bathroom and yelled, "Will you please stop talking about the damned Shakespeare and give me a hand."

'He slammed down his glass and yelled at her, "Will you please stop this bloody nonsense with the horrid little monster and come and talk to this man and if you are lucky you might work with him, so do you think you could be more pleasant to him?"

'She yelled, "I don't care what he thinks of me. All I want is some help to catch my bush baby."

'And on and on it went, and I knew they were Katharina and Petruchio [in *The Taming of the Shrew*]. I thought Richard would definitely be interested, but I wasn't sure about Elizabeth. Then she said to me, "Can you help me? I couldn't get along with someone who doesn't like animals."

'I told her I had dogs and cats, and then I followed her into the bathroom and saw the terrified bush baby, which was so exhausted that it wasn't difficult for me to wrap a towel around my hand so I could reach and hold it without getting scratched. I passed it to Liz and it snuggled in her arms, and from that moment I was Elizabeth's friend and she would be my Katharina.'

The thought of doing *The Taming of the Shrew*, which couldn't begin before late March in 1966, rejuvenated Richard. 'I wanted that film so badly that we waived our fees and agreed only on a percentage,' he told me.

I said, 'Elizabeth too?'

'Yes,' he said with a wry smile. 'I don't think the concept of doing a film for the love of it had ever occurred to her before.'

After filming on *Spy* was completed, the Burtons returned to Gstaad for a two month holiday. In June 1965, Richard heard that Sybil was to marry a member of a pop group called The Wild Ones, and that she was no longer wanting the generous alimony payment Rich had been making. Life suddenly seemed a little brighter, especially as there was another new film project that excited Richard, *Who's Afraid of Virginia Woolf?*, based on the play by Albert Albee. The casting of the Burtons as the arguing married couple, George and Martha, was not what producer Ernest Lehman and Warner Bros. originally wanted. They certainly wanted Elizabeth as the fat, foul-mouthed Martha, but not Richard as the henpecked teacher George.

'I had to talk Elizabeth into doing *Woolf*,' said Richard. 'I told her it could be her Hamlet. So she accepted the role but then she insisted that they cast me as George. They didn't want me. But Elizabeth was very powerful in the motion picture business – she's the best businessman in films I know – and so they reluctantly gave me the part. She also picked Mike Nichols to direct and he'd never even made a film before. She had good instincts.'

Elizabeth was paid $1.1 million plus numerous perks and a good percentage of the profits. 'I would have done it for nothing,' she told me. 'When they offered me a million for *Cleopatra* I took it for the sheer fun of it, and when they offered me over a million for *Who's*

Afraid of Virginia Woolf?, I signed the contract and then told Ernest Lehman, "I took you, didn't I?" '

Richard was paid three-quarters of a million plus profits. But the Burtons actually weren't greedy – by film star standards – because when the film ran more than 30 days over schedule they waived their overtime fee; they were contractually entitled to an extra million dollars between them.

George Segal and Sandy Dennis were also cast in the film. When I interviewed Sandy Dennis in London in 1983, she said, 'Working with [the Burtons] was extraordinary. They were like royalty and yet Richard was so approachable. They called each other names. I think it was in fun.'

Mike Nichols wasn't so sure that it was in fun. 'They said some really nasty things to each other,' he said.

Nichols observed that the filming took a toll on Richard and Elizabeth; perhaps the roles were too close to their real lives. Said Nichols, 'It got to the point where Richard didn't have the nerve any longer to suffer the kind of exposure playing George brought to him. In one scene, Elizabeth had to spit in his face. We had to do a number of takes but Elizabeth burst into tears and just couldn't do it any more. Richard stood there and took it. But finally his nerve cracked and he wouldn't come out of the dressing room until he had had a few drinks.'

No wonder Richard declared, 'I *am* George!'

The film was made at Warner Bros. studios, the first time Richard had filmed in Hollywood for some years, and they set up home in Los Angeles for the duration. But Hollywood was still a place where Rich had little respect from the natives, and although he and Elizabeth were both nominated for Oscars, he lost again; she, however, won, and he was delighted for her.

'I felt that Richard wanted Elizabeth to give her very best,' recalled Sandy Dennis, 'and he really kind of helped her through the part.' Mike Nichols, however, felt that Elizabeth 'wore him out'.

Sandy Dennis also won an Oscar, as Best Supporting Actress. The film won Oscars for its black and white cinematography, black and white art direction and black and white costume design. Again Richard was in a film that won Oscars, but none for him. Richard did, however, win the BAFTA award – the British equivalent of the Oscars – in 1966, but in those days the BAFTAs were not given to actors for any particular film but just for being best actor that year in anything; *Who's*

Afraid of Virginia Woolf? and *The Spy Who Came in from the Cold* both claimed Burton's award. It wasn't until the 1970s that someone finally made the sensible decision that an actor had to win for a specific performance.

Mike Nichols believed that Richard deserved an Oscar, 'if only for one single scene where he sits alone under a tree and tells the story of the boy. He did that in a single take. It was overwhelming. Just that scene was worth an Oscar.' The film kept Richard in the list of the top ten box office stars.

Rich rarely saw his own films – or so he said – but he saw this one. He said that his performance wasn't good enough. I asked him which one of his performances was good. He said, 'There's no such thing. If I'm ever as good as I think I can get, it will be time to stop.'

Chapter Nineteen

HOLLYWOOD vs THE BARD: THE CULTURE CLASH

W HEN THE FILMING OF *Virginia Woolf* was over, early in 1966, the Burtons went to Oxford purely for philanthropic purposes; Rich was to appear in a student production of *Doctor Faustus* at the Oxford Playhouse as a favour to Nevill Coghill who had directed him in *Measure for Measure* back in the Oxford days.

Richard was exhausted from playing George, but he rehearsed ten days straight and then performed for a week. Elizabeth appeared in the play, with no lines, as Helen of Troy.

Some critics had the knives out for Richard's return to the stage in what they saw as something very amateurish. That was incredibly snobbish of them. How many actors would appear on stage with amateurs for a good cause?

Richard decided that he would even make a film version of *Doctor Faustus* with his amateur cast, as well as co-direct it with Nevill Coghill. Rich did it for free and even put some of his own money into the production. Again, Elizabeth appeared as Helen of Troy, although her role was significantly enlarged but still without dialogue. This was a seemingly sound commercial decision although the critics derided her appearance in it. All proceeds were to go to the Oxford Playhouse.

It was no cheap enterprise; it would be filmed partly in Rome after *The Taming of the Shrew* was made and then at Shepperton Studios for just a few days. Despite having had no break since before *Who's Afraid of Virginia Woolf?*, Richard went into *The Taming of the Shrew* with a passion that had been missing from his film work for many years. He wanted this attempt to put Shakespeare on film to be a triumph;

160

Shakespeare on film had not been successful since Laurence Olivier's *Hamlet* in 1948 (Olivier's *Richard III*, in 1956, was not a commercial success).

Richard believed that only one man could ensure that *The Taming of the Shrew* was done right – and it wasn't Franco Zeffirelli. It was Philip Burton.

'Richard insisted I go and meet Philip Burton to ensure we didn't do anything that might offend the purists,' Zeffirelli told me. 'I expected to find myself in an argument but he was charming and knew what he was talking about. In fact, he helped me because I had some problems understanding some of the more difficult parts of the text.

'It was obvious that Richard idolised the man. I met Philip and I left realising how lucky Richard had been to have such a father-figure to rely on when he was young.'

When filming began in March 1966, Richard was unsure about Zeffirelli. 'I really didn't like Franco at first,' said Rich. 'I found him quite dominating to begin with. We had a lot of nonsense about costumes which we all argued over.'

The problem was that Elizabeth insisted that Irene Sharaff, one of the legends of Hollywood, do her costumes. Zeffirelli agreed Sharaff could do Elizabeth's costumes, but he didn't want her designing Richard's. 'I'm bored by costumes,' Rich told me. 'Olivier and Gielgud love dressing up and sorting out their costumes, but I hate costumes. I'd rather play the whole thing in contemporary clothes.'

Despite Zeffirelli's decision about costumes, Sharaff came up with designs for Richard; Zeffirelli turned them down which upset Elizabeth. Zeffirelli was not fluent in speaking English so he wrote all his thoughts down in letters, which made arguing with him very difficult, or so Richard thought. 'I was a pain in the arse to Franco when we started,' he said. 'I thought he was being a bore, and I got angry at him.'

Zeffirelli shrugged off the suggestion that there was tension between him and the Burtons to start with:

'Everyone was getting to know each other, and that can be a very difficult time, especially for people with artistic temperaments. But Richard was so enthusiastic to make the film that he and Liz put up most of the money to make it. It was a Burton–Zeffirelli production.

'For Richard, *The Taming of the Shrew* was a return to his cultural background, but to Liz it was just another film. A lot of their legendary squabbles were quite good-natured. Richard came from the theatre and he called Liz a Hollywood Baby. And she would say, "Yes, a golden baby."

'He'd tell her, "You certainly like gold and you're as plump as a baby." Then she'd say, "There are countries where they like their women to have some meat on them. If the Arabs hadn't banned my films because I'm pro-Israel, they'd all be drooling over me. You better hope I don't meet a rich sheikh." Then she would make some comments about his drinking.'

The Taming of the Shrew was both a meeting and a battle of two cultures; Rich fell back on his Shakespearean background but worked hard to translate it into screen terms. Elizabeth was using all her experience in Hollywood but worked hard to lift her game to do something classical, even if it was a comedy. She even succeeded in ridding herself of her acquired American accent (which marred her performance in *Cleopatra*) and spoke with a fine English accent which sounded far more attractive than the somewhat shrill tones she acquired in Hollywood.

They had some fun working, and they had their fights as well. It might seem that Zeffirelli didn't think of the legendary Burton rows as anything serious, but he shifted his position slightly on the subject when I pressed him and he said, 'I could see that beneath all this banter there was some bitterness. He resented her because she represented the Hollywood that he disliked. She disliked his British actor's superiority.'

But overall, making *The Taming of the Shrew* was a happy time for the battling Burtons. 'They both loved Italy,' said Zeffirelli. 'They loved their beautiful villa, and Rome, and the food and the wine. Elizabeth later told me that this was their only real honeymoon and it was the best time in their lives. Even during this, their best time, they managed to quarrel.'

Zeffirelli learned to roll with the punches:

'Working with Elizabeth was not always easy. Richard turned up at 7.30 every morning and was dressed and made up by the time we were ready to start filming at 9.20. But then we'd have to wait till around eleven for Liz who was having her face massaged and her eyebrows plucked. But Liz compensated for this because she gave her best in a single take, and we only took an extra take for technical reasons. So we made up for lost time. But then we'd lose time again because we'd break for lunch at one o'clock and they would have lunch parties in their dressing rooms. It would go on until four, and then they'd come back and we'd get a couple of shots done which usually weren't so good.

'I wanted to switch to French hours where we would start work at 12 noon and work through until eight in the evening with only a break for tea at around five. But the technicians weren't happy about that because they would still have to be there in the morning to get the set and equipment ready and then not leave until after nine in the evening. So I came up with the idea of starting at eight in the morning and finishing at three in the afternoon with no break. Liz wasn't happy with it, but Richard was, and finally she agreed.

'I saw how they helped each other. Liz knew more about film technique than Richard and she showed him how to play down his sometimes theatrical style. She knows how to achieve the greatest effect with the minimum of movement and expression. She knew how to play to the camera which Richard still hadn't learned by then. But he knew Shakespeare and she didn't, so he helped her to interpret the role.

'We got to the final scene which upsets many people because Katharina makes her act of submission to Petruchio on behalf of all women to all men, and a lot of women didn't like that, so many actresses have tended to do the speech with a sense of irony. But Liz played it straight, as though she meant it, and Richard was so moved by her speech that he wiped away a tear and said, "All right, my girl, I do wish you'd put that into practice."

'She looked him in the eye and replied, "Of course, I can't say it in words like that, but my heart is there."'

Zeffirelli was kind in trying not to remember Richard's occasional savage humour. But Richard didn't forget or forgive himself. 'I should have been totally happy making *Shrew*,' he said. 'But this terrible depression would just descend on me even then. I would throw tantrums and although I knew I was behaving appallingly, I felt helpless to stop myself.' He admitted that often his rows with Elizabeth were started just because he felt 'in a black mood and couldn't find the light'.

There were other pressures on the Burtons; Elizabeth suffered badly from piles and a month into filming she began to bleed so badly that Richard was convinced she would die. She was hospitalised but just a couple of weeks later she appeared to be fully recovered.

Once filming was well under way, Richard came to love Zeffirelli as much as he had loved any director and they remained firm friends, attending social events together and mingling with high society. Towards the end of filming, Zeffirelli learned that he could count on Richard when he needed him most. 'I had to leave for New York for the opening of the new Met [to direct an opera of *Antony and Cleopatra*] with just a few covering shots left to do, so Richard said he would direct them.

'He's a good man, willing to help in a crisis. When the Arno River burst its banks and flooded Florence [in November 1966], I hurried to Florence to film the tragedies and the disaster. Lives were lost and so were great treasures. There was the risk of infection from the sewage and from oil. Richard asked if there was anything he could do to help Florence, and I said that he could narrate my film. I wanted the world to know that Florence needed help. He set to work on it without question and without a fee. I was very grateful to Richard and so were all Italians.'

Zeffirelli's documentary raised over $20 million to aid Florence.

Richard found his short directing stint on *The Taming of the Shrew* a useful warm-up for his next venture – directing as well as starring in *Doctor Faustus*. He and Elizabeth were still in Rome in October for some extra filming for both *Shrew* and *Faustus*.

Those two films were released in 1967; *The Taming of the Shrew* was an enormous success, *Doctor Faustus* was a disaster.

Time said of *Shrew*, 'Zeffirelli has succeeded in mounting the liveliest screen incarnation of Shakespeare since Olivier's *Henry V*.' The *Time* critic thought that Elizabeth gave one of 'her better performances', and that Burton 'catches the cadences of iambic pentameter with inborn ease'.

Hollis Alpert, writing in *Saturday Review*, wrote 'There was never very much doubt about the abilities of Burton. There was more doubt about Miss Taylor . . . She had to contend with her husband at his absolute best in a role for which he is so extremely suited. Well, not only has she managed it; she has come through the ordeal with honour.'

Judith Crist of the *New York World Journal Tribune* was one of the few who didn't care for it or the Burtons; 'It's a shaky and unpoetic contraption, little more than a vehicle for a couple of players to exhibit their talent for merriment and romping in excelsis – and, too often, in excess.'

Doctor Faustus was savaged by the critics. '*Doctor Faustus* is of an awfulness that bends the mind,' said Renata Adler of the *New York Times*.

And *Time* noted, 'Lots of grads bring their wives back to the old school and ham it up for home movies – but this is ridiculous.'

Professionally, Rich was ahead of the field. Privately, he was struggling, especially with his health. He was finding that his body, at the age of 40, was letting him down more and more, and so he exercised to fight the arthritis and what would later prove to be pinched nerves that caused him terrible pain and weakness.

He also managed to stop drinking, mainly because, he said, he simply lost his taste for any alcohol at that time. Elizabeth never joined in with his abstinence and continued to drink as much as ever. He said he didn't mind, but it seems to me that she didn't exactly encourage him to stay sober by drinking heavily in front of him. He didn't stay on the wagon long. He got drunk for two days and said that he thoroughly enjoyed it.

Towards the end of 1966, there were a number of projects he was considering. Sir John Gielgud wanted him to play Caliban in *The Tempest*. Joshua Logan wanted him to play Arthur in the film version of *Camelot* he was to direct, but Richard decided he didn't want to do it and so Richard Harris played Arthur instead. Burton wanted to make *The Fixer* with director John Frankenheimer, and he also hoped to star in MGM's musical remake of *Goodbye Mr. Chips*, but in the end Peter O'Toole played Mr. Chips. What Richard did actually do was make *The Comedians* which Graham Greene had scripted from his own book. Rich didn't see the script, accepting it simply because of his admiration for Greene as a writer. He also wanted to work with director Peter Glenville again. The film had a role for Elizabeth, which seemed paramount to Richard back then.

So in January 1967, Richard and Elizabeth worked together once again in *The Comedians*. It was set in Papa Doc's Haiti but filmed in very effective locations in Dahomey in West Africa, and in the South of France, with interiors shot in studios in Paris and Nice.

For the first time, Richard was paid more than Elizabeth; he got three-quarters of a million dollars, she got half a million. Hers was really a supporting role. They needed the money, having both done *Shrew* and *Faustus* for no upfront fee; it would be a while before they received profits from *Shrew*.

Rich played an Englishman running an empty hotel in Haiti. In between political and sometimes violent events, he has an affair with the wife of a European ambassador; Elizabeth played the wife and Peter Ustinov the ambassador.

'I liked working with Richard and Liz very much,' Peter Ustinov told me. 'But Richard seemed utterly bored by the whole thing, which didn't surprise me because it was a huge bore whenever the Burtons had to make love for the camera. Elizabeth, who was playing a German, affected a French accent which bemused me no end.'

Ustinov was right; watching the film, you find your attention easily distracted by Elizabeth's peculiar accent – which many critics picked up on – and the fact that the love scenes only served to stop the drama whenever something interesting started to happen in this lengthy film.

While Richard walked – almost slept, probably often drunk – his way through the film, Sir Alec Guinness gave the film its brightest moments as a bogus major who was selling arms to Papa Doc. Guinness had been one of the numerous friends who had been unable to get through to Richard on the telephone in the years since he had been with Elizabeth. 'When I worked with Burton [on *The Comedians*], I wondered how he would be towards me,' Sir Alec Guinness said. 'He was, it turned out, genuinely happy to see me, and when I told him about the calls I'd made and the presents I'd tried to send which were returned, he was extremely puzzled. Richard didn't seem to know half of what went on to keep him, Elizabeth and the whole family safe from the world.'

And they still needed to be kept safe; while filming *The Comedians* there were two to three kidnap threats each week. 'It must have been terrible for Richard who is a most gregarious person,' said Sir Alec. 'But he was wonderful to work with. I had to do a long scene – just me, talking, and him listening off camera. He could have just stood there to give me something to look at but he paid complete attention to what I was saying which helped my performance no end. He was incredibly supportive to me, and to all the actors.'

Elizabeth next earned some more much-needed income by starring in John Huston's *Reflections in a Golden Eye* with Marlon Brando. The Burtons now found themselves able to afford to buy a yacht, the *Kalizma*. Rich also invested £100,000 in a new Welsh TV company, Harlech TV.

In July 1967, Richard was so stricken with pain through arthritis that he at last saw a doctor and was given a course of pills which seemed to work. But the effect was only temporary.

The Burtons were back in the sun, this time in Sardinia, to film *Boom!* based on Tennessee Williams' play *The Milk Train Doesn't Stop Here Anymore*. Shortly before filming began, it seems that Richard may have had, or came close to having, a seizure. He was telling me how he came to make *Boom!* against his better judgement. 'The producer was just looking for another Dick and Liz flick,' he told me. 'But Elizabeth was enthusiastic because she had had success with [Tennessee] Williams before [in *Cat on a Hot Tin Roof* and *Suddenly Last Summer*]. We went to Rome on business where everything that was ever bad happened to me. Or so it seems. We got into a *debate* – a howling fight! Then it was like something happened in my head – something went . . . *wrong*.'

I asked him if he had come close to having a seizure. He answered, 'I can fight them off sometimes, if I know they are coming on and I take a pill, or have a drink.' He frankly hated admitted having what he was sure were epileptic fits.

Most of *Boom!* was filmed in a wonderfully designed construction of a villa perched on the Sardinian rocks. Joseph Losey directed against the visual splendour of the blue sky and sea of the Mediterranean, but the screenplay by Tennessee Williams was far too symbolic to attract a mass audience. Richard knew that he and Elizabeth were badly miscast; she was playing a dying older woman and he was playing a young enigmatic poet. He felt the film would have been better served by casting a couple like Bette Davis and Robert Redford, and he was right.

As Foster Hirsch wrote in *Cinema*, 'The film went haywire in casting a voluptuous Elizabeth Taylor as the dying Sissy Goforth and sagging Richard Burton as the strapping ministrant.'

Judith Crist felt that Taylor was '20 years too young and 30 acting eons away from the role,' and that Burton looked 'more like a bank clerk on campy holiday, kimono and all, than a poet'.

But there was praise for Richard from Andrew Sarris of *The Village*

Voice: 'Burton seems at first entrance utterly miscast as the morbid gigolo masquerading as the Angel of Death, but his final Booming exit line caps what turns out to be the most brilliant performance of his career.'

Audiences who had lapped up the delights of *The Taming of the Shrew* weren't fooled into believing that this Burton–Taylor picture was going to be much fun, so they stayed away. On top of the failure of *The Comedians* and *Doctor Faustus, Boom!* proved that the public would no longer go and see Liz and Dick in just anything, and in effect, it brought to an end their reign as the supreme screen team of the 1960s.

Nevertheless, they were rich enough to buy their own private jet plane. They had the money if not the success. Life for the Burtons would never be the same again.

Chapter Twenty

THE DARK SIDE

1968 BEGAN PROMISINGLY. Richard was in *Where Eagles Dare* with Clint Eastwood. It was a boy's own adventure of a war movie, written especially for the screen by Alistair MacLean who had written a number of novels which had been turned into successful films, particularly *The Guns of Navarone.*

Rich seemed not to mind that the film's producer, Elliot Kastner, had set up *Where Eagles Dare* with what he described as 'an off-white lie'. Kastner, according to Richard, had gone to novelist Alistair MacLean and said, 'Look, Richard Burton is keen to make a film along the lines of *The Guns of Navarone.* Can you write an original screenplay for him?' MacLean said he could and began writing *Where Eagles Dare.*

Kastner then went to Burton and said, 'Look, Alistair MacLean is anxious to write a screenplay for you along the lines of *The Guns of Navarone.* Are you interested?' Richard said he was.

Filming began at MGM's Borehamwood Studios in England in February 1968. Richard received a million dollars plus a percentage which, in the case of this highly successful and totally enjoyable action film, was considerable. While Richard made *Where Eagles Dare,* Elizabeth was at another studio in England making *Secret Ceremony* with Mia Farrow and Robert Mitchum. For once, Elizabeth was not on Richard's set every day, but she kept in touch constantly by phone.

Brook Williams had a good supporting role in *Where Eagles Dare.* He told me of the day Clint Eastwood arrived at Heathrow Airport, 'bringing just two bags with him. He went to customs and discovered there was a commotion ahead of him that was causing a huge delay. He asked a policeman what the commotion was and was told, "It's Richard Burton and Elizabeth Taylor. They've just flown in from Geneva in their private jet."

'They had dozens of cases and all their usual personnel, and there was a crowd of photographers around them, and nobody even noticed Clint.'

Polish actress Ingrid Pitt played the vital role of a resistance fighter who helps the film's main heroes. In one scene she had to sit on Richard's lap and then she had to slap his face hard. Richard told me, 'I've never had so much fun being slapped before.'

Ingrid told me, 'Richard was very naughty and Clint enjoyed his sense of humour. Elizabeth would phone him at the studio and he would tell her that I was sitting on his lap which would make Elizabeth furious. On our way home from the studio we would stop at all the pubs. Always there would be someone who would come up to Richard and say, "Aren't you . . . ?" and he would say in a gruff voice, "No, mate." And they would say, "I didn't think you were."'

Mary Ure, then married – though not too happily – to Robert Shaw, was also in the film; it was her biggest movie in some years. When she ran into trouble with the production company, Richard stepped in to help. 'I had been promised billing above the title with Richard and Clint Eastwood but the studio had reneged on the promise,' said Mary. 'I was very upset, and before we began on the film I had dinner with Richard and he asked me what was wrong, so I told him. He went to his agent and said, "Kindly tell MGM that neither Mr. Burton nor Miss Ure will set foot before the cameras until Miss Ure's name is reinstated above the title." The studio changed their mind.'

During filming in England, Richard and Elizabeth were living on a rented yacht on the Thames; their own yacht was being refitted so they had hired another. 'We had to live on the yacht because Elizabeth had so many bloody dogs and we couldn't bring them on to British soil for nine months,' said Rich. 'Elizabeth couldn't be without her dogs. They crapped everywhere. I swear they were all incontinent.'

Clint Eastwood had still not completely cracked Hollywood back then, having been a star for several years in the TV show *Rawhide* and then finding fame in Europe in *A Fistful of Dollars*, *For a Few Dollars More* and *The Good, the Bad and the Ugly*. Richard recognised that Eastwood was destined to be a great screen star. 'Within three minutes of shooting time we all realised we were in the presence of a very remarkable man,' he said, and compared Eastwood to the likes of Spencer Tracy, James Stewart and Robert Mitchum, actors who 'appear to do nothing and they do everything. I enjoyed making that film with Clint. I did all the talking and he did all the killing; it seemed a good match. And he was very easy to work with. We got on very well.'

Eastwood said, 'I just stood around trying to figure out the espionage tricks, or firing my machine gun, while Burton handled the dialogue.'

Richard's role was, in fact, quite physically demanding and he was very happy playing a man of action once more. 'It's a joy to be a hero,' he said. He was comfortable doing action roles, despite the pain in his back and shoulders. He had developed an exercise regime which he tried to stick to, but he noticed that his arms had grown considerably weaker. But he bore up well when the unit moved to the snow-bound location in Austria where, high on a mountain in the Bavarian Alps, stood a magnificent castle where much of the film's action took place.

The only way up to the castle was by cable car, so actors, crew and equipment were ferried from the local village to the castle by cable car. Second Unit Director Yakima Canutt devised some breathtaking action which took place on the cable car using stunt doubles. Eastwood said, 'They gave this film the wrong title. It should have been called *Where Doubles Dare.*'

When Richard finished *Where Eagles Dare*, he started work on another film in London called *Laughter in the Dark* for Tony Richardson who had directed him in *Look Back in Anger*. But after a fortnight of filming, Richard was fired. He told me, 'I was just half an hour late one Sunday morning and Richardson exploded. I didn't mind that but I had brought Liza with me, and she had to put up with me and Richardson yelling obscenities at each other. So Richardson fired me.' Nicol Williamson replaced him.

There followed a brief stint on a sex comedy called *Candy* which somehow attracted Marlon Brando, James Coburn, Walter Matthau and John Huston in cameo roles; Rich was on screen for ten minutes as a Welsh pop poet. The film was panned by the critics, but it was an unexpected hit.

Elizabeth had been unwell throughout the filming of *Secret Ceremony* and finally had to be hospitalised in London and underwent a hysterectomy which had some complications. Rich slept in a room next door to Elizabeth's in the hospital and listened all night to her screaming in agony. 'The drugs they gave her caused her to have terrible hallucinations,' he recalled. 'One night I heard her cry out "Jim!" and we found her in the corridor. She wasn't supposed to be out of bed at all. I put her back to bed and said, "You're a naughty girl.

Now stay there," and she said, "Fuck off!" I said I would stay with her and she said she wanted me to sit in the corridor as she couldn't stand my face. Well, I was used to that sort of talk, but she was out of her mind with all the drugs, so it was really very frightening. I left the room and shortly after I heard her cry, "Richard!" I went back in and a nurse arrived and we found Elizabeth sitting on the end of the bed. She didn't know where she was.'

Elizabeth's health would be poor for some time to come, but as he told me, 'Our marriage was never stronger than when she was ill. There was no fighting. I just took care of Elizabeth.'

While Elizabeth was in hospital, news came that their Céligny gardener, André Besançon, had committed suicide. Brook recalled:

'I went with Rich, Ifor, Gwen, Kate and Liza to Switzerland for the funeral. Afterward Rich insisted that he, Ifor and me should have a few drinks at the Café de la Gare which was near the *Pays de Galles*. Ifor decided he'd go and open the house. But he was very drunk and he caught his foot in a grille. He tripped and fell against a window ledge and broke his neck. For the rest of his life he was confined to a wheelchair, and for the rest of his life Rich felt it was somehow his fault.

'Rich couldn't hold it together after that. He drank more heavily than usual. That's around the time I became closer to him. He really seemed to have no real friends – mates – around him, and he was lost without Ifor. Rich had always treated me well and he was like a hero to me. I was really one of the family.'

Richard told me, 'I rely on Brook. He tells me stories that make me laugh, and he's intelligent, and he likes to drink, and he's loyal.' Another time he told me, 'Brookie is like the son I never had.' He rewarded Brook for his loyalty by getting him work in almost all of his films. Brook was sometimes an extra, sometimes he had a few words to say and sometimes he had a major supporting role. Brook also became his confidant and an unofficial personal assistant. Whatever Rich needed, Brookie would do his best to provide it.

Richard was relieved in a way to escape the depression he was in over Ifor's accident by heading to Paris in September 1968 where he was to film *Staircase* with Rex Harrison. Elizabeth, released from hospital, was also in Paris to make *The Only Game in Town* for director George

Stevens; her co-star was Warren Beatty. If Richard and Elizabeth couldn't make films together, they made sure they were in the same town at the same time to make their respective movies. Elizabeth's film was set in Las Vegas; Richard's in the East End of London. Paris would substitute for both towns.

Harrison and Burton were playing homosexual barbers; Harrison told me, 'The film was a risk. I felt I was old enough and rich enough to take a risk. And I think Richard did too. We discussed it, and it was rather a case of "If you do it, I'll do it." So we did it. It was a mistake. It was a *dreadful* mistake. But that's what risks are all about.'

Vincent Canby of the *New York Times* said that the characters played by Burton and Harrison 'are exploited as freaks. The two stars seem terribly uncomfortable, and I wonder if the apparent discomfort, conscious or not, isn't meant to call attention to the real distance that exists between the actors and their roles.'

But the film shouldn't be dismissed so casually. It was from a play by Charles Dyer and directed by Stanley Donen who, perhaps, was at his best when directing musicals like *Singin' in the Rain*. But it was a bold attempt, for its time, to try to tell a bitter-sweet story of ageing homosexuals living desperate and lonely lives in the late 1960s. That wasn't the kind of story which was easy to tell back then.

'This was one film I cared about,' Rich told me. 'I didn't see it as a story of homosexuals but about two neurotic individuals who needed each other desperately for consolation. I loved its caustic wit, but I think it was lost on almost everyone who thought it was just a campy story about two poofs played by two actors who are rather notorious for being anything but poofs.'

A few critics appreciated it. *Variety* thought that Harrison 'offers a portrait of a bitter, disenchanted man living in terror of being alone. Burton, almost stoic, commands respect and, at the same time, sympathy. Harrison and Burton have dared risky roles and have triumphed.'

But the film was still a flop. Nevertheless, being in Paris gave him and Elizabeth the chance to meet and dine with the highest of society, such as the Rothschilds and Maria Callas.

If the work was not always good, the high living was.

While filming *Staircase* in Paris, Richard had made a tentative agreement to make *Anne of the Thousand Days* for Universal, but when he told them he had decided not to do it, they threatened to sue him.

'I didn't want to make the film,' he told me. 'I thought it was a poor attempt to try and make a "classic".'

As a great fan of the play by Maxwell Anderson (I've played the part of Henry VIII in it myself), I remain mystified by Richard's negativity towards it.

'The words don't sparkle,' he said. 'It's not *Becket*. It's not Robert Bolt, and it isn't anywhere close to Shakespeare.' He couldn't help but make comparisons to some of the greatest play writing; few other plays could therefore satisfy him.

Michael Horden, who was in the film, told me, 'I suspect his indifference had more to do with having to dress up. Richard doesn't like costumes very much. He doesn't wear wigs and false beards. Of course, he grew his own beard to play Henry, but he didn't much like disappearing behind it.'

Although he eventually made the film he tried to hold out against it until, finally, he simply decided to save himself the hassle of being sued. So he went into *Anne of the Thousand Days* with no enthusiasm whatsoever. But before that he had *Staircase* to finish, with the final scenes being shot in London in December 1969. When he returned to Paris he found Elizabeth in pain with her back. She was told by doctors to lie flat on her back for a month, so George Stevens arranged it so she could have time off from filming.

It seems that the marriage was never better than when Elizabeth was ill. 'Elizabeth's many ailments gave Rich something almost tangible to bind them,' Stanley Baker observed. 'They had love and passion and sex, but he was never more doting than when he was her nurse.'

Rich had always blamed doctors for neglecting his mother and causing her premature death; he had always distrusted doctors. Said Brook:

'Rich was afraid they would kill Elizabeth because they told her it was all right to drink while she was taking strong medication for the pain. At least, that's what she told him she'd been told. He was sure that it had to be dangerous to mix alcohol with strong painkillers, and he often discovered her towards the end of the day to be incoherent and barely able to walk. He was sure it was due to the mixture of booze and drugs.

'He asked the docs about it and they said that she was only being given vitamins so he concluded that she really had to be very drunk, and it turned him off drink for a short time. He needed to stay sober to be able to care for her.

'But her behaviour became more erratic, more than that of a drunkard. She often screamed and cried in her sleep. He assumed, and no one ever confirmed it, that she was suffering anxiety attacks from the trauma of the hysterectomy.

'It turned out that she had become addicted to the strong medications she had been on, and she had to return to hospital to be weaned off them. She was given a thorough physical and was told she would have back trouble for the rest of her life. Her liver was in a poor way too.'

After the premiere in London of *Where Eagles Dare* and with Elizabeth's film finally wrapped, they went to Puerto Vallarta in Mexico to try to recover from their ordeals. By then he was drinking heavily again and, for the first time, they actually fought to the point where they nearly separated. He found consolation in writing a feature about Wales for *Look* magazine, and he managed to stop drinking

In April 1969, he sank into one of his unfathomable depressions. He was sure that being on the wagon only made his black moods worse. He was still apathetic about *Anne of the Thousand Days* and avoided learning his lines until early in May; filming was due to start later that month. 'I had rarely begun any film so disinterested,' he said. 'I usually know all my lines long before I start.'

His mood was not lifted upon arriving in England to hear that sneak previews of *Staircase* had proven disastrous.

He finally began to prepare to play Henry VIII in *Anne of the Thousand Days*. He said, 'I saw Henry as quite mad, with great charm and spectacular outbursts of rage and a superb and cynical intelligence.'

I argued with him that he played the part a little too aggressively; there is a lot of sympathy in the part as written in the play. He said, 'I didn't feel too sympathetic about myself at that time, so I couldn't find it in Henry.'

Nevertheless, his Henry VIII is one of his best performances; he just gives the part a different colour to the way I think the playwright intended.

His mood wasn't helped when he discovered that Elizabeth would not be cast as Anne Boleyn as they had both hoped. She had just turned

38 and was considered too old. A French Canadian actress, Geneviève Bujold, had been picked. She was only 28. 'My first impression of Geneviève was of Vivien Leigh,' Richard said. 'I felt that she would work well in the part.'

Although Richard had flown to London, his yacht the *Kalizma* made its way to Princess Steps on the Thames where he and Elizabeth would live with the dogs who still crapped all over the place.

Ifor was in hospital at Aston Clinton, not far from Shepperton Studios where *Anne* was being filmed, so Rich was able to visit him. Ifor was in a motorised wheelchair and able to get himself about. Richard paid for all of Ifor's treatment, and also for Gwen's room at the nearby Bell Inn.

But Rich couldn't quite lift himself out of the doldrums; he continued to be wracked with guilt about Ifor, and he was anxious about how well Geneviève Bujold and their director Charles Jarrott would perform. It was Jarrott's first film, and Bujold's first film in English. He was unable to sleep so he drank lots of vodka. He knew he was drinking too much and tried to slow it down.

He was, however, delighted to find himself working with old friends like Anthony Quayle and Michael Horden, and he particularly enjoyed his scenes with them; there was always a certain amount of competition between them which gave added bite to their scenes.

Michael Horden told me, 'We are devils when we do a scene – people like Richard Burton, Tony Quayle and myself. Tony and I were doing each take differently to throw each other and Richard off. Richard realised what we were doing and he did the same. It's all very childish but great fun, and I think makes for an interesting scene in the end. It's down to the editor and director what versions they choose, but we give them a variety and we have such silly fun in the process.'

Brook Williams had a small part. He said, 'I saw it my duty to try and keep Richard's spirits up. He was very down. But he loved to hear my stories and so I'd make him laugh. He'd have tears running down his face. He loved telling stories, but he loved hearing them too.'

Although she had been passed over for the part of Anne, Elizabeth agreed to be an extra in one scene. It was just as well she didn't have the title role because in June she was ill again; she had piles that seriously haemorrhaged.

Rich found little pleasure in the work. He failed to stop drinking and considered giving up acting altogether. He told me, 'The problem with

Henry VIII is that anybody can play him. Even Robert Shaw played him.' That was a side-swipe at Robert Shaw whose few professional triumphs included playing Henry VIII in the film version of *A Man for all Seasons*. He had little liking for Shaw and didn't like the way he treated Mary Ure.

'When you're a friend of Richard's,' Mary told me, 'he will defend you to the death.'

But he was hard on himself. 'I should have been much better [as Henry],' he said. 'About halfway through filming I suddenly realised – well, not suddenly as I had known but not admitted – that I had treated people I liked enormously with unforgivable disrespect. I knew it was the drink, and so I gave it up. Well, much of it. I eased up on it, although every now and then I couldn't stop myself and got appallingly drunk. But I pulled myself together to finish the film.'

Before the film was over, there were rumours of an affair between Richard and Geneviève Bujold. 'That was all rubbish,' he told me. 'It was a bigger problem for Gin [Bujold] because she had Elizabeth training her sights on her.'

He told Elizabeth there was no truth in the rumours but she apparently didn't completely believe him. 'It was all very tiresome,' he said in 1974. 'I had never betrayed Elizabeth. Not at that point.'

His dissatisfaction with the film and his performance is puzzling. It was a popular and successful film and his performance won him another Oscar nomination. He is completely compelling to watch as Henry, although he lacked the necessary sympathy factor the role required to balance the drama between Henry and Anne, beautifully played by Geneviève Bujold. But I think he was playing the part in a way that reflected his own anger at himself for some of his past sins. He once told me, 'I sinned when I gave Kate up for Elizabeth.' He didn't consider it a sin to give up Sybil, but to give up his daughter Kate for the love of Elizabeth was something he never forgave himself for.

Not that he lost Kate. She often visited him, he loved her being with him. Children from divorced parents can be very resilient if the absent parent is not negligent. Nevertheless, the searing emotional pain Kate and Sybil suffered lasted for many years. In a documentary, *Cleopatra, the Film That Changed Hollywood*, made in 2000, Jack Brodsky, who was one of the publicists on *Cleopatra* as well as an actor and producer, told of the time he was casting in 1992 for a film called *Rookie of the Year*. Kate Burton tested for a role in it. Brodsky told her he had worked on *Cleopatra* and added, 'Of course, you're too young to remember me because you were such a little girl at the time.' She told him that she didn't want to talk about it. 'I've put that part of my life away. It was terrible. It still haunts my mother,' she told him. Thirty years on, Kate and her mother still hurt. Richard must have known that and felt forever guilty.

He also felt tremendous guilt over Ifor; that was another of his sins. He was convinced it was his fault and he couldn't forgive himself. Ifor's condition was deteriorating and early in 1970 he was back in hospital with a serious kidney disease. Rich couldn't bear to see him so helpless and said he actually wished Ifor would die and be out of his agony.

Perhaps in Henry VIII Richard saw something of his own dark side when it came to matters of family, sex and fatherhood; Henry does, after all, reject his daughter Elizabeth, and Richard felt he had rejected Kate and Jessica. Henry was perennially changing wives; Richard didn't actually go that far, but he had given up his first wife for a second. And I believe that by that time in 1969 he had begun to think that he had made a big mistake marrying Elizabeth.

'I can't help loving her,' he told me, even in 1974 after their separation, 'and we had some fine times – really good times – but by God, she was more than I could cope with.'

Henry VIII, then, was the dark side of Richard, to some extent – although, happily, Rich never had any of his wives or girlfriends beheaded – but I think it goes a long way to explaining why he felt so dissatisfied with the film even before he began work on it. 'I was disappointed with the script. Such mediocre rubbish,' he once told me. But it wasn't mediocre.

And perhaps it is the black mood that the film put Richard into which made his performance so succinct and memorable if not entirely in keeping with the original play. In fact, the film critic of the *Observer* picked up on the comparison between Richard Burton and Henry VIII: 'Richard Burton plays Henry like a man who has promised to buy another diamond before Easter, using himself like an acting machine that will, if flogged, produce another million dollars.'

It was a review that seemed to indicate something of a backlash against Burton, not so much, I think, for his acting but more for his all-too-public private life. *Variety* at least noted that 'Burton's portrayal is sensitive, vivid and arresting', but it also picked up on the fact that 'it is still basically an unsympathetic role'.

178

Although it was liked enough to earn him yet another Oscar nomination, he again failed to earn the little gold statuette. It went, arguably undeservedly, to John Wayne for *True Grit*; Wayne gave better performances for films he wasn't nominated for and I think Wayne knew that too because he turned up at the Burtons' own private party, thrust his Oscar at Richard and said, 'Here, you should have won this.' Rich didn't keep the Oscar, but he thought it was a truly thoughtful gesture by Wayne.

The fact that the film was actually put together so fast for release at the end of 1969, just a few months after principal photography had finished, demonstrated how much faith Universal had in it as an Oscar winner. It the end it received only one Academy Award, for Costumes, but it was nominated for Best Picture, Screenplay, Photography, Music, Best Actress, Best Supporting Actor (Anthony Quayle) and, of course, Best Actor.

Curiously, the BAFTAs completely ignored the film. However, Geneviève Bujold did win a much-deserved Golden Globe.

Rich had finished the film relieved but depressed. He and Elizabeth fought. He believed that his marriage was seriously threatened. 'I remember after I'd finished [the film] we had an almighty row and she gave me such a whack around the head. She had all those bloody rings on; it was like being hit with a knuckleduster. I felt like I could have killed her. I had blind rage. But I held myself back. God, what people we were.

'We were both drinking heavily. It was a wonder either of us was still alive; the booze should have killed us both. I noticed one morning that I felt quite calm. I didn't shake. I often did. Still do sometimes. But I didn't have the shakes that morning . . . until *she* came in. And then I began to shake. Nothing was said. She only had to be there and I shook. Scared me to death.'

'She scared you?' I asked him.

'No, the fact that I shook scared me. What did that mean? What did it say about the way I felt about her, or what she was doing to me?'

Then I asked him if maybe it was also fear of a possible seizure. He said, 'I had that thing in my head and I could never figure out what set it off. I managed to keep control and I made up my mind to give up drinking – *again*. I have learned that there have to be times that you *must* stop now and again. So I stopped drinking and we went back to Gstaad where I exercised a lot – playing badminton and walking; the

179

both of us walking. My body was so weak that I'd finish a game or a walk so stiff I hurt all over.'

It was with Brook that he played badminton. 'We played every day,' said Brook. 'I think it hurt him to play, but he wouldn't give up.'

His arms were becoming less mobile and his back and shoulders often hurt.

Brook said, 'I'd gone over [to Gstaad] with my wife, Liz. Rich called her Lillabetta. We brought Maria over with us; we really were all part of the family. While we were there Rich decided to drink. I sat up with him through the night. He drank a bottle of Scotch. I didn't drink much but thought it best to stay up with him. He was fine and after that he stopped drinking for a time once more.'

Richard didn't stop drinking altogether; as he admitted, 'I drank only a little wine with dinner . . . and a vodka before lunch. To me, that was being on the wagon, which I managed to fall off from time to time.'

He wanted to bring Ifor over to Switzerland, so he, Elizabeth and Brook visited a doctor in the paraplegics ward of a local hospital. Brook recalled:

'Anything involving Ifor sent Rich into a deep mood and sometimes a ferocious mood. After going to a hospital to arrange for Ifor's treatment and accommodation, Rich became quite evil. Elizabeth tried hard to calm him but he was vicious, not only with her but with me too. He hated himself for it, and he told me he didn't know why he was like that. There were times when I saw him just very, very scared. He said to me, "You stick by me, Brookie. Even when I'm at my most evil. I don't deserve you." But that's what you do for people you love; you stand by them through thick and thin. It wasn't always easy. But I always knew that whenever Rich sank into a deep depression or whenever his anger boiled over, it would pass and he would be his real self again.'

Richard and Elizabeth returned briefly to England to arrange for Ifor and Gwen to move to Switzerland, and while there Rich secured a 69.4 carat diamond ring for Elizabeth. He had bid on it for a million dollars but had been outbid by Cartiers by $50,000. He got on the phone and haggled with Cartiers over the next 24 hours until he had secured that ring, or as he called it, 'that bloody thing', for $1.1 million.

The ring was brought over from New York by security guards, one of whom was armed with a machine gun. I asked Richard if it had been worth the price. He said, 'I didn't want to be the one to make the marriage end. It was an almost last-ditch attempt to make it work – make *us* work. But we were never going to work.'

The rich and famous couple decided it was time to take a long sabbatical and see what destiny had in store for them that a $1.1 million, 69.4 carat ring couldn't guarantee them.

Chapter Twenty-One

FIGHTING GERMANS AND VILLAINS

THE LAST FEW months of 1969 and the first few of 1970 were spent in peace and solitude in Puerto Vallarta in Mexico. Rich hoped to spend the year writing and even began work on a novel but he never finished it, probably because he didn't think it was any good. But he did write articles for a number of newspapers and magazines, including the *Observer* and *Vogue*.

The Burtons turned up in Hollywood for the Oscars. They spent time with Frank Sinatra who flirted with Elizabeth, and she with him, making Rich so jealous that he was never to forget it. He was convinced that Sinatra purposely ignored his anger which he apparently made no attempt to hide.

'I like Frank,' he told me. 'But only in short doses.'

Rich had promised Elizabeth that he would have a health check-up, and so he promptly checked into the Hollywood Presbyterian Hospital for 24 hours. Doctor Rex Kenemer told him he had to stop drinking for three months because he had an enlarged liver and would have sclerosis of the liver within five years. In fact, his liver would continue to deteriorate, but more slowly, even if he stopped drinking.

So Rich stopped drinking entirely, which surprised everyone. He felt he might have been giving his liver a better chance but he had become, or so he believed, a bore when sober. He also found that things Elizabeth said seemed to hit home more vehemently, such as when she told him that she wished he'd get out of her life. He began to feel that she really did mean it and he accepted that she would, at some time in the near future, leave him.

It didn't help him at all that she continued to drink. He always said he didn't mind, but in 1974 he told me, 'If only she had stopped as well.

Maybe we could have been two decent civilised people at the same time. I had to watch her knock back her booze and pop her prescribed pills and I found she was like a banshee towards me at times. Drunk, I took everything she threw at me. Sober, it all hurt like hell.'

He made another admission to me. 'During that time I lost my libido, for Christ's sake. Can you believe it? I put it down to the withdrawal from alcohol. Maybe it was. Maybe it was the way she made me feel. I hate being made to feel anything less than a man, but somehow with her I sometimes felt like a girl. I didn't have the heart to tell her to fuck off. So we just bickered throughout the first six months of our sabbatical.'

In April they flew from Mexico to Los Angeles for the Oscars. Amazingly, Rich managed to refrain from drinking any alcohol even after he lost to John Wayne. Two days after the Oscars, at the bungalow they were staying in, Elizabeth got very drunk and had a row with her mother. Rich, staying out of it all, went to bed and was alarmed when Elizabeth called him from the bathroom. She was bleeding badly from piles so he called for Dr Kenemer who decided she would need an operation.

In May Richard was offered a CBE; he accepted it but was frankly and honestly disappointed that he wasn't getting a knighthood. A CBE meant they were 'officially posh', as he put it.

A few weeks later, Elizabeth went into hospital for her operation which left her in terrible pain. She had become dependent on strong painkillers, so the doctors managed her pain with milder medication and kept a watchful eye on her in case of withdrawal. Rich was never more at peace in some peculiar way than when she was ill; he could care for her and know that she was more dependent on him than at any other time. When she was well enough, he took her out of the hospital in a wheelchair and back to their Beverly Hills bungalow.

But before long she was bleeding again. He felt he was able to cope only because he was sober; he had been dry for almost three months. She was hospitalised again and it was discovered that one of her stitches had broken. As she was wheeled off to the theatre, she said, 'I love you, Richard,' and he replied, 'I love you too, Baby.'

It had been almost a year since he had worked, which was his intention, but he decided to accept a film offer from Henry Hathaway, a tough director of many action films. It was *Raid on Rommel*, a Second World War adventure set in the North African desert. The picture was basically conceived to make use of a great deal of stock footage from Universal's Second World War blockbuster, *Tobruk*. By comparison, *Raid on Rommel* was a modest enterprise to be shot quickly in three weeks to cash in on Richard's success with *Where Eagles Dare*. He was to be paid around a million dollars.

Brook Williams had a small but vital role in the film as Sergeant Reilly. 'Rich always makes sure there's a part for me and some of his friends,' he told me when he was working on *The Medusa Touch*. 'It's a condition of his that when he agrees to do a film that he can have whatever supporting players he wants. Even his make-up chap Ron Berkeley had a small role in it. That's the kind of loyalty Rich always had to his friends. And he considered his make-up man a friend and not just an employee.'

During the filming of *Absolution* in 1978, Richard, Brook and I sat around in priests' cassocks (I had a day's work as an extra); they reminisced, I largely listened.

'That was a tough film to make,' said Brook of *Raid on Rommel*.

'Nonsense,' said Richard. 'It wasn't so hard. Three weeks was perfect for me. I get to six weeks on anything and I get bored. And this had plenty of action and little acting.'

'But the heat, Rich! We were filming in the desert near a small town in Mexico called San Felipe. It got as hot as 113. None of the locals had telephones, and only the most courageous pilots landed there.'

'It was hard work but fun. But, you know, I did miss Elizabeth.' She didn't go with Richard when filming began in late June of 1970 because she was still recovering from blood loss. But she flew out later. 'We'd hardly been apart all those years,' he said.

'Do you remember that German chap?' Brook asked Rich.

'Oh indeed – Otto!' (They were referring to Karl-Otto Alberty.) 'He was in the film and he also had the task of teaching me to speak German. I liked the challenge of learning to speak German. I wanted him to teach me by just writing down everything I had to say in German phonetically, but he insisted on expatiating every line. "I do not think Chermans would say to a check-point man dese thinks mit deses vords." He drove me mad. It took an hour to learn three lines. I had to keep very calm. And I was on the wagon too. I was tempted a few times. Especially when dealing with Otto.'

'Hathaway was a tough bastard,' said Brook. 'He yelled at actors and called them stupid. I even felt sorry for Otto. Hathaway made him do

50 or 60 takes and before Otto had barely spoken a word on each take, Hathaway cut and yelled at him, "You are the most Goddamnest stupidest actor I've ever known."' Brook's impression of Hathaway made Richard laugh. 'He didn't care about his actors,' said Brook.

'He only cared about the "stars",' said Richard.

Brook remembered, 'One day he kept me and the other supports on a truck for hours with only a break for lunch, and most of the time we weren't even in camera shot.'

'He really didn't care whether he was liked or not,' said Rich. 'I thought that meant he couldn't be all bad. I remember him screaming at one of the actors, "You moved and I hadn't told you to Goddamn move." I said to Hathaway, "You're mistaken. You *did* tell him to move." He yelled, "Goddamn it, I did not." I yelled back, "Goddamn it, you did," and then he suddenly said to the actor, "I apologise."'

'You were a real fucking hero to everyone on that picture,' said Brook.

'I was told Hathaway had never apologised to anybody before,' said Rich.

Richard, it seemed, earned enormous respect from Hathaway who I spoke to by telephone a few times, the last being in 1981 when he told me he enjoyed working with Richard. 'Burton was always very professional. None of the behaviour I was warned about. He was sober throughout, and always early on the set.'

Rich had got himself into relatively good shape for the film and was very active in scenes, jumping in and out of tanks and lorries, running and diving into holes amid controlled explosions. He was in the best condition he had been in for some years, and he was delighted to discover his libido had returned when, in mid-July, Elizabeth was able to visit. Their reunion in the heat of San Felipe was a passionate one.

But there were familiar problems during her visit. 'She drank and complained that I was boring when I didn't drink,' he told me in 1974. (1974 had been a cataclysmic year for the Burtons; it was the year Richard almost succeeded in drinking himself to death and the time Elizabeth decided to finally leave him, blaming his drinking on the failure of their marriage. We were talking shortly after those events.) 'Then we would row. It was really hard work when other people have been drinking and you haven't. I just gave up in the end. After the war film, we got back to Beverly Hills and I began drinking again.'

Raid on Rommel, released in 1971, was not a success, unsurprisingly.

It was shot like an old fashioned B-picture and it looked like one. It also gave critics a chance to pursue the backlash that continued quite undeservedly. The film critic for *Time* wrote, 'Burton's voice remains one of the most distinctive and controlled in the world. But he is no longer in charge of his face. The little piggy eyes glisten and swivel in a seamed and immobile background. Dissipation, alas, now seems less a simulacrum than a portrait.' Apart from the rather cruel and unnecessary 'little piggy eyes' insult, this critic forgot that the film simply required Burton to do little more than fight the Germans in the desert.

When filming on *Raid on Rommel* was finished, life for the Burtons pretty much returned to the way it always was; a holiday in Portofino on their yacht in September resulted in a drunken fight that lasted hours.

In the autumn of 1970 Richard made *Villain* in London at the same time as Elizabeth landed her first film for some time, *X, Y and Zee* (also known as *Zee & Co*), also filmed in London. Michael Caine and Susannah York were her co-stars.

In *Villain*, Richard played an East End gangster. 'I do love thrillers and thought this would make a nice change,' he told me.

I observed on the set of *Villain* that he was liked by everyone in the cast and crew. He would talk to everyone – even me who was just a lowly extra and who he didn't know then – and he called people 'Luv'. He was drinking a lot during the filming.

During my day on location I'd become aware of a few certain types of shady-looking characters observing; I knew the look of them because I'd encountered their type before a few years earlier (under circumstances I have no intention of relating in full here) and was certain that they were citizens of London's underworld. They alarmed me somewhat, so I pointed them out to Rich.

He sent for Brook who turned up and I met him for the first time. He asked Brook to go and talk to the onlookers, which Brook did without any enthusiasm. It turned out they were just curious to see how the great Shakespearean actor was portraying an East End gangster.

'Well,' said Rich, 'there's no law against them watching so long as they stay out of camera range.'

He became increasingly curious about how I was able to spot them and so I told him how, in 1966, I'd found myself among opposing gangsters in a pub in Bethnal Green, an area of London's East End notorious as a haunt for criminals like the Kray Twins. He loved my story (which I told him in full); it seems telling a good story was another requisite of gaining Richard's approval.

Not long after my day on the set, Brook turned up, one lunch hour, in a cab at the offices of Cinerama where I then worked and told me to come with him. We collected Richard and he told me to guide the cab driver to the pub I'd told him about; the cab driver knew it, and before long we had arrived in Bethnal Green.

Rich was hoping to meet an authentic East End villain; I wasn't too keen on the idea myself. But Richard, as well as Brook, had already been drinking; it was the only time I ever saw Richard drunk.

Maybe it was the time of day, or perhaps by 1970 much of the criminal element had withdrawn from public view, but the drinkers all seemed like normal Londoners having a pint in their lunch break. All, that is, except for one man who clearly wasn't impressed to see Richard Burton buying drinks for all. This obvious second-rate villain took some delight in telling Richard that he could call people who would break his knees; I think this small-time criminal merely aspired to bigger and nastier things and wanted to make an impression on everyone. Richard Burton was a perfect target. I was extremely anxious, as was Brook, but Rich showed no fear.

In fact, to my horror he began to goad the villain into a fight. He'd had too much to drink, and even though the prospect of getting his face smashed up was a bad idea with the film still to be finished, he poured scorn on the other man.

'You think you're a match for me?' Rich said to him. 'You're not even man enough to take me on yourself. You stand there and threaten to get your thug friends to break my knees, but you're a fucking coward and won't dare to lay a finger on me. Someone else made the same threat years ago. He was going to have the Mafia break my legs. I showed him he couldn't scare me either.' He was referring to his run-in with Frank Sinatra.

The ambitious villain clearly didn't want to lose face, and I was sure that at any moment all hell would break loose. I was trying to figure out how I was going to get Richard out of there when it did.

Brook said to me, 'It's all right. Rich knows how to use his fists.'

Richard suddenly became more convivial towards the man and offered to buy him a drink. But, perhaps feeling he couldn't afford to lose face any further, the villain decided to say the wrong thing, which was, 'You think you're such a big man 'cos you fuck Liz Taylor. Liz Taylor would fuck any man. She only fucks you 'cos you buy her fucking diamonds. That makes her a fucking whore.'

He had barely finished speaking when Richard smashed a pint beer glass against his head. Down went the villain. I saw some blood oozing through his hair or possibly from his ear.

There was a moment of silence, and then everyone burst into spontaneous applause. Richard bowed. People slapped him on the back and he threw some cash on to the bar and said, 'Give everyone whatever they want.'

I was tugging on his arm, eager to get him out, not knowing if the police would arrive, or worse, reinforcements; there was no knowing who in that pub might have been a friend of the now unconscious villain, and I wasn't keen to find out.

I urged Rich to leave, and so did Brook. 'All right! All right!' he said impatiently. We got outside, into the cab and took off.

Richard's mind began ticking over at speed. He told me that if the story managed to get into the newspapers, I should deny that we had been there. I said, 'You think those people don't know that you are Richard Burton?'

He said, 'All you have to do is deny we were there and I'll organise an alibi.'

He seemed perfectly calm. Brook looked like a nervous wreck. Rich just smiled. But then I noticed his hands were shaking and there were beads of sweat forming on his brow. He looked at me, his eyes suddenly filled with terror, and he said, 'Under no circumstances are you to ever let me do that again.'

I told him I wouldn't.

Then he said, 'Are you all right for cash?'

I said I was. Nevertheless, he tucked £50 into the pocket of my jacket.

When the three of us were together on the set of *Absolution* the subject of that event came up. Brook suggested that Richard had paid everyone off to keep quiet because it never got into the newspapers, but Richard insisted he had done no such thing. I said that it would make a good story. Rich said, 'It's a good story, Mick, but perhaps not one to tell anyone.'

I said it was too late; I had told Ava Gardner. He wanted to know what she had to say. She had laughed and said, 'Well, of course, Rich even decked Francis [Sinatra] so I guess he'll deck anyone.'

After *Villain*, I didn't see Richard again until 1974 in Winchester. But I gather he completed the filming of *Villain* in a drunken gloom, despite receiving his CBE at Buckingham Palace on 10 November 1970, his forty-fifth birthday. Elizabeth and Cis had gone with him. He was still despondent at not getting a knighthood.

Villain wasn't a success in America, but it was in Britain where Richard was voted the number one box office star of 1971.

X, Y & Zee went over schedule and finally finished just before Christmas, 1970. Richard turned up at Shepperton Studios where Elizabeth, Michael Caine and the rest of the cast and crew of *X, Y & Zee* were gathered for the end-of-picture party. Michael Caine said to Richard, 'Happy Christmas.'

Richard said, 'Why don't you go and fuck yourself?'

Caine never knew why Rich had spoken to him like that. But I think it was because Richard was living a life he no longer enjoyed. The fun had gone out of it. The fun had gone out of his marriage. He was drinking heavily and he had found himself at a time in his career when he felt he should have had greater recognition for his contribution to film and theatre.

Maybe in comparison to people like Gielgud and Olivier and in the context of the times he lived, Burton perhaps didn't deserve a knighthood. Yet little more than 20 years after his death, entertainers receive knighthoods for having achieved far less than Richard Burton did – in my humble opinion.

Chapter Twenty-Two

SPIRALLING DOWNWARD

IN EARLY 1971 Richard returned to his Welsh roots for a pure labour of love; the film version of Dylan Thomas' *Under Milk Wood*. It had been performed as a poetic radio play and in stage readings but it seemed an unlikely choice of film material. 'It was a brave thing, a wonderful thing, a beautiful thing to do,' Richard told me in 1978.

Andrew Sinclair, who had directed only one film – *When Winter Comes* – had the vision to adapt the play into a screenplay and also to direct it. He once said, '*Under Milk Wood* was one of the more impossible films to make, and I doubt that I will ever put that sort of thing together again.'

Sinclair first cast Peter O'Toole as Captain Cat; O'Toole had played the part in his student days. Richard was sceptical that a film of the play would work, but he was easily persuaded to play the First Voice – in essence, the narrator – once he knew that his friend O'Toole was on board. 'I'd always hoped to get the role of First Voice if anyone dared to make a film version,' Rich told me.

Glynis Johns, Vivien Merchant and Siân Phillips – Mrs. O'Toole – had important roles, but there was the small but significant role of Rosie Probert to cast. Sinclair knew that it would be a significant coup if he could cast Elizabeth Taylor. The film was being made on a shoestring and Sinclair needed it to be as commercial as possible without compromising the artistic merit of the piece. Producer Jules Buck agreed.

Elizabeth was the only one who thought she was wrong for the part. Ironically it was O'Toole who persuaded her to do it, despite the fact that he and she had not spoken since *Becket*. 'I thought I was very brave,' O'Toole told me. 'They should have given me a medal. Maybe a VC.'

Elizabeth said that her name should not receive equal billing with Burton and O'Toole on the grounds that she was giving a cameo performance and was not the star of the film. Buck needed her name up there with Richard's and Peter's and so she got star billing anyway.

The film was made in just 40 days, shot in the Gwaun Valley in Wales with many of the locals appearing as extras and in small roles. The budget was just £300,000, so to keep costs to a minimum, Burton, O'Toole and Taylor agreed to small fees but large profits. In the event, the film never made much money but it was generally agreed to be an admirable production.

It even managed to win praise from Judith Crist; 'The winning film of the moment is *Under Milk Wood* . . . a triumph of visualisation of the verbal visions and vignettes the poet created. No question but that Burton was born to recite Thomas's luxuriant and flowing poetic realities and lusciously lilting prose; his voice washes over the screen, penetrates to the very heart of the matter.'

Pauline Kael of *The New Yorker*, wrote, 'I enjoyed sitting back and listening . . . Sinclair brings the material emotionally close . . . You feel the affection of the cast and you share in it.'

And that's what *Under Milk Wood* – the movie – is all about; just sharing the experience with the cast.

There was to be one last Burton–Taylor movie – their ninth – a rather obscure but nonetheless beguiling opus, *Hammersmith is Out*, directed by Peter Ustinov who also took a part in the film. He called it 'a crime film with black humour'. It was a sort of modern variation on the Faust legend with Richard as Hammersmith, a somewhat demonic criminal mastermind – a modern-day Mephistopheles – who escapes from an institution for the criminally insane run by a doctor played by Ustinov. Elizabeth played Jean Jackson, a voluptuous blonde waitress in a Southern roadside diner. Beau Bridges, still then an up-and-coming young actor, played Billy Breedlove, a sort of scruffy Faust who promises Jean a fine life and whisks her away on a series of adventures and meeting up with Hammersmith on the way.

'We all knew it wasn't going to be *Bonnie and Clyde*,' Peter Ustinov told me, referring to its commercial value. 'But it was the time of off-beat movies, and this had to be one of the off-beatest.'

He became very aware that the married couple didn't always exude the required chemistry audiences had come to expect. 'Love scenes or even lust scenes between people who you presume have those moments in the privacy of their home are invariably dull on the screen, especially if they happen to be going through a crisis in their domestic life which only makes those scenes even worse.' The Burtons, then, were still having their usual battles, but overall these didn't affect their ability to function on the set. 'That's merely their professionalism,' said Ustinov. 'But my auntie can be very professional and that doesn't make her worth watching.'

Ustinov was critical of Burton and Taylor as a screen team. He said, in 1978, 'Richard is a very fine actor, and Elizabeth has intellect and intelligence that she is rarely given credit for. When they parted ways, I hoped they would find themselves doing better work. Certainly Richard has.'

Richard did *Hammersmith is Out* because, he told me, 'it seemed like a good idea at the time.' I really didn't think the film was bad at all, just very offbeat. The film was released by Cinerama Releasing Organisation, where I was employed at the time, and I worked on the film's publicity. But the picture undoubtedly suffered because although it was filmed in 1971, beginning in May and shot quickly in Cuernavaca in Mexico, not far from Puerto Vallarta, it's release was held up for a year because of a dispute between J. Cornelius Crean, a self-made millionaire who decided to finance the film, and the film's producer Alex Lucas. By the time it came out, the vogue for such off-the-wall films had given way to the likes of more commercial and gritty crime films like *Dirty Harry*.

Nevertheless, Elizabeth picked up a Best Actress award at the Berlin Film Festival in 1972, and the film did well in Europe if not in America.

By the end of July 1971 Richard and Elizabeth were back home in Gstaad. He was looking for interesting film projects – certainly the last two had been interesting if not entirely successful – and he found what he thought was one in *The Battle of Sutjeska*, the story of Marshal Tito and his forces under siege by overwhelming German forces during the Second World War. Rich was intrigued at the prospect of playing Tito but found the screenplay had little to say about the man so he persuaded the producers to rewrite the script using a first-hand account of the battle called *The Embattled Mountain* by F.W.D. Deakin as the basis.

Before starting on the film, Rich was again struck by arthritis which made his left hand and wrist painful and immobile. While writing an article for *Vogue* he was unable to type properly. He was prescribed medication which improved the condition considerably. He also suffered from a touch of gout. Setting off on another health kick, he gave up alcohol again.

In August he met President Tito of Yugoslavia in preparation for portraying him. 'I found I admired the man,' he told me. 'It was a rare opportunity to actually study a living person – a hero in his country – in order to portray him.'

Filming did not start well because of bad organisation and so Richard stepped in to try to sort out some of the problems.

There were also the same domestic problems to deal with. While he battled to keep off the booze, Elizabeth continued to drink. There was also the usual fighting. 'I'd grown so bored of the fighting,' he told me. He was also growing bored with the filming as it dragged on. 'There was an actor who I had a lot of scenes with who didn't speak a word of English,' he said. 'So they asked me to do the whole of my part in Serbo-Croat which I refused to do because it would be impossible to dub well.'

Brook Williams was, of course, out there with Richard in Yugoslavia, and remembered that it was only a miracle that none of them was killed as they were ferried to and from locations by helicopters.

'We had finished filming for the day at a place called Kupari, and we all piled into the helicopter – Richard, Ron Berkeley, Gianni Bozzacchi and our interpreter, a nice lady called Vesna.

'The cloud was so low that the pilot could barely see. Rich, Vesna and I sat behind the pilot and Ron and Gianni sat at the rear. We were barely passing mountain peaks on both sides. Then suddenly there was a complete white-out – nothing could be seen but the cloud. It was terrifying. And then it began to rain – a torrent. Then the pilot realised we were heading straight for a mountain peak. He was a good pilot and flung the 'copter to the right to miss the peak and found we were heading into another mountain. Then we pulled to the left and just missed the rock face. The co-pilot was keeping lookout; we were flying blind. I shut my eyes tight. I couldn't bear to look. Ron had already got himself into a crash position, curled up on the floor in a tight ball. I could hear Richard whispering "Holy shit! Holy shit!"

'Suddenly we seemed to drop – I thought we were going down, but the pilot had decided to get as low as he could as quickly as he could so he could see the mountain road which we followed. It was harrowing. And I'd never been so pleased to see a road in my life.'

The film just wasn't worth all the trouble and fear; it was hardly seen outside of Yugoslavia in 1973 although it got a few meagre showings at the New York Cultural Centre in 1976.

In October 1971, Richard started work on *The Assassination of Trotsky*, another film he hoped would prove interesting. But he had accepted it without reading the script first, putting his trust in the film's director, Joseph Losey. Yet again Rich had chosen a subject he found interesting because of the historical content, and yet again the film flopped.

Producer Joseph Shaftel had been trying for years to get this film made and every star actor he had approached had turned it down. Rich began to realise he too should have rejected it. 'Joe Losey didn't know the bloody script,' he said. 'He just wasn't himself and he was drinking hard. He had some personal problems. I don't think he knew what he was doing, so he wasn't much help to me.'

Filming began in Mexico where Leon Trotsky had been assassinated. Again Richard found himself working with actors who couldn't speak English. But the bigger problem was the Mexican government which, sensitive about the film's subject, had a censor on the set. It was decided that certain scenes couldn't be filmed in Mexico so the unit moved to Rome where Trotsky's Mexican villa was faithfully re-created.

Richard was still not drinking, but one afternoon, at the Grand Hotel where the Burtons were staying, he fell spectacularly off the wagon after meeting up with Peter O'Toole. They drank through the afternoon and into the evening. Rich had to be carried to his suite, furious at being carted away from his little party. Brook told me that the next day he surprised everyone by giving the best day's work he had done since filming began.

At home in Gstaad, while Richard considered whether or not make a spoof horror film called *Bluebeard* in between bouts of cleaning up the dog crap, Elizabeth tried to get him to join her in a martini before lunch because she didn't like to drink alone. He told her he preferred to wait until the evening. 'I had to tell her over and over that when I've had one drink, I have to have another and then another,' he said to me. 'That's what a drunk does.' He always preferred to refer to himself as a 'drunk' rather than an 'alcoholic', although towards the end of his life I did hear him talk about being an alcoholic.

There appears to be a common belief that the reason Elizabeth finally left Richard was because he couldn't control his drinking. But whenever he had given up, she continued to drink. He often said that it never bothered him that she drank, but clearly by 1972 it did bother him. 'She didn't exactly encourage me not to drink,' he said, 'but then she complained that I wouldn't stop drinking.'

The marriage was spiralling downhill, much like the helicopter almost did in Yugoslavia. He made another attempt to give up the booze in December 1972, and found it particularly difficult to stay dry at a ball thrown by the Rothschilds. He managed to get through the entire party without any alcohol passing his lips.

In January 1972 he went to Budapest, Hungary, to make *Bluebeard*, playing a European count who murders his many wives. He decided to do it simply because he had never made a horror film before and was looking forward to it, if only because it was something light following the heavy dramas of Tito and Trotsky.

The film actually had very little horror in it and a fair smattering of soft porn. It also featured several beautiful actresses including Raquel Welch, Nathalie Delon, Virni Lisi, Sybil Danning and Joey Heatherton. That was reason enough for Elizabeth to be constantly present. When she celebrated her 40th birthday, she threw a big party. She had invited 200 guests but when she realised she had also invited the female contingent of *Bluebeard*, she uninvited them. Raquel Welch nevertheless turned up. Among the guests were Michael Caine, Princess Grace, David Niven, Susannah York and Ringo Starr. And plenty of Richard's family.

Richard's birthday gift to Elizabeth was a $50,000 heart-shaped diamond. He was staying dry throughout filming and remained sober through the party. Edward Dmytryk, the director of *Bluebeard*, was among the guests and he told me, 'It was the most wonderful party I have ever been to. There were many Welsh relatives there and a great deal of singing.

'I was sure Richard would drink, but he didn't. And he was as endlessly fascinating sober as he was when drunk. He also knew

195

instinctively how to make a woman feel special. The diamond made Elizabeth feel special. But another young lady felt so special after talking to him casually for about five or ten minutes that she ran across the room telling everyone, "He loves me." I don't know what he said to her, but whatever it was – and the way he said it – she was convinced that he had fallen in love with her.'

Dmytryk recalled plans Richard had at that time; 'He talked like someone who was seriously thinking of almost giving up making films – just make the occasional one. He had earned all the money he could hope for and he wanted to have a house in Oxford where he wanted to teach. He wanted to do *King Lear* at Stratford. He was going to establish close links with the best stage directors. It seemed that he was striving for something that was within his reach, but somehow he couldn't quite grasp it. Elizabeth would undoubtedly follow because her career was not in good shape, and neither was she. She was always ill. I think these plans rejuvenated him. I know *Bluebeard* didn't turn out well for any of us, but we were happy making it.'

Then the day came when Richard drank. He could easily be forgiven. News reached him in Budapest that Ifor had died. Richard and Elizabeth travelled to Wales for the funeral. Dmytryk told me, 'When they came back, he was a different man. He looked older. As he carried on with the filming, he seemed agitated, frustrated, desperate.'

Rich was in great emotional pain. He told me, 'One of the worst things that ever happened to me was losing Ifor.' He had once wished for Ifor to die so he would no longer suffer. But when the time actually came, Richard had a hard time accepting it. 'Ifor was more than a brother to me. He was a hero.'

Trouble now brewed on the set of *Bluebeard*. 'We had a scene – a romp – Richard and one of our young actresses,' said Dmytryk. 'Richard and the actress were enjoying it, and Elizabeth saw what was happening. Well . . . she landed one on the girl.'

I asked Dmytryk if he meant a punch. He said, 'Maybe it was more of a slap. It was terrible to see. Richard was behaving very oddly. It was like he was trying to goad Elizabeth. Or maybe he had just lost interest in her.'

Something had certainly happened to Rich, and it had much to do with Ifor's death. When I talked to him about it, he said, 'I reached a point where I wondered if it was all worth it.' I asked him what he meant, and he said, 'Trying to make the marriage work. Trying to be the best actor I could be. All the plans I had.' He reached that point when Ifor died.

There was more trouble on the set. Dmytryk recalled:

'All Richard had to do was walk Nathalie Delon down a street. It was a night shot. We did the scene, and Richard and Nathalie went around a corner. We waited for them to come back. Eventually I had to send an assistant to find them but they had gone. I found out that Richard had told his chauffeur, Gaston, to wait for them with his Rolls, and then he took Nathalie off for dinner.

'Elizabeth retaliated. She flew off to Rome to have dinner with Ari Onassis when Jackie wasn't around. Then when Elizabeth got to her hotel room she phoned through to the Intercontinental Hotel in Budapest where we were all staying, and she screamed down the line, "Get that woman out of my bed!"

'The next day Burton said to me, "How could she have known?" and I said, "Richard, don't you know? You're surrounded by her spies." He'd not known that. There wasn't a move he made that she didn't know about. I think that only made things worse.'

Richard and Elizabeth had been invited to the British Embassy for an official dinner. He remembered it: 'Oh, that was something I hadn't the heart for. I hadn't the heart to pretend Elizabeth and I were the happy, glamorous couple. I behaved intolerably.'

'What did you do?' I asked him.

'Well, first of all I insulted two ambassadors, then I insulted their wives, I said something obscene to the British Ambassador and then walked out, leaving Elizabeth there on her own.'

He told me he had wished that he and Elizabeth would go their own ways but he had promised himself that he would never leave her. 'I was on a mission to destroy what we had,' he said, and then added, 'Well, no, it was already destroyed. It was only a matter of time. She was always telling me she would leave me. I just wished she would without any further help from me.

'I was broken into tiny pieces and I had no idea how to fix myself. I scared my daughter Kate and my stepdaughter Liza. They begged me to stop drinking, and I promised them I would. But I couldn't even keep my promise to my Kate.

'I felt like I had no control of my life. Even now I look back and don't think I could help myself. I was attracted to other women and couldn't help it. I knew then the game was up.'

He hated to say it but he finally told me, 'I loved Elizabeth but I couldn't be happy with her. When she loves you, she must own you . . . your very soul. I must have my own way. I made my own decision that I would be faithful to her. But it was all too suffocating. I had to go my own way in the end.'

The end hadn't come quite yet, but it wasn't far off. And when it did come, it was almost terminal for Richard.

Chapter Twenty-Three

THE END OF THE ADVENTURE

A FTER *BLUEBEARD*, RICHARD returned to Yugoslavia in a drunken haze to finish the Tito film which had gone through some seemingly necessary rewrites but which still failed to make the film work.

After that he decided on his most prophetic work, a two-part television film about the breakdown of a marriage called *Divorce His, Divorce Hers*, made for Harlech Television. The first episode was from his point of view, the second from hers. She was played by Elizabeth.

John Osborne had written the teleplay and had set it in England, as originally planned. But Richard, now seemingly unable to control not only his work but also his life, decided the film should be filmed out of the UK to avoid paying tax. Osborne refused to rewrite it, believing, probably rightly, that Rich had lost all sense of what was right or wrong. It was rewritten by a good television writer, John Hopkins.

The production was marred by the many Burton–Taylor rows over drunken lunches which held up the work many afternoons. The film was not only a self-fulfilling prophecy but also undoubtedly a nail or two in the coffin of their personal lives and their careers. Richard was uncharacteristically unprofessional, leaving when he felt like it and cold-shouldering the director, Waris Hussein.

It was an eagerly awaited event for television, but it was disappointing and really quite painful to watch. *Variety* said watching the two episodes 'holds all the joy of standing by at an autopsy'.

Rich returned to Rome in early 1973 to portray a real-life Second World War German SS colonel in *Massacre in Rome*. It was produced by Carlo Ponti and directed by George Pan Cosmatos who later had more commercial success with *Rambo: First Blood* and *Tombstone*.

Massacre in Rome is based on an actual event when Italian partisans attacked an SS troop in Rome in 1944, killing 32. As a reprisal and on Hitler's direct orders, 320 Italians were shot. Rich played Colonel Kappler of the SS, ordered by his superior, played by Leo McKern, to find the 320 Italians and then carry out the mass execution.

The Germans were played by British actors, all of whom avoided the clichéd German accents. George Pan Cosmatos told me, 'I remembered that the best Roman epics had British actors playing the Romans and Americans played the Jews or the slaves. I thought it would work just as well to have good British actors play Germans and we had real Italians to play the Italians. It was an interesting concept and I thought it worked.

'Richard Burton was amazing. Always very professional. Very interested in the historical background and quite fascinated by the character he played. He wasn't afraid to be unsympathetic but he wanted to see if he could find what the Nazis would have considered their own sense of humanity.'

Leo McKern recalled, 'Richard took his work very seriously. He was amused that for once he was not required to give vent. I was. I had to shout and cry and frankly I went a little over the top. He watched me, laughed and said, "You're doing a *Burton*." And I told him, "But not as good as you do it."'

Brook Williams had a good supporting role in the film. 'We all went to Rome,' he told me, 'Elizabeth too. She didn't have a film to make. They both loved Rome. They had gone through hell in Rome when making *Cleopatra* and then fell in love with the city when they did *The Taming of the Shrew*, although Rich always said that the worst things happened to him in Rome. But he still loved going there.'

Leading the contingent of Italian actors was Marcello Mastroianni as an art-loving priest who has developed an uneasy friendship with Kappler. Cosmatos and Carlo Ponti insisted that Mastroianni and even the supporting Italian actors, who all played their parts in English, were *not* revoiced as Italian actors usually are for the American market. Perhaps that's partly why the film failed to get a full release in America. It only just managed to get a limited release in Britain in 1975; I must have been one of the few who saw it. I found it to be a shocking and compelling film with an excellent performance by Burton. In fact he was quite surprised when I asked him about it. 'I didn't think anyone ever saw it,' he said:

'It was a fascinating study of this real-life SS officer. Germany knew the war was lost and the BBC was already announcing names over the radio of the Nazis who were to be tried as war criminals. I was fascinated by Kappler because he had just enough humanity in him to decide that he would find the men he had to execute from the prisoners among those who were already condemned rather than take random and innocent people. But it was also a political move because he knew the reprisal would outrage the Allies and he didn't want to be seen as a war criminal. But he did eventually go to trial after the war and was imprisoned as a war criminal.

'When he couldn't find enough condemned men he widened the search to those who *might* face execution if found guilty. He then filled the quota with Jews and did so without conscience; to him that was the practical solution. To us it is an outrage. He was a complex character to play. I tried to show there was a spark of humanity there but also trying to demonstrate that while the idea of shooting Italians appalled him, he not only carried out his orders as clinically and as efficiently as he could but that the lives of Jews meant nothing to him as an SS officer.

'I was also intrigued that Colonel Kappler had never killed anyone before. He had to include himself among the executioners and that also appalled him, and yet he was a "good" SS officer and carried out his duty.'

When *Massacre in Rome* was finished, Elizabeth worked on *Ash Wednesday*; it was the first time since they had been together that she had work to do and he didn't. Brook Williams said, 'That really irritated him. He wasn't used to waiting around for her to finish work. He got very bored and got drunk a lot. He thought the film [about a middle-aged woman who gets a face lift – very prophetic] was rubbish. He said to me, "Brookie, I wouldn't mind if she was playing Lady Macbeth."'

In the summer of 1973 the Burtons arrived in America, and while he went to Long Island, she visited friends in California, including Roddy McDowall. 'She went to California to visit her mother who was sick, but she was really just getting away from Richard,' said McDowall. 'I knew the marriage was all but over because Rich was supposed to meet her in California but he refused to come and so he called her up and told her to get over to Long Island. She went and he met her at the airport, but they fought all the way to Long Island so she left him there and went to New York and stayed on her own at the Regency Hotel.'

I asked McDowall if he was able to see exactly what the causes of the breakdown were. 'It was so many things,' he said, 'But the one thing I can say with some certainty is that I knew back in Rome when we were making *Cleopatra* that it would never work. Elizabeth doesn't just *love* someone; she *possesses* them. And Richard isn't a man to be possessed. I'm surprised it lasted as long as it did. But, really, it was over long before it really was over.'

The end seemed to come in July when Elizabeth made a prepared public statement in the newspapers: 'I am convinced it would be a good and constructive idea if Richard and I separated for a while.' She went on to say, 'I believe with all my heart that the separation will ultimately bring us back to where we should be – and that's together.'

As McDowall commented, 'When Elizabeth sent out that newspaper release, you just knew it was the end. Nobody separates temporarily. Not in this business.'

Richard told me he had felt relieved that it all appeared to be over. 'She didn't waste time finding that used-car salesman,' he said, referring to businessman Henry Wynberg. 'I thought, "Let him drop everything and devote himself to all her problems." I'd had enough.'

He also had a new and more serious battle on his hands: his health. On doctor's orders, he gave up drinking and started a detoxification regime. He was due to film *The Voyage* with Sophia Loren in Rome, to be directed by Vittorio De Sica. He called Sophia and asked if he could come over and stay with her and her husband Carlo Ponti for a month. 'I needed to escape everything, and I needed to get in shape, and I didn't want to stay in a hotel where I would be harassed by the paparazzi,' he told me.

Loren was happy to oblige. 'I had not met Richard before,' she told me when she was making *Brief Encounter*, 'but I was very happy to have him stay in our guest house.'

Sophia recalled that he arrived with a small entourage; a doctor, a nurse, a secretary and two bodyguards. 'It was very sad because he was still so in love with Elizabeth,' she said. 'He wanted to talk about her and I always listened.'

Before filming on *The Voyage* began, he spent a little time in New York so he could visit Philip Burton but also took the opportunity to see a pretty young actress. Philip noted how Richard found walking painful.

Apparently there was a phone call from Richard to Elizabeth but there seemed no hope of a reconciliation. Personally, I'm not convinced Richard wanted one. But he was going through the motions, probably from a sense of guilt more than anything else.

Over a short period of time, Philip Burton saw how Richard's condition, psychologically and physically, deteriorated. Philip also spotted Richard with another young woman. Even with a back and legs that were so painful he had trouble moving, Richard could still charm the young women.

Then he returned to Italy and on to Sicily to make *The Voyage*. Elizabeth also arrived in Rome, to make a film, *The Driver's Seat*. Richard said, 'As usual, we had planned our careers around each other. It was stifling. And so we had a *tender* reconciliation.'

Rich emphasised the word 'tender' with the irony he saw in the whole sad episode. Elizabeth moved in with him in Sophia's guest house. 'She stayed just nine days,' said Brook Williams, 'then she moved out of Sophia's house and into the Grand Hotel in Rome.'

The reconciliation was not going well.

'Just before Christmas [1973],' said Brook, 'Elizabeth had to return to Los Angeles for an operation. She telephoned Rich and told him she didn't want to live and die alone, and asked if he could come over to be with her. Typical Elizabeth! She publicly announces their separation and then when she's about to have an operation, she asks him to drop everything and go back to Los Angeles.'

Richard did fly from Sicily to Los Angeles; he couldn't resist Elizabeth when she was ill and pathetic. He couldn't resist being needed. When he walked into her hospital room he said, 'Hello, Lumpy,' and she replied, 'Hello, Pockmarks.'

He stayed that night in the hospital and the next morning he wheeled her out and on to the plane for Italy so he could finish his film – which was hardly seen in the USA or the UK – and then home to Puerto Vallarta for Christmas.

'He was a mess,' said Brook. 'It was all too much for him. He believed they were going to be reconciled.'

Well, it all seemed like a happy ending, but before long Elizabeth was accusing Richard of having had an affair with Sophia Loren. I saw for myself the friendship between Richard and Sophia on the set of *Brief*

Encounter in 1974, and saw no sign of anything other than a very warm, mutual friendship between them.

It's true that Richard and Sophia had spent a great deal of time in each other's company back in Rome before filming on *The Voyage* began, but much of it was taken up with playing Scrabble, at which Sophia invariably beat him, and having long talks about Elizabeth. 'Richard never blamed Elizabeth for the failure of their marriage,' said Sophia, 'which I really admired him for. He took all the blame himself.'

Sophia told me, out of earshot of Rich, 'Richard needed to be reassured, and to be listened to, and his ego boosted. I took all that on. I became genuinely fond of him. But an affair? Never.'

Rich was not one to hide his passions. He told me, 'Sophia is a wonderful, warm and loving person, but I could never be the man for her. But Elizabeth was adamant. She was still suffocating me. Sophia tried to reason with her; she told her nothing had happened. But there it was. Elizabeth, one of the most beautiful women the world has ever known, threatened by Sophia, one of the great classical beauties of our time and one of the loveliest people to walk the Earth, and she couldn't accept that nothing had happened.'

The first few months of 1974 saw Richard and Elizabeth seeming to make a go of it. 'But it was hopeless,' said Rich. 'I didn't know what the hell I was doing.'

That is certainly true when it came to choosing films. He picked another disaster. It is remembered not for its qualities, of which there are very few, but for being the film on which Richard almost died.

It was called *The Klansman*. It seemed to have its heart in the right place. But Rich was badly miscast as a Southern liberal landowner who opposes the Ku Klux Klan.

Also starring was another of the world's great drinkers, Lee Marvin, playing the sheriff trying to maintain law and order between the Klan, the local Negroes and Burton.

Directing the film was Terence Young, a Brit who had managed to bring a sense of style and slickness to the first two James Bond movies but somehow never was able to do the same with most of his other films. A better director and someone other than Burton cast in his role might have made for a reasonable film. As it is, *The Klansman* is by far the worst film Richard – or Lee Marvin – ever made.

However, what took place off the screen has always been more fascinating than what occurred on it. I was given good accounts of it, first by Terence Young when he was making *The Jigsaw Man* in 1981, and then by Lee Marvin one rainy day in the English countryside in 1985 when the weather was holding up filming on *The Dirty Dozen: The Next Mission*.

Young went into the project believing, maybe with good reason, that the film could be a winner. He told me:

'It sounded great on paper but it was a recipe for disaster. Like a powder keg. Richard was at his all-time low and on the verge of drinking himself to death, and Lee was doing his best to catch up.

'Lee arrived in the North Californian town of Oroville, which resembled a Southern town, with his wife Pamela, and hardly anybody noticed them. The press seemed disinterested, which suited Lee fine. In fact, they were all waiting for the Burtons and when they arrived complete with the usual entourage, they didn't disappoint – especially Richard.

'He gave the press what they wanted to hear; his thoughts on love, life, Wales, politics and booze. Then Lee was brought in so he and Richard could meet for the first time with the world's press looking on.'

Marvin recalled that first day: 'It was a circus. The producers needed to sell their picture, and Richard and I were the ones to sell it. So we did what we had to do to make headlines. We put on a verbal sparring match for the reporters. I said, "I suppose you know I get top billing in this."

'"Yes," said Richard, "but I'm getting more money." We were putting on a performance for the press so they could tell the world we hated each other, but that was all bullshit.'

Young recalled, 'After the Press Call, we broke for lunch and Burton and Marvin succeeded in knocking back 17 martinis each.'

Of that event, Richard told me, 'I never counted.'

Lee said, 'However many he drank, I matched him.'

Once drunk, Lee was *not* on his best behaviour. Young told me:

'Lee was too drunk to greet Elizabeth [Taylor] when she tried to wish him luck, even though they had worked together [in 1956 on *Raintree County*]. He said to her, "Why don't you fuck off, sweetie?"

'And Liz just said, "I see you haven't changed a bit, Lee."

'They didn't speak to each other for the rest of the filming – or possibly ever again.

'We began shooting that very day, but Lee's voice was slurred. He was just awful. I couldn't use anything we shot. But it was the only scene of Lee's I couldn't use. His lovely wife Pamela kept him from drinking most days until after we stopped filming.

'I think Liz tried to keep Richard from drinking, but it didn't work. One morning he knocked back an eight-ounce tumbler of vodka in one go – *before* breakfast.'

Out-of-work hours were usually spent at the Prospectors' Village Motel where local women tried to get the attention of both Richard and Lee. 'Every night two girls ran naked through the bar and out to the pool,' said Young. 'You knew for sure something was going to happen. There was a very determined 17-year-old girl called Kim Dinucci, a waitress; she went up to Richard and demanded he kiss her. He did, on the forehead, and said, "How's that, dear child?" It wasn't what she had in mind and she kissed him hard on the mouth. Not long after that she was on the set at Burton's invitation. That started one of the famous Burton quarrels. He continued drinking, Liz left the location, and Kim became the proud owner of a $240 ring, a gift from Burton.'

Lee told me he thought the ring cost $480.

Young continued: 'There was one evening when the husband of a local woman stormed into the motel bar declaring he was going to shoot Burton for messing around with his wife. Fortunately, Richard wasn't there that night. Well, who knows if Richard was playing around with the man's wife? With Elizabeth gone he didn't pass up any opportunity the young ladies presented him with.'

Richard admitted to me, 'I went a little off the deep end. The young women were throwing themselves my way. I was like a hungry bear with salmon jumping into my paws.'

Marvin, meanwhile, was demonstrating his very unique sense of humour by firing a rifle loaded with blanks at the crowd who came to watch the filming. 'Well, I warned them to clear off or I'd fire,' he told me. 'They didn't, so I did.'

Terence Young said that he felt like throwing himself 'under a bus at times. In our first week Elizabeth had left Burton, and he was running around with a waitress, and an angry husband wanted to shoot him, and Lee was scaring the locals to death with a rifle.'

There was also a *Playboy* centrefold, a beautiful black model, called Jeanne Bell, who caught Richard's attention. She wasn't in the film, but he thought she should be and told Terence Young he should give her a part – so he did. This might simply seem like another of Richard's ploys to win over a beautiful woman, but he did do that kind of thing for people he felt could make a career in films. And once you were his friend, he would always get you work in his films. He did the same not only for Brook Williams but also his dresser Bob Wilson and make-up man Ron Berkeley who both often turned up in minor roles.

In the film, Richard walks with a limp. He made it a part of his character but the fact was he was in terrible pain caused by acute sciatica. He also had pain in his left arm. 'It was a wonder he could move at all,' said Marvin, 'but you have to hand it to him, he had guts, and I admired that. He never complained of being in pain. I'd say, "Rich, are you okay?" and he'd say, "Just a little discomfort." *Discomfort*! Jesus, the guy was in fucking agony.'

For a while, Lee and Richard passed jibes back and forth, and nobody could tell if they were in jest. Lee told me:

'Hell, *I* didn't know if we were just joking. But, you know, I soon began to see something in Richard Burton that troubled me. He wasn't just having a drink or playing around. He was going to self-destruct. It was plain to see. Well, it was to me. I'd gone that way in the past, and someone had been there to help me. But Richard had no one. Elizabeth was gone, his waitress girlfriend was of no help, and nobody had time. So I stepped in. I had to. He was drinking not for the pleasure of it but because he had a great need, and I doubt he knew what that was himself. Maybe it was for Elizabeth. But whatever it was, he was in pain, and he drank to kill that pain. I used to do it too.'

Richard recognised that Marvin was suddenly the best friend he had on the set. 'I wouldn't have survived without Marvin,' he told me. 'I would have drunk a hell of a lot more a whole lot quicker and wound up dead a whole lot sooner.'

Terence Young was relieved that Lee 'made it his business to handle Richard. One afternoon we stood around waiting for Richard. We were all set to go. I knocked on his [caravan] door but got no response. Nobody could get him to respond. Lee turned up. He wasn't scheduled to film, but there he was, and thank God, because he went up to Richard's door, knocked quietly and simply said, "Richard!"

'Richard recognised that gravel voice and said, "Yes?" He opened the door and Lee went in. We didn't film anything the rest of that day because the two of them stayed in that caravan, and we could hear them laughing and singing songs, telling each other raucous stories. And they didn't even have a drink.'

Rich told me, 'Lee Marvin was my salvation.'

But it almost came too late.

There were just a few of Richard's scenes left to film. Lee recalled:

'Richard was having trouble walking on to the set and had to be helped by two aides. He tried to sit in his chair but he couldn't manage it. It was obvious he was a seriously sick man. They shouldn't have tried to even continue but I guess they figured they had to get their money's worth. Money is more important than lives, I suppose. Finally Young saved him from this indignity and asked him to go straight to his mark and stand there ready for the shot. But he was unsteady, and Young gave up and got Burton's stand-in to do the shot.

'The next day we had a scene, and I'd give him the cue line, and he'd start giving his line and he'd get a word wrong. Young would say, "Cut", and then tell the script girl to give Richard the line. Then I gave him the cue again, and he got a different word wrong. Young looked like he would explode, and again the script girl gave him the line. We'd do it again. Same thing. "Cut!" Then Burton pointed a finger at Young and said, "Got you, Terence!" It was a game. It kind of relieved the tension because he knew he was giving us all hell.

'I just felt terrible for Richard. The next day he couldn't remember his lines. So Young gave them to him, line by line, and he repeated them parrot fashion.'

Young's version of that event was, 'Richard just couldn't get a single line right. He tried again and again but it just wouldn't come out right. He was so desperate. It was painful to see this great actor disintegrating before all our eyes. He was in tears.'

Marvin recalled, 'I said to him, "Rich, you can't go on like this." He gave me that defiant Welsh look of his and said, "Just watch me", but I could see tears in his eyes. He was crying out for help and I couldn't do anything for him.'

The end of the film was almost in sight. There was Burton's death scene to shoot. Young said, 'He was so sick. He was lying there and I looked at him, and I told the make-up man, "You've done a great job with Richard." He said, "I haven't touched him."'

'Richard was making a great effort, but his head was shaking and he kept changing colour: blue, then white, then yellow. When I saw how bad he was I decided we'd better stop filming and called for a doctor. He told me, "This man is dying. He'll be dead in three weeks."'

'I said, "You must be kidding."'

'He said, "No. His blood has to be changed. I don't think he's quite got cirrhosis of the liver yet, but he's in the last stages of getting it. His kidneys are diseased. He's dying."'

Lee Marvin wasn't impressed by what happened. 'The man's lying there doing his death scene and a doc's just told the director he really is dying, and the director decides they'd better get the goddamn scene finished, so they keep going. They finished the scene before getting a car to take him to the airport to get him on a plane and to a private hospital in Los Angeles. Jesus, they could have *waited*. Let the guy get well first. I just think Young was scared Burton would die and not come back to finish his scene.'

Burton was diagnosed with influenza and tracheobronchitis. When he was told he had three weeks to live, he told the doctors, 'I am amused that you think I can be killed off that easily.' It was a typical show of Welsh bravura. He was given blood transfusions and remained gravely ill for a week. Terence Young told me, 'I think I saved his life. If we hadn't moved that fast, Richard would be dead today.'

Marvin's opinion was that Young nearly killed him. And if anyone saved Richard, it might well have been Ifor. Richard told me that during his time in hospital, he barely slept and when he did he had recurrent dreams about Ifor. 'I could only sleep maybe 45 minutes at a time. I'd wake up and I swear I could see Ifor in the room with me, and he was perfectly well. Standing and walking, smiling and talking to me. He was still my hero, and maybe he had come to me in spirit to tell me not to give up. I think Ifor may have saved my life. It's all nonsense, of course. Maybe!'

While Rich was convalescing, Elizabeth announced she was divorcing him. Lee Marvin was staggered. 'There he was, almost at death's door, and he's been there God knows how many times for her – he told me she was always ill, always having operations and he was there to nurse her – and when he was almost at death's door she told the world she was divorcing him. Well, fuck her!'

When Richard was discharged, he returned to the unit where Young was finishing up Lee's scenes. Young recalled, 'Burton was completely changed. He was on the wagon, of course, and he seemed so in control. He had a nurse with him. We had lunch and we all drank Frescas and Pepsis. He said, "Good God man, I know you want a bottle of wine. I know the moment my back is turned you'll go off and have one. So go ahead and drink." And we did. Burton didn't touch a drop.

'He had been through hell. The divorce from Elizabeth had hit him harder than any of us realised.'

Rich said of his near-death experience, 'I was close to self-destruction. I'm so very lucky to have deliberately and brutally destroyed my career with my own hands and then be given the chance to come back again. That was an interesting week in hospital waiting to find out if I had cirrhosis of the liver.'

Richard had survived. But the film had put his career well and truly on the rocks. *Variety* said that the film 'is a perfect example of screen trash that almost invites derision'. It said Burton's performance was 'as phoney as his Southern accent. There is not a shred of quality, dignity, relevance or impact in this yahoo-oriented bunk.'

Richard began 1974 sober. He drank a little white wine at first, but stayed off the vodkas. He recuperated at Puerto Vallarta and may have been happy to have not worked at all except that he was offered the role of Winston Churchill in a BBC–NBC full-length television film, *A Walk with Destiny*.

On 16 June 1974 he and Elizabeth were divorced. It had been on the cards for a long time but it was a shock to his system nonetheless. He didn't fight it and was happy to take the blame. Elizabeth certainly blamed him, saying that she had divorced him because of his heavy drinking.

Ava Gardner confirmed that Elizabeth had certainly told her that was the reason.

But when I talked to Brook Williams about the divorce and the reasons for it, we both agreed that any woman who wanted her husband to give up drinking heavily should surely also give up drinking heavily herself. 'She never supported him when he tried to stay dry,' said Brook. 'How could he stay dry when she was drunk so very often?'

So what killed the marriage?

I believe it had so little going for it to start with. Rich began married life filled with guilt about the way he had treated Sybil and the girls. He obviously deeply loved Elizabeth – he never stopped loving her or at least being incredibly fond of her – but they were at war with each other from the beginning. Their rows were legendary. They both claimed that they enjoyed the arguments. If they did, Richard certainly grew bored with them.

I wondered what need Elizabeth really had of Rich; Brook had his opinion. He said, 'She had started their relationship almost like a mother, but he didn't need a mother, and before long, he was more like the parent and she the demanding child. She demanded his time and attention.'

She never had his time and attention more than when she was ill. And Rich felt never more needed than when he could care and nurse for her. I think that if Elizabeth had been a strong healthy woman, the marriage would have ended much sooner.

The irony was that when Rich was so sick that he literally had only a few weeks to live without immediate treatment, she decided to divorce him.

As Ava Gardner said, 'He gave her love, he gave her sex, he gave her diamonds, he gave her the sweetest care when she was sick and in pain. I never figured out what she gave him.'

When I asked Rich what it was Elizabeth had given him, he replied, 'She gave me the adventure of a lifetime.'

I think he was relieved when that adventure came to an end.

Chapter Twenty-Four

BEEN THERE, DONE THAT

JUST BEFORE PLAYING Churchill, Rich was asked to follow it with a TV remake of *Brief Encounter* with Sophia Loren. Robert Shaw had originally been cast but he was unable to begin as he was held up making *Jaws*.

Sophia Loren had the part originally played by Celia Johnson in the David Lean-directed 1945 classic, that of a married woman who meets a stranger at a station and embarks on a brief affair. It was Loren's idea that Burton be offered the part of the stranger, originally played by Trevor Howard in the film. He accepted for a fee of £200,000 plus expenses.

It meant a return to England for Richard; the film was shot in August 1974, on location at Winchester, with interiors at Twickenham Studios. For me it was a wonderful opportunity to moonlight from my regular job at Warner Bros. and Columbia to visit Rich in Winchester, do a day's work as an extra and spend a day alone with him – all at his expense; he paid for my petrol and my B&B. He also paid me out of his own pocket for my meagre participation as an extra since I wasn't on the payroll.

He called me Mick and I called him Dick to start with, which alarmed people. 'You can't call him Dick,' I was told.

'Want to bet?'

But it was always a joke that was short-lived each time we met, and I always called him 'Rich', or 'Richard'. He still called me Mick; he could have called me anything he liked.

I wondered why he had taken the role which he clearly found boring. He was his usual professional self, but it seemed clear to me that he wasn't relishing the part. 'Elizabeth has taken me to the cleaners,' he told me. 'So the money is helpful.'

But I knew Rich was rich enough to withstand Elizabeth's demands which included all the jewellery; some of it had been bought as a joint investment but she was wanting it all and he was letting her have it.

'Why do you let her do that to you?' I asked him.

'Because it makes life much easier. Life has been bloody difficult and I want it to be easy for a little while. Besides, the money doesn't mean so much to me. There's only so much it can do. It doesn't do much more than make life comfortable, but it can't *make* life. I've been given back my life. I feel like it's sort of . . . one more time and get the best out of it.' He had realised that all the money in the world couldn't save Ifor.

Brief Encounter isn't a bad picture; it just didn't stand a chance up against the David Lean original. As a TV movie it works well enough and is enlivened by the star power of both Rich and Sophia. Critics felt that he was not at his best, which isn't surprising because the material doesn't demand too much of him. But it does display his natural charm and, after the disaster that was *The Klansman*, it was easy on the eye and ear.

Loren is also her usual warm self, and having watched the film again recently I was struck by how much it is simply a showcase for the personalities of the two stars. The only thing missing was sexual chemistry, but then, oddly, Richard seemed to lack sexual chemistry with most of his leading ladies, including Elizabeth Taylor.

'I dislike love scenes,' he told me. 'I find kissing for the screen quite embarrassing.' It seemed an odd admission for this womanising actor to make, but it is obviously true; I've noticed that his screen kisses are surprisingly tame. Even when he kissed Elizabeth Taylor in *Cleopatra* and *The Comedians* it never looked totally convincing. The only time I've felt that one of his screen kisses came alive was when he kissed Claire Bloom in *Look Back in Anger*.

Brief Encounter was shown on American TV, was somehow overlooked in Britain and had a theatrical release in Europe in 1976.

Richard wasn't without female companionship around this time. He was seeing Princess Elizabeth of Yugoslavia who had been a long-time friend of Rich and Elizabeth. Quite suddenly, his engagement to Princess Elizabeth was announced.

Throughout the filming of *Brief Encounter* Rich had been sober. But suddenly he fell off the wagon and got very drunk just as he was about to start the Churchill telemovie *A Walk with Destiny*, and failed to turn

213

up for the first day's shooting. He was there for the second day and every day thereafter but he was often drunk.

There is no great mystery or any particular reason why Richard was drinking again. Although he didn't like to call himself an alcoholic, he was one, and a single drink, as he had said, would have to be followed by another and another. It wouldn't be the wine that did it, but the vodka. Not even his dice with death the previous year kept him from drinking now.

Shortly before the film was due to air on American television, the *New York Times* asked him to write a piece about Churchill for them. To everyone's surprise, what he delivered was a diatribe on Churchill. 'I realise afresh that I hate Churchill and all his kind,' he wrote. He had long studied Churchill and had met him a few times, but suddenly he was writing, not as an honorary member of the British aristocracy but as an angry Welshman from the valleys who had not forgotten the historic English oppression.

'I was writing about the fear I find in men who have such overwhelming power and what they do to it,' he told me a few years later.

Politicians and even his friends protested. Robert Hardy sent him an angry telegram. Members of Parliament condemned him. But the result was that NBC got one of its biggest-ever audiences when the film was aired.

'It's no good looking at everything through rose-tinted glasses,' said Rich. 'And look what it did for the viewing figures. I'd say I did the producers a big favour.'

With his new fiancée, Princess Elizabeth, he went on a tour of Morocco where, to his great surprise, he was greeted by people as 'Saint Becket' and 'Major Smith'. Later, John Huston told him, 'That's because *Where Eagles Dare* is a favourite picture in Morocco and plays continuously, and *Becket* is a picture they keep re-releasing.'

Terence Young had another picture for Richard called *Jackpot* in 1975 and so he turned up promptly on the Riviera to start work on the film. When I asked Young why he had decided to work with Richard a second time after the first disaster, he said, 'I'd heard Richard was sober and, besides, it was his name that got us the money to make the film.' But the picture didn't get made in the end because the money ran out.

Before the film had its terminal crisis, Rich had secured a part for Jeanne Bell, the model he had managed to get a small part for in *The*

Klansman. Back in London, Princess Elizabeth saw a photograph of Rich and Jeanne walking arm in arm. She called him and demanded an explanation, so he went to London to persuade her that he and Jeanne really were just good friends.

Princess Elizabeth took no chances and joined him in Nice. Terence Young recalled:

'I threw a party in a restaurant and both Jeanne Bell and Princess Elizabeth were there. Without a word, Richard left the restaurant and shortly after that his chauffeur, Gaston, came in with a message for Jeanne. Richard was waiting for her to join him. Jeanne sent a message back that she wouldn't go. The driver came back a second time to try again and this time Princess Elizabeth went out, got into Burton's car and found him asleep. He slept all the way back to the hotel. Then something happened the next morning; I don't know what, but he snubbed her, and she got on a plane and went back to London.

'When Rich had realised what he'd done, he felt terrible and flew to London to try and make it up to Elizabeth. The problem as I saw it was that Richard, who I had thought was on the wagon, was drinking heavily again. He'd become really very irrational and unpredictable. I knew he wanted to quit but he just couldn't. And he didn't know what he was doing.'

In July 1975 Richard and his co-stars James Coburn and Charlotte Rampling took action to have the film's backers, Irwin Trust Company Ltd, wound up. The film was shut down and Rich went back to London, to the Dorchester Hotel, to try to patch things up with Princess Elizabeth. He waited in the bar for two hours while she prepared herself. He spent those two hours drinking. Richard, at that stage, would have done nothing else, so she shouldn't have been surprised to have found him drunk when she finally arrived. She told him their engagement was off.

Brook Williams recalled, 'Rich took Jeanne [Bell] and the 13-year-old son she had, called Troy, to Switzerland where she tried to help Rich stop drinking. He did slow down considerably, but it didn't help when Elizabeth [Taylor], who'd heard his engagement to Princess Elizabeth was off, began phoning him from Leningrad.' She was there making the Russian–American co-production *The Blue Bird*. One of her co-stars and confidante was Ava Gardner. Henry Wynberg was there too, but Elizabeth, apparently, wanted Richard back.

'She was still in love with him,' Ava Gardner told me. 'I got pretty sick and tired of hearing her go on about him. I said, "If you want him, go and get him." But I thought that if she did, it would be a big mistake. I just wanted her to shut up.'

In August Elizabeth arrived in Geneva with Wynberg and met with Richard. The next morning Wynberg flew to Los Angeles while Jeanne Bell moved out of the house.

'I just suddenly found myself with Elizabeth again,' he told me. 'What the devil was I thinking of? She wanted to get married again. I didn't. But I married her again all the same. What Liz wants, she gets. We went to South Africa where Elizabeth had sponsored a hospital project. She kept giving me notes – "I love you. Please answer." Everyone knew about these damn notes. I found her irresistible, and in the end I found myself on one knee – literally – proposing to her. I'd actually stopped drinking by then, so I should have been sober enough to know what I was doing, but I didn't. So after she accepted, I got drunk.'

They were married in Botswana on 10 October 1975 by an African District Commissioner from the Tswana tribe. Typically, Rich bought her an expensive diamond as a wedding gift.

'I remember going through the ceremony like it was a dream,' he said. 'I kept asking myself; what the devil am I doing here, getting married in the bush, by an African gentleman to a woman who destroyed me? I even managed to catch malaria which should have been an omen.'

They flew to London for his 50th birthday. He drank only mineral water but was very tired and it showed. It might have been because he married Elizabeth again against his better judgement, or the malaria – or both.

Elizabeth was suffering again with neck and back pains, but this time Rich refused to stay in hospital with her. 'It was the same as before,' he told me. 'I had to be there for her the whole time. I had to be her nurse. I had been there, done that. I knew it was over before it had begun.'

Brook Williams revealed to me that at this time Rich was very ill with malaria and drink-related problems and was in a London clinic for treatment. He was exhausted and depressed when he wheelchaired Elizabeth out of hospital and took her back to Gstaad for Christmas,

1975 so they could both recuperate. Family and friends came over; Brook Williams was there too. 'I went skiing with Rich and on a ski lift he spotted a tall, beautiful young woman who I happened to know,' said Brook. 'I told him she was Susan Hunt and was married to but about to be divorced from racing driver James Hunt. He wanted me to introduce him to her, so I did. After that she began visiting the house which alarmed Elizabeth.'

Richard said, 'Elizabeth knew that Suzy was something special.'

Suzy was a stylish, middle class, 27-year-old Englishwoman who was attracted to Richard, and he to her.

He had made a brave decision to save his ailing career: to go back to the stage. He hadn't done a play since 1964, not counting *Doctor Faustus* in Oxford, and chose to make his return by going to New York to be in Peter Shaffer's *Equus*. It was going to be a difficult, physically taxing role; he was often in pain in his arms, neck and back.

The idea to do the play came from Shaffer because Richard had already been signed to do the film version, and Shaffer thought the play would be perfect preparation to do the film. The play had been running successfully for some time, first with Anthony Hopkins and then with Anthony Perkins, so Rich was stepping into a play that other fine actors had left their mark on. He was signed to do a 12-week run, starting in February 1976, but the producers were anxious because of the tales of his drunkenness. So he brought with him a secret weapon – Susan Hunt; he always called her Suzy.

He told me in on the set of *The Medusa Touch*, as he lay in bed for a scene set in a hospital, 'If I had taken Elizabeth to New York with me, I would only have got drunk and it would have been a nightmare. But Suzy was different. She didn't stop me drinking. She didn't hide bottles. But she encouraged me not to drink because she knew I didn't want to drink. She steadied me. She may have even saved my life. Booze would have killed me, I am sure, if it had not been for Suzy.'

Brook Williams helped Rich rehearse in his suite at the Lombardy Hotel. 'I played all the other parts and Suzy provided milk to drink,' said Brook. 'Rich was off the booze throughout rehearsals.'

He wouldn't allow himself to give in to the full power of the role in rehearsals; that was something he could do only in performance. Towards the end of the rehearsal period, Elizabeth came to New York; they quarrelled for two days.

The play was a huge test for him and he asked if he could begin with a Saturday matinee as a warm-up with a live audience. He was, by his own admission, 'never so bloody scared before in my life', but he fought the urge to have a drink. He shook, forgot some of his lines but was helped by the rest of the cast, and somehow staggered through it.

When he went on on Monday night, he was sensational. Walter Kerr, writing in the *New York Times*, called it 'the best work of his life'. John Barber of the *Daily Telegraph* reported, 'He made a fine play seem even finer.'

He received standing ovations and it was decided to extend the run by two weeks. He received a special Tony Award which had the inscription, 'Welcome back to Broadway'.

Richard Burton was back on top. And he was in love with a new woman, Suzy Hunt. He told Elizabeth he wanted a divorce so he could marry Suzy. Elizabeth knew she'd lost him. Brook said, 'She delayed the divorce until publicity about the maintenance she wanted made her give in. She took all the jewellery – again – and even took ownership of the *Kalizma*, and all the artworks. Rich let her have the lot for his freedom. Besides, he didn't care about art. He cared only about Suzy. She was, I have to admit, the best thing that happened in his life at that moment.'

Like Rich had said, he'd been there, done that. Now things were about to change.

Chapter Twenty-Five

ROCK BOTTOM BUT NOT OUT

I N 1976 S IR Stanley Baker was ill with lung cancer. Richard telephoned him and said, 'Why don't I see you any more.' Baker said that he had tried often to call but had never been able to get through; so many friends from the past had long given up trying to contact Richard. It shook him.

A week or so later, on 28 June 1976, Stanley died. Richard sent his widow, Ellen, a telegram saying how devastated he was to have lost his friend and that if he could help her in any way, he would.

He then wrote a tribute to Sir Stanley in the *Observer* entitled *Lament for a Dead Welshman*. It was a meant to be a tribute to a hero, as Welshmen like Baker were. Rich described him as being uncultured and lacking a sense of poetry which seemed unflattering. He also strayed often from the truth with anecdotes about events that never happened. There were reports that Lady Baker was outraged; she was certainly puzzled and called the editor of the *Observer* who explained that he had cut much of it because of its inflammatory nature.

Richard told me, 'I wrote what I felt. I have never held back. I wrote what I thought of Churchill, and I wrote what I thought of Stanley. I don't think he would have objected. I suppose it wasn't the kind of tribute people expect of someone who has just died. I was sorry if it offended Ellen. But I wanted to show that Stanley come from nothing and made everything of himself. He had what I haven't had and probably never will – a knighthood.' Richard was unrepentant about his article, and from his point of view, as harsh as it may seem, there was no need to be.

He still had the film version of *Equus* to make, but before that he was a Catholic priest in *Exorcist II: The Heretic*, the first sequel to the phenomenally successful *The Exorcist*. It's a film that at best can be said to be not as bad as *The Klansman*, and I once asked Rich, with all the sincerity I could muster, 'What possessed you to do it?'

It was an intended joke and he laughed loudly. When he stopped laughing, he said, 'I can't resist playing priests. I have a fascination for them. What makes them tick? And what is it in me that film directors see that makes for a priestly figure? What do I see in myself that makes me think I can play them? Because I'm a Christian, perhaps? Well, I'm not. Maybe it takes a good atheist to make a convincing priest.'

'And so what interests you about priests?'

'How can they go through life without sex? That makes no sense to me. Not that I can accept that they are all celibate. It isn't in man's nature to be celibate. I find a wondrous sense of irony in the fact that I, who love to fuck, get chosen to play men who can't.'

Peter O'Toole once told me that he thought that Richard displayed a 'tremendous sense of religious fervour whenever he performed, especially on the stage. He comes from a Methodist background and when he sings his songs are full of religious and spiritual emotion and sincerity. It's in the voice, so when he speaks it is beautiful like a song. That is why he was so bloody good as *Becket*.'

But I still wanted to know why Richard chose to make such a disastrous film as *Exorcist II*. He said, 'It looked a whole lot better going in than coming out. It had a good director [John Boorman] but he was lost with the material. He said, "I made the wrong film." Well, didn't we all? It seemed like a certainty to be a success because of the original, but nobody was fooled this time. I could have done with a hit film. My agent thought it a wise move, maybe because the money was good.' He was originally paid $750,000 but that apparently turned into a million when the film ran over schedule.

Newsweek found Richard's performance to be a 'dispiriting spectacle'. *Variety* put it mildly: '*Exorcist II* is not as good as *The Exorcist*. It isn't even close.'

During filming of *Exorcist II* in New York, his divorce from Elizabeth finally came through, on 1 August. So Rich and Suzy got married on 21 August 1976 in Virginia. He was sober and the bride was on time.

She saw how much he hated making *Exorcist II* and told him, 'You must never do anything like that again, not even for a million dollars.' She began to take an interest in his work, aided by Valerie Douglas who had often worked as his personal assistant since *Alexander the Great*. At first it was just advice Suzy offered. In time she was reading all the scripts sent to him.

After *Exorcist II* wrapped, he went to Canada to film *Equus*. *Variety* summed it up best: '*Equus* is an excellent example of film-as-theatre. Peter Shaffer's play, which he adapted for the screen, has become under Sidney Lumet's outstanding direction a moving confrontation between a crudely mystical Peter Firth and the psychiatrist (Richard Burton) who is trying to unravel the boy's mind.'

Burton, Firth and Lumet were all Oscar nominated; none of them won. It was Richard's last hope of an Oscar. 'I believe I am the most nominated actor in film history not to have won,' he said. (Currently Peter O'Toole is the most Oscar-nominated actor not to have won – with eight nominations.)

Colin Blakely, who co-starred in *Equus*, admitted to me in 1979 that he was in awe of Burton. 'The power of the man is overwhelming,' he said. 'I suppose it helped that he had done the play because he had these long monologues and he was word perfect.' There were eight monologues in all. 'They were all shot in a single day. And he wasn't well. He was in some pain because of a bad back and I think he has some pinched nerves, but he never complained. He was good humoured, he didn't get drunk, and he told some lovely stories. I would have loved for him to have won the Oscar. But I heard that the Americans don't much like him. I think he never won an Oscar because he didn't fit in with Hollywood. How could Richard Burton have never won an Oscar? That's ridiculous.'

It is odd that despite proving time and again what a rich and powerful actor he was – when he was at his best – Hollywood just wasn't breaking his door down. It seems that remarks he had made back in the 1950s about the Communist witch hunts had not been forgotten.

John Huston had another theory; he told me, 'Hollywood doesn't like actors who are British classical actors. They like Michael Caine because he's a sort of English Everyman. But the Laurence Oliviers and John Gielguds and Richard Burtons are not and can't be an Everyman. They have some quality of aristocratic greatness that Hollywood finds threatening. Hollywood doesn't like those who don't conform. I should know because they don't much care for me because *I* don't conform.'

Lee Marvin put it more succinctly. 'Hell, Hollywood wouldn't know what to do with Richard if he said to them, "Give me anything and I'll do it." They don't have that kind of intelligence. He told me on *The Klansman* that sometimes he'd just like to play a New York cop who only has to shoot a few people and arrest the bad guys, and then he said, "But I can't do a good New York Accent." I said, "Jesus Christ, Rich, you're a great actor. You can *learn*." He was really touched by that.'

Fortunately for Richard, he didn't need a film like *Dirty Harry* to prove what he could do; *Equus*, though not a huge commercial hit, proved he could still deliver and he was able to go back to Céligny with Susan feeling satisfied and happier than he had been in a long time. He also spent a little time in England narrating a 26-episode series called *Chronicles of an English Crown* for BBC Radio. He enjoyed that kind of work, where he could just rely on his voice; he never knew what to do with his body. Even when his arms had been more mobile, he tended to let them hang down by his sides because he never had learned enough technique to know what to do with them. But his voice was his prize gift.

Some astute people made good use of his voice, such as Stanley Baker who asked Rich to narrate the opening and closing scenes of his remarkable epic *Zulu*. The narration, although brief, was so effective that when John Barry's score was released as a soundtrack album, Richard's narration was included. Musician Jeff Wayne recognised the magic of the Burton voice and asked him to narrate his rock musical concept album *War of the Worlds* in 1978.

Susan redecorated *Le Pays de Galles* and they discussed having children. He at last seemed settled. But it was never going to be that easy.

Richard was back in England in 1977, making *The Medusa Touch* at Shepperton Studios. He played a man with a gift for causing disaster with just the power of his mind. I was on the set for the hospital scene. Rich was, for a while, relieved to be lying down in bed to do all his acting, although after a while he got bored and wanted to get up.

We started with the usual gag that had some second assistant director ready to throw me off the set.

'Hello Dick!'

'Hello Mick!'

'Still staying at the Dorchester?' I asked him.

'No, Mick. We've rented a house in Windsor. Come over some time.

It's so much cosier for Suzy and I than the Dorchester which Elizabeth loves and where she wants to be waited on hand and foot. At Windsor we wait on ourselves. It's perfect.'

Then he added, like it was an important footnote, 'And I'm off the drink.'

'Seems like you always are when I see you.'

'So I am. That means you must be the only person in the world who's never seen me drunk.'

I said that I had, but only the once, and reminded him of our escapade in the East End of London when he was making *Villain*. 'Oh my God!' he said. 'I'd forgotten about that. I can barely remember it.'

Then he called out, 'Hey, Brookie, come over here.' And there, in the uniform of a male nurse, was Brook Williams who made it his business to get me into some kind of medical uniform to look busy doing something or other in the scene.

Over lunch, I sat with Rich and Brook and we talked – or rather, they talked and I listened. At one point, Rich said to Brook, 'Careful what you tell him. He's a reporter now.'

I was, at that time, a journalist at *Photoplay*, but I wasn't there to report on anything; I was just having fun being an extra in a Richard Burton film. And until I wrote this book, I never wrote about what Richard or Brook told me, or about the times I spent with Burton and some of the crazy things that seemed to happen when we were together.

Brook was at Pinewood when I turned up for a couple of scenes as an extra in *The Wild Geese* in 1978. He wasn't in the same scenes as I; he had the fun part of the job, going on location with Rich, Roger Moore and Richard Harris to South Africa where they were playing at being mercenaries, led by Colonel Allen Faulkner – played by Burton – on a daring mission to free an imprisoned black leader.

The Wild Geese was an attempt by British producer Euan Lloyd to make a film in the mould of *The Guns of Navarone*; it was never as big or as good as that film but it was a huge success and made Richard bankable again at the box office.

But it had been a difficult film for him to make. Brook told me, at the time of the film's release in 1979, 'He was in constant pain but he never complained. "Just a little discomfort," he'd always say. But he had pain in the shoulders and in the arm, and he had very strong shots to kill the pain. He was told they might even cure his arthritis.'

He was treated by a professor whom Euan Lloyd had flown from Pretoria when the unit filmed on location in South Africa. The treatment seemed to do the trick, but some years later Brook said that he thought the treatment did more harm than good. 'He didn't know it at the time,' said Brook, 'but he had a nerve trapped in his spine, so just relieving the pain only made him think he was better, and when he was very active, it did more damage.'

Sir Roger Moore said that Richard 'was feeling rather low because it was a strenuous film for him to do, and he couldn't drink because he had a bad shoulder and a bad hip'. The painkillers he took, it seems, were a major reason why Richard didn't drink. But there was also a proviso that Richard *couldn't* drink if he were to make the film – and he kept his word. In fact, Richard was quite desperate to do this film. Stephen Boyd was to have taken the lead role but died of a heart attack. Richard got his agent, Robert Lantz, to call Euan Lloyd and ask if he would consider Richard. Lloyd was anxious about using him because of his drinking, but when he discovered that Richard was staying sober and that he was being supported in his efforts by Suzy, he decided to take the gamble. Then he found he couldn't get insurance for Richard because of his back problems.

He also took a gamble on casting Richard Harris who promised that he wouldn't drink even though Lloyd couldn't get insurance for Harris because of his drinking problems. The producer was taking a chance with both Richards.

John Glen, the film's second unit director responsible for shooting the action sequences, had to find ways to give the impression Richard Burton in his role was fit and active. Glen told me, 'Burton's movements were restricted. We did get him running on a couple of occasions but he wasn't fit enough to sustain that for very long. We were lucky enough to have a very good stunt arranger, Bob Simmons, who was a perfect double for Richard Burton and we used him whenever we could.'

The film was inspired by the exploits of mercenary Colonel 'Mad' Mike Hoare who served as technical adviser on the film. Richard didn't like him. 'I dislike mercenaries,' Rich told me. 'I saw no saving grace in him at all.'

Nevertheless, Richard based his character directly on Hoare. But he was not at all amused when he was told by Euan Lloyd that Mike Hoare was going to give all the actors drill instruction, and that all those playing mercenaries were to report to him. Brook Williams recalled:

> 'Richard stormed into Euan Lloyd's office and said, "What's this all about? I'm not in the fucking army."
>
> 'Euan explained that Mike Hoare thought it would be a good idea if all the actors had proper drill instruction. Rich said, "I don't give a damn what he thinks." Rich came to me and was grumbling and swearing about it. He said, "What do you think, Brookie?" I said, "I think if Mike Hoare can make us look like a crack unit, then it's a good idea." He said, "Well, I don't."
>
> 'The next morning we all reported for drill instruction, including Richard Harris and Roger Moore. I don't think Harris liked it any more than Rich. Anyway, out on to the parade area walked Rich and he just quietly took his place. I said to him, "I thought you weren't going to do this," and he said, "I changed my mind." And he bloody well did the drill, even though he was in pain.'

Rich stayed dry throughout filming, but Brook Williams recalled what he called 'The Night Richard Harris Fell off the Wagon with a Loud Crash!':

> 'The unit had turned this shack in South Africa into a pub and christened it the Red Ox. One night Richard Harris went on one – a pretty spectacular bender. Roger Moore was drinking, but Rich stuck to Tab which is a soft drink popular in the States. Poor Euan Lloyd got very worried and was calling "Time gentlemen, please."
>
> 'The next morning Harris turned up very sheepish and said to Euan, "Sorry, governor. It won't happen again." And it didn't. But Rich was furious with Lloyd and told him he should read everyone who got drunk the riot act. There was quite an argument. Rich was staying dry and he thought it was pretty poor that the others hadn't done the same. I know there's a sense of irony in Richard Burton getting furious because actors had got drunk, but Rich was trying very hard to keep his act together.'

Helping him keep his act together was Susan, which Euan Lloyd thought a very good thing. Brook Williams wasn't so convinced. He became gradually alarmed at the influence Susan was having on Richard's career. A few years after *The Wild Geese*, he told me:

'She was on location with us [for *The Wild Geese*] and he loved having her there. She fussed over him all the time. Brought him so many cups of tea he couldn't drink them and soup he never touched. But he loved having her around. The trouble is, she'd made a lot of us who've been with Rich such a long time unwelcome. His publicist [John Springer] gave up because he couldn't get close to him, and Ron Berkeley who'd been doing Rich's make-up and hair for ever had gone because Susan did all that herself.

'I think she wanted to get rid of all his old pals, and that has, I'm sure, made him feel very isolated. She and Valerie Douglas were reading all the scripts that came in and agreeing on the contracts. Andrew McLaglen [director of *The Wild Geese*] wanted to get as many of the same bunch together for *The Sea Wolves* in Goa. Rich would have loved that but Suzy wouldn't let him. The money was good and we all had good fun. But instead of Rich, Andy McLaglen got Gregory Peck. Such a shame. Still, we sent him lots of postcards from Goa.'

A film Richard chose for himself was *Absolution*, written by Anthony Shaffer, brother of Peter Shaffer. He had been interested in the project for some years and just before he started work on the Tito film there were plans to make the film with Christopher Miles – brother of actress Sarah – directing, but by the time the film finally got into production in 1978, Anthony Page was directing it.

Richard played (yet another) priest who teaches at a Roman Catholic school. He hears about a murder in confession and sets out to solve the murder. Like *Sleuth*, written by Peter Shaffer, there are some twists and turns before the truth is unravelled.

Some scenes were shot at Ellesmere College in Shropshire where I met up with Rich again, and Brook Williams who was also playing a priest. I ended up in a priest's cassock and the three of us had some fun sitting in our priest cassocks reminiscing in a most un-priest-like way.

The film was not a big hit but it satisfied Richard's need to play a character part, and he was good in it; he was often amazingly effective as a priest although they tended to pale when compared to the time he played the Archbishop of Canterbury. 'When it comes to playing a man of the cloth,' he joked, 'there's nowhere to go but down after you've been the Archbishop of Canterbury.'

'Unless you play the Pope,' said Brook.

'I must make that my life's ambition – to be Pope. If Tony Quinn can do it [in *Shoes of the Fisherman*], so can I.'

I can't be sure how much influence Susan had over Richard's choice of films over the next year or so, but he made some of the poorest pictures of his career. He played the King of Cornwall in *Tristan and Isolt*, then a First World War German sergeant in *Breakthrough* which was a poor sequel to the successful *Cross of Iron*, and *Circle of Two*, playing a 60-year-old artist in love with a 16-year-old schoolgirl, played by Tatum O'Neal.

While he was filming *Circle of Two*, I did my one and only formal interview with him; this was for *Photoplay* – it was a shame it had to be done by transatlantic telephone. It was also a personal shame for me because the editor took my name off the published piece as he tended to do often, and edited to make it seem like Burton was being inter-viewed actually on the set – so here it is, in full, under my own name.

Richard said to me, 'Okay, Mick, let's play the game. You ask me the questions and I'll try and give a straight answer. I'd like this film to be a success so I won't give you any of the usual interview bullshit.'

I asked him first of all how he was getting on with Tatum O'Neal; he replied, 'It's great fun working with Tatum. She has terrific vitality and enthusiasm. Sort of matches my own, I hope. It's so much better than working with someone who knows it all and is very blasé about it.'

I asked him how he felt about playing a man who was actually several years older than his real self and having to wear make-up to age him.

'I said to Jules Dassin, our director, "Here I am looking fitter and younger than I have in years and everybody's going to say *Look how he's gone to the dogs again*."'

At that time Richard was very contented with his private life and he said – and I think he meant it – that getting older didn't worry him. 'As a man you can go on being a top-ranking figure virtually forever. Look at Larry Olivier; he's what? Seventy-two? Life is harder on actresses. The odd thing is, with every film my leading ladies are getting younger and younger, and I'm required to look older and older. The last one was 34. That was Kate Mulroon in *Tristan and Isolt*. And this one, Tatum, is nearly 16. I've never worked with anyone so young.'

I asked him if it bothered him playing an older man having an affair with a young girl? He said, 'It makes a change. I'm forever being offered princes or kings or spies with a very nasty case of angst! I believe that *Circle of Two* is a delicately balanced story. The two personalities have to complement each other very much and be totally believable or they run the risk of being just a dirty old man with a beautiful young girl. It's a tremendous job for the director.'

Since Richard was playing an artist, and knowing that he had little interest in art, I asked him, for the record, what sort of art interested him. He laughed and said, 'A trick question! I wouldn't recognise a Rembrandt from a hole in the wall. I'm really quite a Philistine.'

As I wrote in the article, if you asked him to sing, write, play the piano or simply asked if he'd read any good books lately, he would quickly dispel any notion of being a Philistine.

And that was my only formal interview with Richard Burton. Brief but a special moment for me. Now I have published it under my own name.

Unfortunately, *Circle of Two*, nor the other two films, were seen much anywhere, and the only benefit he got from them was being paid $750,000 for each. Brook Williams, who believed that it was Susan who was choosing his projects, was bewildered that Rich had allowed Susan to agree on such poor material for him. He had reached rock bottom. But he wasn't out for the count just yet.

Maybe it was simply a matter of Rich being too old – and ill – an actor in a business dominated by younger and more virile male stars and there simply wasn't much in the way of good material around for someone like Richard Burton. It was the time of Clint Eastwood and Burt Reynolds. Sylvester Stallone was just making a name for himself, and so was Robert de Niro. The word was out that Richard Burton was physically deteriorating and becoming increasingly unemployable. He knew he had to prove them wrong.

And despite what Brook thought of Suzy, she helped him make a decision that would put him back on top. Not many actors get the chance to spring from rock bottom to the top of the heap too often, but Rich did.

Chapter Twenty-Six

TOP OF THE HEAP AGAIN

A LAN JAY LERNER had long been trying to get Richard to do a revival of *Camelot*. Rich had often said he would do it if Julie Andrews would also do it. But it didn't happen.

In 1980 there was a successful revival of *My Fair Lady* with Rex Harrison in the part of Professor Higgins which Harrison had made his very own, and its success spurred Lerner on to resurrect *Camelot* and to do it with Richard Burton.

It was a good time for the offer to come Richard's way. 'The key to getting Rich to agree was Susan,' Alan Jay Lerner told me. 'I went over to Switzerland with the two producers [Don Gregory and Mike Merrick] and we had lunch with Susan and Richard. I think it was Suzy who convinced him that he should return to *Camelot*.' Lerner also thought the offer of $60,000 a week helped swing the vote.

Richard decided that *Camelot* might prove he could still deliver, despite his many ailments. He was only 54, but he seemed so much older. Nevertheless, he grasped the role of King Arthur with amazing strength, despite his lack of it, and opened triumphantly in Toronto in June 1980 at the O'Keefe Centre. The show received standing ovations at every performance.

'I was carried by the power of the show,' Rich told me. 'I find it endlessly fascinating that it's a show which makes seemingly intelligent people speechless with emotion.' But he was happy to take some of the credit himself, and rightly so. 'I've learned through personal experience that a supple voice speaking lovely sounding banalities such as *Camelot* possesses can break down even the most cynical of audiences.'

His voice had always been his richest gift and he knew he could always find some way of creating the required emotional impact with

229

just his voice. He hardly ever relied on technique, or so he said, but there was definitely technique in the way he used his voice to manipulate an audience.

Soon after the opening in Toronto he developed problems with the tendons in his right arm and shoulder and was given cortisone treatment which only served to make his arms weaker than ever. He could hardly raise his right arm, so he used his left arm to wield Excaliber.

A few weeks later doctors discovered he had a pinched nerve at the base of his neck and he was put on a course of medication. He was already taking something he told me was called 'Antabuse' which was to help keep him from drinking. 'Susan was with him to make sure he took all his medication,' said Lerner. 'She was his nurse.'

She was also his make-up artist and his dresser; Ron Berkeley and Bob Wilson were no longer needed.

When the show came to New York, the reception was as extravagant as it had been in Toronto, and some critics lavished personal praise on Richard. 'Burton doesn't merely command the stage,' wrote Frank Rich in the *New York Times*. 'He seems to own it by divine right . . . He remains every inch the King Arthur of our most majestic storybook dreams.'

But there were just a minority of critics who were underwhelmed. Clive Barnes of the *New York Post* described the show as 'a knight to forget'.

The public didn't care what the critics thought; they loved the show and they loved Burton. He felt highly gratified by the personal second solo calls he received. 'I would just stand there, feeling the audience supporting me and feeling the affection and warmth from them all. It was one of the most extraordinary experiences I have ever had in the theatre.'

There was just one disaster of a show. Richard staggered around on stage, unable to deliver any kind of performance. Someone yelled out, 'Give him another drink.' His understudy went on instead, but hundreds walked out. People thought he was drunk. He wasn't. It was the combined effect of all the medication and two glasses of wine he had taken when he spent time with Richard Harris who had arrived to catch up.

He promised there would be no more alcohol, and he kept his word. He also appeared on *The Dick Cavett Show* on television and gave an honest explanation about his one-night disaster.

The moment he stepped on stage the following night he was given a three-and-a-half minute ovation and it lifted him. 'That night I gave what was probably the best performance I ever gave as Arthur,' he said.

There was further triumph in Chicago in September. While he was there, he heard about the roasting Peter O'Toole had been given by the critics back in London for his performance in *Macbeth*. O'Toole told me, 'Rich phoned me from Chicago and said he'd heard about the reviews, and he said, "How are the houses?" I said, "Packed." He said, "My boy, just remember that you're the most original actor to come out of Britain since the war. Fuck the critics." I said, "Thank you." Then he said, "Just think of every four letter word and twelve letter expletive and ram them all up their envious arses in which, I am sure, there is ample room." I said, "Thank you, Rich." Then he said, "I love you Peter," and I said, "It's mutual."

'I think he was more furious with the critics than I was. It was a lovely thing for him to do.'

In October *Camelot* played in Dallas; both his shoulders were extremely painful. The show, and the part, were marathons, and from what I can gauge, everyone who saw him or was with him was astonished at the staggering punishment he endured and survived.

The show was in Miami in time for Richard's 55th birthday in November. It seems he made sure the show played there because Philip Burton was then living and working in Key West and he wanted Phil to see the show. Brook told me, 'Phil was there for the extravagant birthday party Susan threw for Rich [on 10 November] in an expensive Miami restaurant. The whole company had been invited. The owner of the restaurant invited Rich to visit his wine cellar and see their famous collection. Well, Rich couldn't resist trying the wine and before long was drunk. Well . . . it was his 55th birthday, after all.'

The last city on the tour was Los Angeles where they opened in March 1981. Since Toronto, Rich had dropped from 170 to 142 pounds. Shortly after the opening he fell ill with flu and pain in his arms, and was sent to St John's Hospital in Santa Monica for tests. A top neurosurgeon was flown in from Florida who diagnosed severe degenerative changes of the cervical spine and recommended urgent surgery. But Richard needed to recover first from the flu and gain some weight.

The show literally had to go on, and it did. Between scenes Richard raced to the men's room to vomit and then returned for the next scene.

Only after he gave his final performance in February 1981 did he undergo surgery, during which the doctors discovered that his entire spinal column was coated with crystallised alcohol. It had to be scraped off and then they set about rebuilding the vertebrae in his neck, a dangerous operation that could have caused paralysis. The delicate five-hour operation was deemed a success.

Brook Williams didn't think the operation was the success it was made out to be. Some years later he said to me, 'They should never have put him under the knife. It did him no good. He was in terrible pain and the neck muscles were permanently damaged for the rest of his life. He couldn't raise his arms up in the air, or reach across the table for the marmalade. But you never, ever heard him complain.'

But at the time the news seemed good, and many people, including Elizabeth Taylor, sent flowers. Susan was with him day and night, and two weeks after the operation, he left hospital. They remained in Beverly Hills for a while until he was given the all clear to fly back to Céligny to convalesce. He continued with the medication to try and kill the pain, and he had a physiotherapist. He also had Suzy constantly doing everything for him. 'It wore him down,' said Brook Williams. 'He'd been suffocated by Elizabeth's constant need for attention, and with Suzy he was suffocated by being the one getting all the attention.'

What really went on behind closed doors, only Suzy knows, but the strain was definitely there in their marriage although Rich probably tried not to let it show. He was doing well and putting on weight, but in October of 1981 he collapsed with a perforated ulcer and was rushed back to St John's in Santa Monica for an emergency operation. Suzy was with him constantly, and again Elizabeth Taylor sent flowers.

'It was impossible for him,' Brook told me, 'because he couldn't take the painkillers for his back due to the ulcer so he was in more pain. It's no wonder he was irritable. He was losing his temper with Suzy. It was all getting too much. I think he might have even been physically abusive to Suzy when he was at his worst.'

Richard convalesced at the Hermitage Hotel in Beverly Hills where he received a script for a TV mini series on the life of Wagner. Director Tony Palmer wanted Richard to play the title role. Said Brook:

'It was an awful lot to expect of a man who was so sick but he loved the idea and the challenge, and Suzy encouraged him. Tony Palmer and the producer [Alan Wright] went out to Beverly Hills, where Rich and Suzy had bought a new house, to discuss it. They arrived to find Rich surrounded by books about Wagner, and he told them, "I am Wagner. I will play Wagner."

'He was fascinated by Wagner, enjoyed his music and felt there were a lot of similarities between Wagner's life and his own, although Rich would say, "Wagner was a genius. I am not."

'Some years earlier, Rich had met Peter Hoffman who was probably the world's best Wagnerian singer and he had made every effort to befriend Hoffman.

'Palmer and Wright were delighted to have Rich but had nagging doubts about his health. It was going to be a very long shooting schedule – seven months – and the film was going to result in possibly as much as ten hours screen time. [In the event, there was a nine-hour version and a six-hour version.] Getting insurance to cover Rich was proving to be difficult.

'He tried hard to show that he was fit and well. He wanted to *feel* like he was fit and well, and he didn't care to have Suzy sitting by him all the time, asking him if he felt all right. She would run her fingers through his hair. She meant well, but it only irritated him.

'There was also Valerie Douglas who somehow became his agent, and when Alan Wright discussed terms with her for Richard's services, she told him, "Richard doesn't do anything for less than a million and a quarter dollars, even if it's five minutes in a film."

'Alan Wright said, "I'm afraid we don't have that kind of money." They finally agreed on a million which wasn't bad. But I was afraid that it would take a terrible toll on him physically.'

Brook managed to secure some work for himself in the film, and he did all he could to watch Richard from a discreet distance. 'Valerie Douglas didn't like having me around,' Brook told me. 'She told Richard she didn't want me there. I called her on the telephone and told her that Rich needed a stand-in and I would do it, and wash the dishes and anything else that had to be done. I wasn't going to let Rich be gone all those months without someone who really cared.'

That might suggest Susan didn't care; she did. I think Brook felt very protective of Rich and was sure he knew what was best for him. Personally, I think Richard had reached a stage in his life where his physical wellbeing was so poor that nobody could have done the very best for him single-handed. Richard's greatest strength was his own sense of conviction and his need to prove himself.

It was just as well Brook did insist on going because before filming started on *Wagner*, Suzy announced she was going to Mexico to sort out some problems with the house there. 'I did feel sorry for her,' said Brook. 'She meant well but she got on Richard's nerves and he gave her a difficult time. You just can't smother Rich. In the end he just told her to leave him alone. He could be terrifying when he yelled. So she decided she *would* leave him alone as he'd asked. It was a separation, although neither would admit it.'

There was a tremendous supporting cast in *Wagner*, including Vanessa Redgrave as Wagner's second wife, and most exciting of all for Rich was the famous trio of knights – Sirs Ralph Richardson, John Gielgud and Laurence Olivier (although by then Olivier was a Lord). They were all to appear in a single scene together.

Filming began in January 1982, in Vienna. Rich started taking charge of his own requirements which had previously been dealt with by Suzy, and he brought back his regular make-up artist Ron Berkeley. He also had a new personal assistant; a young lady in her mid-thirties. 'Bob Wilson had retired by then,' Brook Williams said. 'He was in his seventies and lived on Long Island; Rich was taking care of him financially. And Rich was taking control of his life again.'

A physiotherapist also went at the insistence of his doctors; that was the only way Richard could be insured for the duration of the filming. Said Brook, 'The physio was a really great guy. Very funny. He said, "The last time I was in Europe I was seven thousand feet up bombing the shit outa the place." But the last thing Rich needed at the end of a ten or sometimes twelve-hour day was to be pummelled for a full hour. He was exhausted at the end of each day and wanted only to put his feet up. But he had agreed with the hospital and he kept his side of the bargain.'

Twice during the seven-month schedule he felt a seizure coming on and went to hospital both times. He also drank on occasions. In fact, I had heard that he was drunk much of the time he was making *Wagner*, but on the set of *1984* he told me, 'I drank quite heavily. I didn't get drunk. I was too *ill* to be drunk.'

He found himself quite enchanted by a young lady called Sally Hay who was working on the film. She had been a production assistant at the BBC and Thames Television, had also been a PA, and she had worked with Tony Palmer before, so she was a good choice to work on the film's continuity. Because scenes are usually shot out of order and sometimes half a scene can be shot days or even weeks after the first half had been filmed, someone had to keep tabs on the continuity; that's what a continuity girl does. (Although why it is invariably a female for that job I've never been able to fully understand.) And so Sally Hay was with Rich every day on the set, taking photographs of him in costume and checking the script constantly.

'Rich was very taken with Sally,' said Brook. 'But he didn't try it on with her. He was more likely to tell her, "I must go and phone my wife." But he told me, "I like that Sally. She has a quiet, calm sense about her." I think he felt he needed calm about him.'

The great day came when Richardson, Gielgud and Olivier arrived for their participation in the film. Rich recalled:

'There was the greatest rivalry between them. They all gave a great dinner for each other – three dinner celebrations by three great actors for each other, and they did it only to outdo each other. They were all disasters of varying degrees. Larry had given everyone the wrong arrival time and he spent two hours on his own waiting for everyone to arrive. Gielgud had a stand up argument with his chef, and Richardson hired incompetent waiters who were slow, sloppy and probably more drunk than I was.

'I expected so much more of the three of them. Ralph couldn't be bothered to learn his lines so they had to be written on idiot boards for him. Gielgud was easily the best of the trio, doing his scene without a hiccup and then heading for home when he had finished.

'But I was disappointed with Larry. He was consumed with technique. There was no room for spontaneity so there was no emotion. He was a caricature of an actor.'

Well, that was Richard's version. Brook Williams said that Rich had got drunk and had verbally laid into the trio, calling Olivier 'a grotesque exaggeration of an actor', then made tasteless references to Gielgud's sexuality and ended by telling Richardson he couldn't even remember his lines.

'Richardson just said, "Poor Richard". John Gielgud said nothing but looked rather disgustedly at Rich who was, perhaps, his most famous pupil. Outside, as he got into his car, Laurence Olivier said to Tony Palmer, "Now I know why you chose Richard to play Wagner."

'Rich was mortified with himself. He said, "Oh God! I went too far." But none of them spoke of it again. I don't believe there was any ire between them.'

During week four of the schedule, Suzy publicly announced that she was divorcing Richard. 'I knew it was coming,' said Brook. But many others were taken by surprise. Rich took all the blame, saying that she had good reason to leave him and that their quarrels had become violent; it seems he had lost his temper in the worst way possible. 'The thing was, he really loved Suzy,' said Brook, 'but he knew he was bad for her.'

Richard never spoke to me about his reasons for the marriage breakdown except to say that they had talked of wanting children when they were first married, 'but,' he said in 1984, 'I was not getting younger and I had felt too many times like I was going to die. I didn't want to have children and then leave them without a father.'

Elizabeth Taylor was quickly on the phone to Richard. 'She'd just divorced Senator Warner and she was clearly still in love with Richard,' said Brook Williams. 'She never stopped loving him. So as soon as she heard Susan was divorcing Rich she was back on the phone to him. She even wanted to come out to Venice where we were then filming, but Rich didn't want her there.'

But they weren't kept apart for very long. It just so happened that Richard had an arrangement to go to London to do a one-off charity performance of *Under Milk Wood*. It coincided with Elizabeth being in London for a play, *The Little Foxes*. She was also about to celebrate her 50th birthday – in grand style, of course. He called her on the phone and she asked him to be her escort to her party; he agreed. Maria was there and so was Liza. It was a highly emotional experience for him, and he got terribly drunk.

He returned to *Wagner* sober and ultimately delivered a powerful performance in a superior television production. But before *Wagner* was completed he turned his attentions towards Sally Hay. While filming at one of Wagner's castles, there was a hold up, and Sally went to Richard to explain the situation. He asked her to have dinner with him. She did, and a few days later she moved into his hotel suite.

'She never expected it to last longer than the filming,' said Brook. 'But he was really taken with her. Before long he asked her to marry him. He still had a divorce to sort out, and he told Sally they should give it a year and talk about it again.'

Brook Williams certainly approved of Sally. 'She was what he needed,' he said. 'Someone who was efficient but calm. And she's very pretty. Not really beautiful like Elizabeth Taylor or Suzy. In fact, she reminded me a lot of Sybil, and I think that's what he saw in her too – those same qualities Sybil has: clever, cheerful, attractive and a good homemaker. He said to me, "She can do everything – cook, type, do shorthand. She looks after me so well. Thank God I found her, Brookie."

'She also knew how to cope with Richard's drinking because her father was an alcoholic.'

Filming finally ended. It had been a feat of endurance for Richard. They had spent seven months filming in Vienna, Munich, Venice, Siena, Germany and Hungary. Rich was in pain, exhausted and short tempered. Sally went with him to Los Angeles where doctors told him he needed another operation on his lower spine. He refused the operation.

Despite all that, he somehow managed to find the time and the strength to appear in *Alice in Wonderland*, a filmed adaptation of a stage production in which his daughter Kate had the title role. Richard played the White King.

He had other plans: appearing in a film called *Herself Surprised* produced by Mike Todd Junior in the autumn of 1982; in the spring of 1983 he would star in *A Long Day's Journey into Night*. Neither project happened.

He was also hoping, as he had long hoped, to do *King Lear* in New York. He felt he just needed to build up enough strength for the scene in which Lear carried the body of his daughter Cordelia.

What he did end up doing was a stage production of Noël Coward's *Private Lives* with Elizabeth Taylor. She had set up the Elizabeth Theatre Group and planned to do three plays, the others being *The Corn is Green* and a third not yet decided. *Private Lives* appealed to Richard because it was actually intended only to be a taped stage production for television, but somehow it not only didn't get taped but it became the play to launch Elizabeth's theatre company and was going to run for seven months.

But before that Richard and Suzy had to get divorced. They did so in Haiti in February 1983. It was a very amicable divorce and while he was there she helped him to learn his lines for *Private Lives.* He also exercised by swimming, but because he couldn't do a crawl due to his painful and immobile arms, he developed what he called 'the underwater butterfly.'

In March 1983 rehearsals began badly. Said Brook Williams, 'Elizabeth not only didn't know her lines but she couldn't read them properly. She was also constantly late and sometimes she was drunk. Rich would have been happy if she had dropped out and they'd had to find someone else. He and I worked with her on her lines. We went over and over the second act with her, but when she came to rehearse it, she couldn't remember a single line.'

Rich was remaining dry. Elizabeth was drinking. She also relied on prescribed drugs.

But a miracle appeared to happen. Said Brook, 'It's the way with Elizabeth to make a drama out of everything, and then deliver when she had to. She just didn't work the way other actors do because she wasn't used to working in the theatre. But on the opening night the audience simply loved it. Or maybe they loved seeing Rich and Elizabeth again. Anyway, she was ready for the opening night, knew all her words; she just *had* to be half an hour late for the first performance. And then she had an interval that was longer than the first act. But the magic worked.'

The critics savaged the play and the players. 'We can do little but anticipate the intermissions,' said the *New York Times.*

The *New York Post* joked that it had 'flashes of mediocrity'.

But the public couldn't keep away; the advances were phenomenal. The show was a commercial if not an artistic hit. 'But he quickly tired of it all,' said Brook Williams. 'He would always be there over an hour before curtain up, and each time she was late. That made him irritable. She'd arrive with only minutes to spare. It drove him crazy, and he said, "I now know that I could never get together with that woman again." I think she was jealous because Sally was there. Rich and I had fun, and we had friends. I think Elizabeth was lonely.'

Brook's job was to field unwanted phone calls because Rich hated using the phone. He also liked to be in bed before midnight and he didn't want to be disturbed by Elizabeth's calls which could come at any time of the night.

Brook recalled:

'One night she called and she said, "Can I speak to Richard?" I said, "I'm terribly sorry, Elizabeth, but he's asleep." She said, "Oh!" and paused. Then I heard sobbing. "Brookie?" "Yes?" "I've gone blind." "Oh, how very upsetting for you Elizabeth." Then I heard a loud crash and she yelled, "Shit! Hell!" I said, "Are you all right?" She said, "Alvin knocked my Jack Daniels over." Alvin was her parrot. "What am I going to do, Brookie? I'm blind." I said, "Well, you could call your doctor. Or maybe you can call Sammy Davis's doctor." That made her giggle. I said, "Or you could have a Jack Daniels and go to sleep and see what happens in the morning." I found out it was just her eyelash that had got stuck. She was really on form and could be very funny. But Rich just didn't need that in the early hours of the morning.'

When Elizabeth fell sick in July, the play had to be cancelled for five days, so Richard said to Sally, 'Let's get married.' She thought he was joking, but he wasn't, so they went to Las Vegas and were married on 3 July 1983 in the Presidential Suite of the Frontier Hotel; Brook was the best man and he and Valerie Douglas were the witnesses. Brook recalled, 'Elizabeth didn't know about it, but when she heard she sent flowers and then got engaged to a Mexican lawyer [Victor Luna].'

The run of the play continued; it played New York, Philadelphia, Washington, Chicago and Los Angeles. The famous Burton–Taylor rows were reignited and continued for the duration. Rich grew bored with the play and with Elizabeth. It was a huge relief for him – for all concerned – when it ended.

But it had been a major success. Richard Burton had gone from the heady heights of *Camelot* to a hugely impressive television series to the commercially successful *Private Lives*. He was back on top. Not many actors, once they nose-dived, got that chance. But it was all, though he didn't know it, his last series of triumphs. I'm sure that had he realised that, he would have been content. The talent was still there and had been spectacularly showcased.

'I'm the luckiest bugger alive,' he would tell me.

Chapter Twenty-Seven

THE PRINCE IS DEAD

ICHARD AND SALLY went to Haiti to rest, read and swim for the next five months; Brook went with them. I suggested to Brook that it was odd that he should have gone on honeymoon with them. He laughed and said, 'Rich insisted I go. So go I did.'

Rich barely touched alcohol, considered retirement and talked of writing his autobiography. When I saw him in 1984, the following year, I asked him if he was ever going to write his life story. He said, 'I should. But I couldn't be sure I'd ever finish it.' I think he meant that he wasn't sure if he would survive long enough to write it.

In Haiti he was called by Euan Lloyd who wanted to make *Wild Geese II* with Richard reprising his role of Colonel Allen Faulkner. Brook called Lloyd and said, 'Rich sends his love but he's having terrible problems with his back.' Brook said to Lloyd that the only person who was ever able to help Richard's bad back was the professor in South Africa and asked Lloyd if he could find the professor and get him to contact Richard's doctor in Haiti and tell him what he did so that the doctor could do the same thing.

Lloyd traced the professor and had him speaking to Richard's doctor in Haiti, talking him through the procedure; the result was, according to Brook, remarkable. But it wasn't a cure, and Brook was sure, in hindsight, that it only made his condition worse.

Another offer came through while Richard was in Haiti, to play the part of the interrogator O'Brien in a new version of George Orwell's *1984*. Paul Scofield was originally going to play the part but had broken his leg. Sean Connery turned the role down, as did Marlon Brando. Richard was far from even being second choice. But he said he would read the screenplay which was sent to him in Haiti.

Rich seemed fit and well when he and Sally returned to Céligny where they remained until May 1984, by which time he had shrugged

240

off all thoughts of retirement with *Wild Geese II* in the offing and the prospect of filming *The Quiet American* from the book by Graham Greene (it was finally made in 2002 with Michael Caine). He read the screenplay of *1984* and agreed to do it and also accepted, with reluctance, a brief appearance in an American mini-series, *Ellis Island*; he did it only because daughter Kate had the leading role, and it was an important break for her.

He was soon back in the UK, making *1984* at Shepperton Studios where I saw him for the last time. 'I rather liked the idea of bringing some humanity to the character who is something of a monster in the book,' he told me. 'And it's a good part. Not the star part, but one that I felt I could make something of.'

A good deal of footage had been shot before Richard came on board and director Mike Radford showed him what had so far been filmed. Rich liked what he saw. 'You know, Mick,' he said to me, 'I think this is going to be a good picture, and I might actually be adequate in it.

'I like Mike [Radford]. He's about the only director in recent years who's actually directed me. Most of them are too scared to, you know. I *am* directable. Maybe I will even be bloody good.'

He was bloody good, with Mike Radford's help. Richard said that on his first day of filming he felt like he was just an 'old actor' among a group of enthusiastic young film makers and actors who suddenly had him thrust upon them. He was extremely nervous and kept forgetting his lines. There were 29 takes of his first set-up and 35 takes of his second set-up.

But Radford guided him through the scenes and wasn't afraid to bring him down when he characteristically started going over the top. 'Oh yes,' Rich would say, 'I'm doing a Burton.' Mike Radford kept Richard's performance quite subdued, which Rich had hoped for, and he told Radford, 'I've been waiting 20 years to do a film without the "Richard Burton voice" and I can see this is going to be the one.'

The film is something of an oddity, being filmed and released in 1984 because it didn't reflect the times at all as George Orwell had predicted. But today it comes across as an intense, frightening drama which still has a ring of prophecy about it; a state in which everyone must toe the line or pay the penalty. Big Brother is watching us ever more with satellites in the sky and CCTV cameras everywhere. Today we are aware that governments don't always tell us the truth. *1984* is, perhaps, getting closer.

Once Richard had settled in among the younger film makers and had told a few of his old stories to amuse and entertain the obviously beguiled young cast and crew, he was in fine spirits. But I saw that he looked thin and drawn. He had deteriorated physically a great deal and wore a neck brace some of the time. His hair was now completely white, although he had some of it dyed but, as usual, kept his temples and sideburns untouched.

He couldn't raise his right arm. I recall that his left arm was weak also. When he was shot in medium close up, someone hunched down out of shot and literally held his arm to raise it when necessary. If Richard was embarrassed by this, he didn't show it. For the most part, he made sure that his hands were the least important part of his performance. He relied more than ever on his voice, keeping it quiet, calm, casual, even using it to show sincere interest in the man he was torturing, played superbly by John Hurt.

I was a black-clad guard in a scene and had fun roughing up John Hurt a little. Richard, asked me, as he always did, 'Still going to be a director, or have you decided to try acting yet?'

This time I said, 'I think I'm going to try acting. Olivier gave me a few lessons when he was making *Clash of the Titans.*'

'Did he now? Well, what can I teach you?' And so he chose to teach me how to use my voice. 'The way to do it is to do radio,' he said. 'You have nothing but your voice for that. That's why I love doing radio more than anything else.'

My lessons took place in his dressing room where he said, 'I'm sorry I can't offer you a drink. I'm dry – well, mostly.' And then he added, very casually, 'I'm an alcoholic, you know.' I had never known him to admit to that before.

'That's okay,' I said, 'I'm dry too.'

'Are you also an alcoholic?' he asked.

'No, I'm a Mormon,' I replied.

He laughed. 'Well, that's just as bad.' (I was going through my Mormon phase back then. I got over it.)

'I still smoke too much,' he said. 'I'm sure it gives the voice an edge.'

When we had our goodbyes, I said, 'See ya Dick!'

'Be seeing you, Mick!'

I had the feeling I would never be seeing him again.

In May of 1984 he went to America to film his few scenes for *Ellis Island.* Brook Williams told me that Rich and Kate spent the time really

242

getting to know each other. He was quite honest to her about his life, his mistakes, and how he had come to feel ashamed about his drinking. 'They became closer than they had ever been,' said Brook.

He returned to Céligny before starting work on *Wilde Geese II*. Elizabeth was phoning again. 'She never stopped trying,' said Brook Williams. 'She wanted to work with Rich again. And he was, he admitted, still fascinated by her. You could have forgiven Sally if she had been feeling insecure, but she was *very* secure. They were both very content with each other. It was back to basics for Rich; just him and Sally – and I was back and forth a lot to help him organise things. I went on ahead to Berlin to start work on *Wild Geese II*. Rich was looking forward to that. "Should be easy, Brookie," he said. "And this time we're going to rescue Larry Olivier [as Rudolph Hess].'

Just before Richard was due to join Brook along with Euan Lloyd and director Peter Hunt in Berlin, John Hurt came to visit him in August. Rich, Sally and Hurt went over to the Café de la Gare where they drank; Rich had too much and got drunk.

The following morning, 4 August, he told Sally he had a headache and she gave him two aspirins. John Hurt had stayed the night so she drove him back to his hotel in Geneva.

That evening Rich went to bed at around ten. Brook told me:

'He was writing something. Sally showed me what it was. It read,
    The multitudinous seas incarnadine,
    Making the green one red.
    Tomorrow and tomorrow and tomorrow . . .
    Our revels now are ended . . .
    Cap a pi . . .
'He never finished it – and I've never forgotten it. At that moment he had a cerebral haemorrhage. When Sally went to bed she thought he was just sleeping. But the next morning when she woke up she heard him breathing heavily and couldn't wake him. So she called the doctor and he didn't think it was serious but got an ambulance anyway to take him to a hospital in Geneva.

'They told Sally he had had a cerebral haemorrhage, that they were going to operate and she should go home because it would be a long operation. She had only just got back to the chalet when the hospital called and told her to come back.

'She arrived to be told that Rich was dead. As soon as I heard,

RICHARD BURTON: PRINCE OF PLAYERS

I flew back to help Sally. Valerie Douglas also flew in from California.'

With Brook's and Valerie Douglas's help, the funeral was arranged as well as the succession of memorial services which followed. Said Brook:

'He had written into his will that he wanted to be buried in Switzerland beside the fast-moving mountain river. The funeral was held in a small church up the hill from the house. I read, "And death shall have no dominion." Kate also read: Dylan Thomas – "Rage, rage against the dying of the light." The Welsh contingent sang a rugby song. Rich would have loved that.

'Sally, rightly I thought, felt it was best if Elizabeth didn't come for the funeral because it would only attract the press, and Elizabeth was good about it. She came on her own, later, about two weeks later.

'Then there were memorial services in Los Angeles which Suzy came to. Richard Harris delivered, "Let us sit upon the ground and tell sad stories of the death of kings," and then he broke down and had to leave the stage for a short while so the Welsh choir sang "We'll Keep a Welcome in the Hillsides". Richard Harris came back and said, "If Rich had seen me a minute ago he would have howled with laughter." Frank Sinatra was there, and so was John Huston to deliver eulogies.

'Elizabeth had stayed away from the Los Angeles service, and she stayed away also from the New York memorial service because she didn't want to have the press intruding at such a time.

'There was another service in Pontrhydyfen, and then in London where Sally was surprised to see Elizabeth sitting with the Jenkinses which, I think, rather upset Sally. Sally knew Susan would be there; she had told her she would, but Sally didn't know Elizabeth was coming. I got there early and sat in the seat reserved for the widow; I didn't want anyone but Sally taking her rightful place, but she sat next to me. I felt very honoured.

'I think Rich would have laughed at some of what went on. My dear father [Emlyn] was there and gave a talk; he was old and not well. Some of it was a little duff. John Gielgud was expected to read from *Hamlet* but he was late because he got lost. He hurried in finally and gave his speech. Rich would have loved that; Gielgud late for Richard's memorial service.'

Kate read from Shakespeare, and so did Paul Scofield. It was the final farewell to Richard Burton who had died at the age of 58. Laurence Olivier, upon hearing of his death in Berlin while filming *Wild Geese II*, said, 'He was so young . . . so young.'

Sally was a widow at the age of 34; her time spent with Richard was all too brief. But she came to accept Richard's death as something of a blessing. She said that Richard's death was a tragedy for all but Richard. She told Melvyn Bragg, 'My feeling was that Richard had many lives in him, but not that of an old man.'

Show business being what it is meant that the show had to go on; in this case it was *Wild Geese II*. Richard's role was taken by Edward Fox. The film was poor; a cheaper, pale imitation of the original. Richard, frankly, was well out of it.

Over the years, and certainly immediately following his death, people have spoken or written about what they considered to be his failure because, they said, he squandered his talent. But I think they are wrong. Richard's great talent was for living, and he did that with abandon. And as for acting, he achieved much more than many of his contemporaries such as Robert Shaw and James Mason. The trouble is, he has been likened so much to Gielgud and Olivier, and probably also to Richardson, that it was almost impossible to match up to their achievements.

Richard did the great classic parts, and he often rejected lucrative film offers to do them. What's more, he came at them having never gone through any kind of formal training as an actor. What he had was a natural gift which he honed; people said he had no technique, but he developed it over time, usually by trial and error. On stage he took on Henry IV, Henry V, Hamlet (twice), Sir Toby Belch, Coriolanus, Caliban, Othello, Iago and King Arthur. Had he been fitter he would have undoubtedly played King Lear eventually.

He also gave some wonderful performances on screen: Jimmy Porter in *Look Back in Anger*, Mark Antony in *Cleopatra*, the title role in *Becket*, the Reverend Laurence Shannon in *Night of the Iguana*, Alec Leamas in *The Spy Who Came in from the Cold*, George in *Who's Afraid of Virginia Woolf?*, Petruchio in *The Taming of the Shrew*, Henry VIII in *Anne of the Thousand Days*, First Voice in *Under Milk Wood*, Martin

Dysart in *Equus*, the title role in *Wagner* and O'Brien in *1984*. That's not such a bad legacy; try comparing it to that of many other notable actors.

I think what people seem to remember mostly is the fact that he was married to Liz Taylor and that they managed to make a lot of money doing films that, with a couple of exceptions, were not generally very good. He was seen as someone who worked only for large sums, and by and large he did command big fees, but he used his wealth for the benefit of his family and friends. He was generous to a fault.

The last time I saw him, after my priceless voice lesson and just before we said our final goodbyes, he asked, as he always did, 'How are you for cash?'

It was a time in my life when I was struggling, and I told him so. 'Here,' he said, handing me a stash of notes. I didn't count them until I got outside the studio. It was around £500. He didn't count the cash either; he just picked up a handful of notes without concern for how much it was and stuffed them in my jacket pocket.

'This may help,' he said.

Richard Burton wasn't a man who squandered his talent or wasted his life. He *shared* it all, as evenly as he could.

Maybe if he had lived longer he might have received that knighthood he coveted. He played kings and made Arthur of Camelot very much his own, and while he may not have reached the heights of Gielgud, Olivier and Richardson, which perhaps prevents him from being a true king of theatre, he was without doubt a prince – a king in waiting who just didn't quite last the course.

Having achieved all he did, escaping the pre- and post-war mining valleys of Wales to a life that was rich in so many ways, I think he settled for that. He was definitely and definitively the Prince of Players.

THE PLAYS, FILMS AND TELEVISION WORKS OF RICHARD BURTON

The Plays

The Druid's Rest, as Glan; written and directed by Emlyn Williams; Royal Court Theatre, Liverpool, November 1943; St Martin's Theatre, London, January 1944

Measure for Measure, as Angelo; directed by Nevill Coghill; Oxford University Dramatic Society, Christ Church Cloisters, Oxford 1944

Castle Anna, as Mr. Hicks; directed by Daphne Rye; Lyric Theatre, February 1948

The Lady's Not for Burning, as the orphaned clerk; directed by John Gielgud and Esme Percy; Globe Theatre, London, May 1949

A Phoenix Too Frequent, as Tegeus; directed by Christopher Fry; Dolphin Theatre, Brighton, 1950

The Boy with a Cart, as Cuthman; directed by John Gielgud; Lyric Theatre, Hammersmith, London, January 1950

The Lady's Not for Burning, as the orphaned clerk; directed by John Gielgud; Royale Theatre, New York, November 1950

Henry IV Part I, as Prince Hal; directed by Anthony Quayle and John Kidd; Shakespeare Memorial Theatre, Stratford-upon-Avon, 1951

Henry IV Part II, as Henry IV; directed by Michael Redgrave; Shakespeare Memorial Theatre, Stratford-upon-Avon, 1951

Henry V, as Henry V; directed by Anthony Quayle; Shakespeare Memorial Theatre, Stratford-upon-Avon, 1951

The Tempest, as Ferdinand; directed by Michael Benthall; Shakespeare Memorial Theatre, Stratford-upon-Avon, 1951

Legend of Lovers, as the Musician; directed by Peter Ashmore; The Plymouth Theatre, New York, December 1951

Montserrat, as Montserrat; directed by Noel Willman with Nigel Green; Lyric Theatre, Hammersmith, London, April 1952

Hamlet, as Hamlet; directed by Michael Benthall; The Old Vic Company, Assembly Hall, Edinburgh, September 1953

Hamlet, as Hamlet; directed by Michael Benthall; The Old Vic, 1953–54 season

King John, as Philip the Bastard; directed by George Devine; The Old Vic, 1953–54 season

Twelfth Night, as Sir Toby Belch; directed by Denis Carey; The Old Vic, 1953–54 season

Coriolanus, as Caius Marcius; directed by Michael Benthall; The Old Vic, 1953–54 season

The Tempest, as Caliban; directed by Robert Helpmann; The Old Vic, 1953–54 season

Henry V, as Henry V; directed by Michael Benthall; The Old Vic, 1955–56 season

Othello, alternating as Othello and Iago; directed by Michael Benthall; Old Vic, 1955–56 season

Time Remembered, as Prince Albert; directed by Albert Marre; Morosco Theatre, New York, November 1957

Camelot, as King Arthur; directed by Moss Hart; (US tour) Majestic Theatre, New York, December 1960

Hamlet, as Hamlet; directed by John Gielgud; (US tour) Lunt-Fontanne Theatre, New York, April 1964

Doctor Faustus, as Faustus; directed by Neville Coghill; Oxford University Dramatic Society, Oxford Playhouse, February 1966

Equus, as Martin Dysart; directed by John Dexter; Plymouth Theatre, New York, March 1976

Camelot, as King Arthur; directed by Frank Dunlop; (US tour) New York State Theatre, Lincoln Center, New York, 1980–81

Private Lives, as Elyot Chase; directed by Milton Katselas; (US tour) Lunt-Fontanne Theatre, New York, May 1993

The Films

The Last Days of Dolwyn (London/DLPA) with Edith Evans, Emlyn Williams, Richard Burton, Hugh Griffith. Directed by Emlyn Williams. 1948

Now Barabbas Was a Robber (Warner/Anatole de Grunwald) with Richard Greene, Cedric Hardwicke, William Hartnell, Kathleen Harrison, Leslie Dwyer, Richard Burton, Kenneth More. Directed by Gordon Parry. 1949

Waterfront (GFD/Conqueror) with Robert Newton, Richard Burton, Kathleen Harrison, Susan Shaw. Directed by Michael Anderson. 1950

The Woman with No Name (US title ***Her Panelled Door***) (IFP/APB) with Phyllis Calvert, Edward Underdown, Helen Cherry, Richard Burton, Anthony Nichols. Directed by Ladislas Vajda. 1950

Green Grow the Rushes (ACT Films) with Roger Livesey, Honor Blackman, Richard Burton, Frederick Leister. Directed by Derek Twist. 1951

My Cousin Rachel (20th Century Fox) with Olivia de Havilland, Richard Burton, John Sutton, Audrey Dalton. Directed by Henry Koster. 1952

The Robe (20th Century Fox) with Richard Burton, Jean Simmons, Victor Mature, Michael Rennie, Jay Robinson, Torin Thatcher. Directed by Henry Koster. 1953

The Desert Rats, (20th Century Fox) with Richard Burton, James Mason, Robert Newton, Robert Douglas, Torin Thatcher, Chips Rafferty. Directed by Robert Wise. 1953

Prince of Players (20th Century Fox) with Richard Burton, Eva Le Gallienne, Maggie McNamara, John Derek, Raymond Massey, Charles Bickford, Elizabeth Sellars. Directed by Philip Dunne. 1954

The Rains of Ranchipur (20th Century Fox) with Lana Turner, Richard Burton, Fred MacMurray, Joan Caulfield. Directed by Jean Negulesco. 1955

Alexander the Great (United Artists) with Richard Burton, Fredric March, Danielle Darrieux, Claire Bloom, Peter Cushing, Harry Andrews, Stanley Baker, Michael Horden. Directed by Robert Rossen. 1956

Sea Wife (20th Century Fox) with Richard Burton, Joan Collins, Basil Sydney. Directed by Bob McNaught. 1957

Bitter Victory (Columbia Pictures) with Richard Burton, Curt Jurgens, Ruth Roman, Raymond Pellegrin. Directed by Nicholas Ray. 1958

Look Back in Anger (ABP/Woodfall) with Richard Burton, Mary Ure, Claire Bloom, Edith Evans, Gary Raymond. Directed by Tony Richardson. 1959

The Bramble Bush (Warner Bros.) with Richard Burton, Barbara Rush, Jack Carson, Angie Dickinson. Directed by Daniel Petrie. 1959

Ice Palace (Warner Bros.) with Richard Burton, Robert Ryan, Martha Hyer, Carolyn Jones, Jim Backus. Directed by Vincent Sherman. 1960

The Longest Day (20th Century Fox) with all-star cast including John Wayne, Robert Mitchum, Henry Fonda, Roddy McDowall and Richard Burton. Directed by Ken Annakin, Andrew Marton, Bernhard Wicki and Darryl F. Zanuck (uncredited). 1962

Cleopatra (20th Century Fox) with Elizabeth Taylor, Richard Burton, Rex Harrison, Roddy McDowall, Pamela Brown, George Cole, Hume Cronyn, Martin Landau. Directed by Joseph L. Mankiewicz. 1963

The VIPs (Metro-Goldwyn-Mayer) with Elizabeth Taylor, Richard Burton, Maggie Smith, Rod Taylor, Margaret Rutherford, Louis Jordan, Orson Welles. Directed by Anthony Asquith. 1963

Becket (Paramount) with Richard Burton, Peter O'Toole, Sir John Gielgud, Sir Donald Wolfit, Marita Hunt, Pamela Brown, Siân Phillips. Directed by Peter Glenville. 1964

The Night of the Iguana (Metro-Goldwyn-Mayer/Seven Arts) with Richard Burton, Ava Gardner, Deborah Kerr, Sue Lyon. Directed by John Huston. 1964

The Sandpiper, (Metro-Goldwyn-Mayer/Filmways) with Elizabeth Taylor, Richard Burton, Eva Marie Saint, Charles Bronson, Robert Webber. Directed by Vincente Minnelli. 1965

The Spy Who Came in from the Cold (Paramount/Salem) with Richard Burton, Alec Leamas, Claire Bloom, Oskar Werner, Michael Hordern. Directed by Martin Ritt. 1965

Who's Afraid of Virginia Woolf? (Warner Bros.) with Elizabeth Taylor, Richard Burton, George Segal, Sandy Dennis. Directed by Mike Nichols. 1966

The Taming of the Shrew (Columbia Pictures/Royal Films International/F.A.I. Productions) with Elizabeth Taylor, Richard Burton, Cyril Cusack, Michael Hordern, Michael York, Natasha Pyne. Directed by Franco Zeffirelli. 1967

Doctor Faustus (Oxford University Screen Production/Nassau Films/Venfilms/Columbia) with Richard Burton, Elizabeth Taylor,

Andreas Teuber, Elizabeth O'Donovan. Directed by Richard Burton and Nevill Coghill. 1967

The Comedians (Metro-Goldwyn-Mayer/Maximilian Prods/Trianon Prods) with Richard Burton, Elizabeth Taylor, Alec Guinness, Peter Ustinov, Paul Ford, Lillian Gish, Raymond St Jacques, Roscoe Lee Brown. Directed by Peter Glenville. 1967

Boom! (Universal) with Elizabeth Taylor, Richard Burton, Noël Coward, Joanna Shimkus. Directed by Joseph Losey. 1968

Candy (Selmur/Dear/Corono) with Ewa Aulin, Richard Burton, Marlon Brando, James Coburn, Walter Matthau, Charles Aznavour. Directed by Christian Marquand. 1968

Where Eagles Dare (Metro-Goldwyn-Mayer/Winkast) with Richard Burton, Clint Eastwood, Mary Ure, Patrick Wymark, Michael Hordern, Donald Houston, Ingrid Pitt. Directed by Brian G. Hutton. 1969

Staircase (20th Century Fox) with Richard Burton, Rex Harrison, Cathleen Nesbitt, Beatrix Lehmann. Directed by Stanley Donen. 1969

Anne of the Thousand Days (Universal) with Richard Burton, Geneviève Bujold, John Colicos, Irene Papas, Anthony Quayle, Michael Hordern. Directed by Charles Jarrott. 1969

Raid on Rommel (Universal) with Richard Burton, John Colicos, Clinton Greyn, Wolfgang Preiss. Directed by Henry Hathaway. 1971

Villain (EMI/Ladd/Kanter) with Richard Burton, Ian McShane, Nigel Davenport, Joss Ackland, Cathleen Nesbitt. Directed by Michael Tuchner. 1971

Under Milk Wood (Timon Production) with Richard Burton, Elizabeth Taylor, Peter O'Toole, Glynis Johns, Vivien Merchant, Siân Phillips. Directed by Andrew Sinclair. 1971

Hammersmith is Out (A.J. Cornelius Crean Films Inc) with Elizabeth Taylor, Richard Burton, Beau Bridges, Peter Ustinov. Directed by Peter Ustinov. 1972

The Battle of Sutjeska (Bosna Film/Filmska Radna Zajednica/Sutjeska Film) with Richard Burton, Ljuba Tadic, Velmir Zivojinovic, Irene Papas. Directed by Stipe Delic. 1972

The Assassination of Trotsky (Dino de Laurentiis/Shaftel/Cinetel) with Richard Burton, Alain Delon, Romy Schneider, Valentina Cortese. Directed by Joseph Losey. 1972

Bluebeard (Barnabé/Gloria/Geiselgasteig) with Richard Burton,

Raquel Welch, Joey Heatherton, Virna Lisi, Nathalie Delon, Sybil Danning. Directed by Edward Dmytryk. 1972

Massacre in Rome (Compagnia Cinematografica Champion) with Richard Burton, Marcello Mastrioanni, Leo McKern, John Steiner, Anthony Steel. Directed by George Pan Cosmatos. 1973

The Voyage (C.A.C.A.P/Compagnia Cinematografica Champion) with Sophia Loren, Richard Burton, Ian Bannen, Barbara Pilavin, Renato Pinciroli. Directed by Vittorio De Sica. 1974

Exorcist II: The Heretic (Warner Bros.) with Richard Burton, Linda Blair, Louise Fletcher, Kitty Winn, Max von Sydow. Directed by John Boorman. 1977

Equus (United Artists/Winkast) with Richard Burton, Peter Firth, Colin Blakely, Joan Plowright, Harry Andrews, Eileen Atkins, Jenny Agutter. Directed by Sidney Lumet. 1977

The Medusa Touch (ITC/Bulldog/Citeca) with Richard Burton, Lee Remick, Lino Ventura, Harry Andrews, Alan Badel. Directed by Jack Gold. 1978

The Wild Geese, (Rank/Richmond) with Richard Burton, Roger Moore, Richard Harris, Hardy Kruger, Stewart Granger, Jack Watson. Directed by Andrew V. McLaglen. 1978

Absolution (Bulldog Prod) with Richard Burton, Dominic Guard, Dai Bradley, Billy Connolly, Andrew Keir. Directed by Anthony Page. 1978

Breakthrough (aka *Sergeant Steiner*) (Palladium/Rapidfilm) with Richard Burton, Robert Mitchum, Curt Jurgens, Rod Steiger. Directed by Andrew V. McLaglen. 1979

Tristan and Isolt (Clar Productions/Castle Hill) with Richard Burton, Kate Mulgrew, Nicholas Clay, Cyril Cusack. Directed by Tom Donovan. 1980

Circle of Two (Film Consortium of Canada) with Richard Burton, Tatum O'Neal, Nuala FitzGereld, Kate Reid. Directed by Jules Dassin. 1980

1984 (Umbrella/Rosenberg/Virgin) with John Hurt, Richard Burton, Suzanna Hamilton, Cyril Cusack. Directed by Michael Radford. 1984

Television

The Corn is Green, as Morgan Evans, for BBC Television Productions. 1946

Wuthering Heights as Heathcliff, with Yvonne Furneaux as Cathy. Directed by Daniel Petrie. 1958

The Fifth Column, also with Maximilian Schell, Sally Ann Howes. Directed by John Frankenheimer. 1960

The Tempest as Prospero, with Lee Remick, Roddy McDowall. Directed by George Schafer. 1960

A Subject of Scandal and Concern, also with John Freeman, George Devine. Directed by Tony Richardson. 1960

Divorce His, Divorce Hers, also with Elizabeth Taylor, Carrie Nye, Barry Foster. Directed by Waris Hussein. 1973

A Walk with Destiny as Winston Churchill, with Virginia McKenna. Directed by Herbert Wise. 1974

The Klansman (Paramount/Atlanta) with Lee Marvin, Richard Burton, Cameron Mitchell, O.J. Simpson, Lola Falana. Directed by Terence Young. 1974

Brief Encounter, also with Sophia Loren, Jack Hedley, Rosemary Leach. Directed by Alan Bridges. 1976

The Fall Guy guest-starring as himself, with Lee Majors. 1982

Alice in Wonderland, as the White King, with Kate Burton as Alice. Directed by Kirk Browning. 1983

Wagner, in the title role, with Vanessa Redgrave, Laurence Olivier, Ralph Richardson and John Gielgud. Directed by Tony Palmer. 1983

Ellis Island, as Senator Phipps Ogden, with Kate Burton, Claire Bloom, Faye Dunaway. Directed by Jerry London. 1984

ACKNOWLEDGEMENTS, SOURCES AND SELECTED BIBLIOGRAPHY

Acknowledgements

I would like to give my heart-felt thanks to a few important people: to Jeremy Robson for his faith in me over the past 22 years; to Lynn Bresler, who edited this book; and to my partner Jane for her immeasurable support.

The first-hand quotes in this book come from the following, listed alphabetically, who I formally interviewed and talked informally with over the course of many years.

Sources

Dawn Addams, London, 1974

Harry Andrews, Shepperton Studios (filming *SOS Titanic*), 1979

Sir Stanley Baker, London, 1970, and in Wales (filming *How Green Was My Valley*), 1975

Colin Blakely, Shepperton Studios (filming *Little Lord Fauntleroy*), 1979

Claire Bloom, Pinewood Studios (*Clash of the Titans*), 1979

Sir Michael Caine, the Dorchester Hotel, London, 1976

Joan Collins, London, 1978

George Pan Cosmatos, Elstree Studios (post-production on *Escape to Athena*), 1979

Sir Noël Coward, Claridges, London, 1972

Sandy Dennis, London, 1983

Edward Dmytryk, London, 1975

Clint Eastwood, Cannes Film Festival, 1988

Bryan Forbes, Pinewood Studios (where he was directing *The Slipper and the Rose*), 1975

Ava Gardner, London between 1969 and 1987

Sir John Gielgud, Norfolk (*Tales of the Unexpected*), 1979

John Glen, Pinewood Studios (post-production of *For Your Eyes Only*), 1980

Peter Glenville, London, 1976

Stewart Granger, Pinewood Studios (*The Wild Geese*), 1978, and in London, 1981

Sir Alec Guinness, London (press screening of *Tinker, Tailor, Soldier, Spy*), 1979

Robert Hardy, BBC rehearsal rooms, Acton, London (*All Creatures Great and Small*), 1978

Richard Harris, Pinewood Studios, (*The Wild Geese*) 1978

Rex Harrison, Norfolk (*Tales of the Unexpected*), 1982

Henry Hathaway, by telephone, 1981

Sir Michael Horden, BBC Studios, London, (*King Lear*), 1981

Donald Houston, Elstree Studios (*Voyage of the Damned*), 1975

John Huston, Ava Gardner's home, London, and Claridges, 1974

Martin Landau, Elstree Studios (*Space 1999*), 1979

Alan Jay Lerner, London, 1983

Euan Lloyd, London (*Who Dares Wins?*), 1981

Sophia Loren, Winchester, 1974

Roddy McDowall, Shepperton Studios (*The Thief of Baghdad*), 1978

Leo McKern, Pinewood Studios (*Candleshoe*), 1976

Andrew V. McLaglen, Pinewood Studios (pre-production on *North Sea Hijack*), 1979

Joseph L. Mankiewicz, Pinewood Studios (*Sleuth*), 1972

Lee Marvin, England (*The Dirty Dozen: The Next Mission*), 1985

James Mason, Shepperton Studios (*Murder by Decree*), 1978

Warren Mitchell, Elstree Studios, (*Stand Up Virgin Soldiers*), 1976

Sir Roger Moore, The Athenaeum Hotel, London, 1980

Mike Nichols, by telephone, 1983

Peter O'Toole, The Old Vic, London, 1980

Ingrid Pitt, London, 1985

Sir Anthony Quayle, Shepperton Studios (*Murder By Degree*), 1977, and Pinewood (*The Last Days of Pompeii*), 1983

Martin Ritt, London, 1979

Jean Simmons, Shepperton Studios (*Dominique*), 1977

William Squire, Pinewood Studios (*The Thirty Nine Steps*), 1978

Rod Steiger, London, 1970, and again in London, 1984

Elizabeth Taylor, Twickenham Studios, (*The Mirror Crack'd*), 1979, and press call, London, 1980

Mary Ure, London between 1969 and 1972

Peter Ustinov, Shepperton Studios (*The Thief of Baghdad*), 1978

Brook Williams, London, 1970, Pinewood Studios, 1977 and 1978, Ellesmere College, Shropshire 1978, and in London, 1987

Emlyn Williams, London, 1975

Robert Wise, by telephone, 1979

Michael York, London, 1978

Susannah York, Devon (*The Shout*), 1977

Terence Young, Pinewood Studios (*The Jigsaw Man*), 1981

Franco Zeffirelli, London, 1977

Most important of all is **Richard Burton** who I knew between 1969 and 1984.

Selected bibliography

Bragg, Melvyn, *Rich: The Life of Richard Burton*. Hodder & Stoughton, 1988

Burton, Philip, *Richard and Philip: Burton – A Book of Memories*. Peter Owen, 1992

Caine, Michael, *What's It All About?*, Century, 1992

Geist, Kenneth L., *Pictures Will Talk: The Life and Films of Joseph L. Mankiewicz*. Charles Scribner's Sons, 1978

Junor, Penny, *Burton: The Man Behind the Myth*. Sidgwick & Jackson, 1985

Morley, Sheridan, *The Authorised Biography of John Gielgud*. Hodder & Stoughton, 2001

Nolan, William F. *John Huston: King Rebel*. Sherbourne Press, 1965

Quayle, Anthony, *A Time to Speak*. Barrie & Jenkins, 1990

Shipman, David, *Movie Stars 2: The International Years*. Macdonald & Co., revised edition, 1989

Strasberg, Susan, *Bittersweet*. Putnam Publishing, 1980

Vermilye, Jerry with Mark Ricci, *The Films of Elizabeth Taylor*. LSP Books, 1978

INDEX